Race, Ethnicity, Crime, and Justice

For Monica Renee Gabbidon

Race, Ethnicity, Crime, and Justice

An International Dilemma

Shaun L. Gabbidon

Pennsylvania State University, Harrisburg

Los Angeles • London • New Delhi • Singapore • Washington DC

For information:

 SAGE Publications, Inc.
2455 Teller Road
Thousand Oaks, California 91320
E-mail: order@sagepub.com

SAGE Publications India Pvt. Ltd.
B 1/I 1 Mohan Cooperative
    Industrial Area
Mathura Road, New Delhi 110 044
India

SAGE Publications Ltd.
1 Oliver's Yard
55 City Road
London EC1Y 1SP
United Kingdom

SAGE Publications Asia-Pacific
    Pte. Ltd.
33 Pekin Street #02-01
Far East Square
Singapore 048763

Printed in the United States of America.

Library of Congress Cataloging-in-Publication Data

Gabbidon, Shaun L., 1967-
Race, ethnicity, crime, and justice: an international dilemma/by Shaun L. Gabbidon.
    p. cm.
Includes bibliographical references and index.
ISBN 978-1-4129-4988-0 (pbk.)
    1. Crime and race. 2. Criminal justice, Administration of. 3. Discrimination in criminal justice administration. I. Title.

HV6191.G35 2009
364.2'56—dc22   2008049622

This book is printed on acid-free paper.

09   10   11   12   13   10 9 8 7 6 5 4 3 2 1

Acquisitions Editor:	Jerry Westby
Editorial Assistant:	Eve Oettinger
Production Editor:	Karen Wiley
Copy Editor:	Jovey Stewart
Typesetter:	C&M Digitals (P) Ltd.
Proofreader:	Ellen Brink
Indexer:	Gloria Tierney
Cover Designer:	Glenn Vogel
Marketing Manager:	Christy Guilbalt

CONTENTS

ACKNOWLEDGMENTS

———————◆———————

There are numerous persons who I would like to thank for making this work possible. First and foremost, I want to thank Jerry Westby, senior acquisitions editor at SAGE Publications, for continuing to see value in my projects. Over the years, he has not only supported my projects but also served as my mentor in the book publishing industry. Thanks, Jerry. I also thank Eve Oettinger and Karen Wiley for their assistance during the publication process. For her fine work editing the manuscript, I thank Jovey Stewart. At Penn State Harrisburg, I thank Steve Peterson, director of the School of Public Affairs, for his continuing support of my research efforts. And, as usual, I thank the library staff at Penn State Harrisburg for locating every foreign, dated, and obscure source that was required to complete this project. On the home front, I thank my wife, Monica and our three boys, Jini, Jalen, and Julian, for putting up with me being secluded in my office for long periods of time to write yet another book. I love you all very much and, hopefully, one day you will understand why I felt a need to write this series of books on race, ethnicity, and crime.

I also would like to thank the following reviewers for their insightful comments:

Dr. Tim Berard, Kent State University

Dr. Lori Guevara, Fayetteville State University

Dr. George E. Higgins, University of Louisville

Dr. David A. Jenks, University of West Georgia

Dr. Paul Knepper, University of Sheffield

Dr. Ihekwoaba Onwudiwe, Texas Southern University

Dr. Ernest Uwazie, California State University, Sacramento

Dr. Patricia Warren, Florida State University

PREFACE

U p front, I must acknowledge my intellectual debt to three scholars whose work opened my eyes to both the international nature of race, ethnicity, and crime and to the significance of the colonial model to contextualizing that issue. First, a decade ago I was introduced to Ineke Marshall's pioneering volume, *Minorities, Migrants, and Crime: Diversity and Similarity Across Europe and America* (1997). The edited volume examined, in detail, several European countries and how race and ethnicity influenced justice system outcomes. For someone who thought that race and crime issues in the United States were the most pressing ones globally, I quickly realized how wrong I was and became fascinated with the international nature of the issue. In short, the book was my initial glimpse into the magnitude of the problem.

A few years earlier, I was exposed to Becky Tatum's work on the colonial model (see Tatum, 1994), which I was first introduced to through the work of Frantz Fanon during my early exposition into Black history (see Fanon, 1963, 1967a, 1967b). But, for the most part, my initial introduction to the model was shortsighted and did not look past its application to Black involvement in crime in America. More recently, through the work of Biko Agozino (see Agozino, 2003), I have continued to be enlightened concerning the role that colonization has—and continues to play—in the fate of racial and ethnic minorities in justice systems around the world. Collectively, I view the work of these scholars, along with the increasing body of international scholarship that I uncovered during my last book project (Gabbidon, 2007), as the impetus for the current volume.

As for my specific aims with this project, I had two. First, I sought to determine the depth of the race and crime problems facing countries around the world. That is, I wanted to explore the "international dilemma" related to race, crime, ethnicity, and justice. So, what is this "dilemma"? In the most basic sense, this terminology represents the fact that racial and ethnic minorities are often overrepresented in justice systems around the world. Ah, but it is really not that simple. Too often those observing these patterns engage in simplistic, shortsighted, and ahistorical analyses to contextualize this issue (Rushton, 1995). In reality, the real "dilemma" is that because of early European colonization based on White supremacy, racial and ethnic minorities have been and continue to be the populations often targeted for justice system attention. This notion is developed further throughout the chapters by providing an expanded historical analysis for each of the countries profiled. Why spend so much time on history? Well, because in some ways colonization and its brutal processes have much to do with explaining the status of racial and ethnic minorities. And no, this is not about making excuses for modern day criminals; it is more about understanding why, in many instances, racial and ethnic minorities are in disadvantaged positions within their societies, and Whites are more often than not in privileged positions. And if one follows the criminological literature, societal conditions and one's status within society have seemingly always played a role in who becomes enmeshed in justice systems (Gabbidon, 2007).

Second, as Marshall and her contributors did in her earlier volume (for another important early volume, see Tonry, 1997), I wanted to examine the similarities and differences of the experiences of racial and ethnic minorities in the profiled countries. In short, does the role of colonization impact all societies the same? Or, are some racial and ethnic minorities able to "recover" from colonization and other forms of oppression (e.g., apartheid). And, if so, what were the factors associated with such a recovery.

Before I move on to the contents of the work, I must admit, to date, this was my most challenging book project. Why? Because I had to learn about countries I knew very little about. In all honesty, for some reason, because of my diverse background as a naturalized American citizen who was born in Wolverhampton, England, to Jamaican parents, I was under the illusion or, more correctly, delusion, that I had an advantage in writing this work. I was wrong. In fact, considering that much of my formal education has been American-centered (for an early discussion of this limitation, see Friday, 1973, p. 155), the sobering reality is that I was likely at a disadvantage writing this work. Nevertheless, it has been a labor of love that has been both challenging and draining. The work has been the most draining because I'm human, and reading about the plight of Black people around the world is, at times, depressing. There is no other way to describe it. The fact that I can get on an airplane and fly to any one of the countries profiled herein and become the target of criminal justice attention—just because of the color of my skin—makes me angry but also sad that color matters just about everywhere. There is no escaping it. Thus, if anything, writing this book has made me a bit more cynical. After reading the book, I suspect some readers might also feel the same way. While this was not my intent in writing this work, I also do not see a reason to "sugar coat" the daily reality of countless people of color who interact with justice systems around the globe.

BOOK CONTENTS

In terms of the content and scope of the book, it was never my intention to write the "definitive" work on the topic. Rather, I saw this effort as, hopefully, serving as a bridge to continue the dialogue on the international nature of race and crime concerns (see most recently, Bosworth, Bowling, & Lee, 2008; Kalunta-Crumpton & Agozino, 2004; Phillips, 2008; Saleh-Hanna, 2008; Weber & Bowling, 2008; Webster, 2007). To do so, I concentrated on the following five countries: Great Britain, United States, Canada, Australia, and South Africa. I selected them for two key reasons. First, colonization and/or some other repressive system previously were a part of or remain a chief characteristic of each society. More specifically, since I was curious about the role of colonization and/or other repressive forms of government and their initial and long-term effects on crime and justice for racial and ethnic minorities (especially Black people), I decided to examine the said countries. Second, in the absence of being able to visit the countries, I needed to select ones where national official data were accessible via the Internet. Further, I wanted to focus on countries where there had been some discussion about race and crime issues. As such, there would be ample scholarship available to gauge the nature of the problem in each respective country.

There are seven chapters in the book. Chapter 1 introduces and provides background information on the colonial model, which is the theory used to contextualize race and crime in each of the countries. It is important to note that this book is not a formal test of colonial theory. In my view, the perspective simply serves as the best criminological theory to understand the development of race and crime issues in the countries profiled herein. The next five chapters profile the individual countries, each starting with a deep, historical

review of the society, followed by a presentation of contemporary demographic information on the citizens of the country. Each chapter concludes
with a discussion of race and crime-related issues specific to each country.
Finally, Chapter 7 concludes with some general thoughts on the international
nature of race and crime issues as well as noting some similarities and differences of the challenges being faced by each country.

REFERENCES

Agozino, B. (2003). *Counter-colonial criminology: A critique of imperialist reason.*
    London: Pluto Press.
Bosworth, M., Bowling, B., & Lee, M. (2008). Globalization, ethnicity and racism: An
    introduction. *Theoretical Criminology, 12,* 263–273.
Fanon, F. (1963). *The wretched of the Earth.* New York: Grove Press.
Fanon, F. (1967a). *Black skin, white masks.* New York: Grove Press.
Fanon, F. (1967b). *A dying colonialism.* New York: Grove Press.
Friday, P. C. (1973). Problems in comparative criminology: Comments on the feasibility
    and implications of research. *International Journal of Criminology and Penology, 1,*
    151–160.
Gabbidon, S. L. (2007). *Criminological perspectives on race and crime.* New York:
    Routledge.
Kalunta-Crumpton, A., & Agozino, B. (Eds.). (2004). *Pan-African issues in crime and
    justice.* Aldershot, UK: Ashgate.
Marshall, I. H. (Ed). (1997). *Minorities, migrants, and crime: Diversity and similarity
    across Europe and America.* Thousand Oaks, CA: Sage.
Phillips, C. (2008). Negotiating identities: Ethnicity and social relations in a young
    offenders' institution. *Theoretical Criminology, 12,* 313–331.
Rushton, J. P. (1995). Race and crime: An international dilemma. *Society, 32,* 37–41.
Saleh-Hanna, V. (Ed.). (2008). *Colonial systems of control: Criminal justice in Nigeria.*
    Ottawa: University of Ottawa Press.
Tatum, B. L. (1994). The colonial model as a theoretical explanation of crime and delin-
    quency. In A. T. Sulton (Ed.), *African American perspectives on Crime causation,
    criminal justice administration and prevention* (pp. 33–52). Engelwood, CO: Sulton
    Books.
Tonry, M. (Ed.). (1997). *Ethnicity, crime, and immigration: Comparative and cross-
    national perspectives.* Chicago: University of Chicago Press.
Weber, L., & Bowling, B. (2008). Valiant beggars and global vagabonds: Select, eject,
    immobilize. *Theoretical Criminology, 12,* 355-375.
Webster, C. (2007). *Understanding race and crime.* Berkshire, UK: McGraw-Hill/Open
    University Press.

ONE

INTRODUCTION

——•◆•——

After studying race and crime for more than a decade, one thing has become apparent to me: The colonial model is vastly underappreciated as a potential perspective to contextualize the overrepresentation of racial and ethnic minorities in justice systems around the globe—particularly in post-colonial societies. This short introduction first provides an overview of the terms *race* and *ethnicity* and then briefly discusses the perils of using crime statistics to examine race and crime cross-nationally. An overview of the colonial perspective is next. As noted in the Preface, though not a direct test of the perspective in the countries profiled in the subsequent chapters, only those readers wearing blinders will miss the connection between colonialism and race, ethnicity, crime, and justice.

RACE AND ETHNICITY

The terms *race* and *ethnicity* are both used to classify groups. Race is seen as the more distinctive marker, by some. The term has a long history and was created by the Swedish botanist Carolus Linnaeus. Johan Fredrich Blumenbach built on Linnaeus's work by separating the people into five races: Ethiopian (African or Negroid), Mongolian (Asian), American (Native American), Malaysian (Pacific Islander), and Caucasian (White). This division set off an infinite debate as to whether there are truly distinct races. That is, do the differences between the assorted groups make them so distinct that they warrant a different classification? DNA research suggests that there are some slight biological differences between groups; as examples, mostly Blacks get sickle-cell anemia, and some drugs have been found to be more effective for some groups than others (Soo-Jin Lee, 2005). However, this does not prove that the use of racial distinctions is appropriate, especially considering that the Human Genome Project has found "that humans share 99.9% of their genetic makeup" (Soo-Jin Lee, 2005, p. 2133).

In light of the existing scientific evidence, social scientists have tended to view race as a social construct or a manufactured term simply used to identify people based on their color. In the United Kingdom, for example, scholars use inverted quotes when they use the term race to signify that it has no scientific meaning (e.g., "race"). Other countries, such as Canada, minimize the use of race altogether, especially in government documents. In a similar vein, residents in the United States referred to as "people of color" or racial and ethnic minorities, are considered "visible minorities" in Canada. As you will see in subsequent chapters, countries tend to handle the use of the term differently. In addition, each country has its separate racial classification scheme for who is deemed a racial minority.

Ethnicity also is a term used to classify groups. However, rather than being based on color or rooted in biological notions, although genetic inheritances and certain traits are characteristic of ethnic groups, the term ethnicity relates more to a group's cultural traditions, geographical ties, common language, and other commonalities. Both terms are imprecise and have their limitations. Nonetheless, over time, they have been used as a means to better understand the experience of assorted groups across the globe. Hence, the terms are reluctantly used herein under a similar guise.

CRIME STATISTICS

In his recent work, *A Suitable Amount of Crime* (2004), Criminologist Nils Christie discusses the numerous problems with the term "crime." He writes: "Crime does not exist. Only acts exist, acts often given different meanings within various social frameworks. Acts, and the meaning of them, are our data" (Christie, 2004, p. 3). While Émile Durkheim would certainly take issue with this statement, one can see where Christie's insight would be particularly useful when examining crime cross-nationally. Thus, the way one society defines or views a certain offense could influence the extent of the problem, as compared to another society. So, if one country is obsessed with marijuana use and criminalizes it while another country does not, there could be a "wave" of crime noted in one country, whereas in the other country because of its different approach, no crime "wave" would exist. Taking this example one step further, if one country decided to crack down on street crimes in communities heavily populated by racial and ethnic minorities, as opposed to crime in other areas where the majority group tends to predominate in crime commission, then statistics will distort the nature and scope of the crime problem (see Chambliss, 2004). In this case, "the crime problem" will be translated into the "minority crime problem." Scholars around the globe have noted this racialization of crime (Brewer & Heitzig, 2008; Chan & Mirchandani, 2001; Covington, 1995; Hall, Critcher, Jefferson, Clarke, Roberts, 1978; Knepper, 2008). However, Christie's important work reminds us of this important consideration, as we try to make sense of race, ethnicity, and crime across the globe. The next section provides an overview of the colonial perspective.

THE COLONIAL MODEL

So why provide an overview of the colonial perspective? The answer is simple: Because criminologists have excluded the perspective from the criminological canon, and though most students of crime and justice reading this text are likely to have heard of the word colonialism, they likely have never been exposed to a criminological perspective based on it. Colonialism, as defined in a recent dictionary, refers to "control by one power over a dependent area or people" (*Merriam-Webster,* 2004, p. 142). Several decades ago, the work of Frantz Fanon (1963, 1967a, 1967b) popularized the perspective among scholars seeking to contextualize the relations between Blacks and Whites in colonial and post-colonial societies (Agozino, 2005; Blackwell, 1971; Hall et al., 1978; Killingray, 1986; Onyeozili, 2004; Saleh-Hanna, 2008). In the United States, for example, the perspective caught on because of its adoption by those associated with the Black power movement (Carmichael & Hamilton, 1967). But it was the early work of Blauner (1969) and Staples (1974, 1975) who applied the theory to Blacks and the work of Moore (1970) and Mirande (1987) who applied it to Latinos in America. More recently, several scholars have revived the colonial perspective (Agozino, 2003; Bosworth, 2004; Bosworth & Flavin, 2007; Saleh-Hanna, 2008).

So how does colonialism help contextualize race and crime? Well, to answer that question, one has to first understand the nature of colonialism. In recent years, the work of Becky Tatum (1994, 2000a) has served as one of the best articulations of the perspective because it addresses more traditional forms of colonialism and also the notion of internal colonialism, which represents another way that colonialism takes hold and transforms a society, and from the native's perspective, usually for the worse.

Tatum's Articulation of the Colonial Model

Drawing on the work of Fanon, Tatum's (1994) conception of the colonial model, classifies it as a socio-psychological perspective. That is, it combines sociological factors with psychological factors to explain the etiology of crime and justice in society. More specifically, the perspective examines the intersection of "structural oppression, alienation and three adaptive forms of behavior—assimilation, crime or deviance, and protest" (p. 34). Early in her articulation of the model, Tatum (1994) points to the connection between colonialism, race, and crime:

> Individuals who are the victims of social, economic and political oppression are likely to perceive that oppression and as a result, develop feelings of alienation in which the commission of crime is an adaptive response. In the colonial model, race or color is the ascriptive criterion for differences in subjection to situations of oppression. (p. 34)

Taking a holistic view of colonization, Tatum breaks the process down into four phases. The first phase usually involves the invasion of one racial group into the country of another. More often than not, this involves a minority group (typically Whites) who takes control of the majority population (typically people of color). Here, as aptly noted by Tatum, "The primary objective of the outsiders is to obtain valuable economic resources" (p. 35). Initially, though, the foreign group seeks to trade with the natives, but at some point they dupe the natives into settling for things of minor value in exchange for more valuable resources (e.g., gold). In some instances, when the natives refuse to trade with the foreigners, they decide to pursue brutal measures (e.g., torture, biological warfare) to extract the desired resources (see Crosby, 1972; De Las Casas, 1992 [1552]; Smolenski & Humphrey, 2005).

Following the initial phase of colonization, it becomes apparent that the colonizers have their minds set on controlling the country. But to do so, they have to think of a strategy that will allow a small minority (of foreigners) to rule over a society mostly composed of native people. The answer, which is the second phase of colonization, is the formation of a colonial society. So what does such a society involve? Tatum (1994) argues that colonial societies "can be characterized by three interrelated processes of cultural imposition, cultural disintegration, and cultural recreation" (p. 35). Once a colonial society is in place, there is the presumption that the culture of the colonizer is superior to that of the colonized. As such, the colonizer spares no expense in minimizing the culture of the colonized. Going even further, the colonizer uses their resources to constrain, transform, and destroy native customs, culture, and values (p. 35). In fact, as part of this phase, the colonizer "paints the native as the quintessence of evil" and uses "Zoological" terms to describe the natives (p. 35). It makes no difference whether the natives are rebelling against the colonizer to secure the most basic rights. The colonized remains "the problem." Finally, during this phase, the society's history is rewritten and the language is changed to that of the colonizer. And, in the end, any reference to native culture and history is seen as referring to "primitive societies" and reference to the colonizer is considered a reference to a more "advanced society" (for an excellent discussion of this phenomenon, see Ani, 1994). By this point in the colonization process, White supremacy has firmly taken hold and has become a key aspect of the colonial "machinery."

Tatum's (1994) third phase of the colonial process involves the governing of the natives by "representatives of the colonizer's power" (p. 36). Thus, even though the colonized represents the majority population, the colonizer uses the police and military as the maintainers of the peace or, more accurately, as controlling "agents of the state." The final phase of the colonization process, as outlined by Tatum (1994), involves "the development of a caste system based on racism" (p. 36). With White supremacy firmly in place, the development of such a caste system is imminent. Such a caste system results in a society where all those in the privileged groups (typically Whites) have access to the best jobs and other opportunities that assist them in flourishing within the colonial society. On the other hand, the worst jobs and least stable opportunities are reserved for those in the non-privileged groups (typically people of color). This, in the end, secures the place of the colonized at the lowest stratum of society. Tatum, though, clearly notes the role of class in the colonial structure. Tatum (1994) writes:

> All colonized individuals do not suffer from the oppressive conditions of the social order to the same extent. In fact, the bourgeois faction of the colonized

people represent the part of the colonized nation that is necessary and irreplaceable if the colonial machine is to run smoothly . . . Although their position in society is lower than the colonizers of any status, in regards to the natives, they enjoy more privileges. As a result, there is an antagonism which exists between the native who is excluded from the advantages of colonialism and his counterpart who manages to turn colonial exploitation to his account . . . The colonialists make use of this antagonism by pitting one against the other. (p. 37)

During the implementation of the four phases of the colonial process, there are psychological consequences for the colonized. The late psychologist Bobby Wright addressed the role of psychology in the context of Black people in oppressed situations. In doing so, he coined the term "mentacide" to describe the use of psychology to destroy a group (particularly Black people around the world). In his words, mentacide is the "deliberate and systematic destruction of a group's minds with the ultimate objective being the extirpation of the group" (Wright, 1994 [1984], p. 20). Fanon, in his classic volume, *Black Skin, White Masks,* provides additional foundation for understanding the consequences of what amounts to psychological warfare. From the need of Blacks to prove that they are not intellectually inferior to Whites, to the desire of Black women for White men and Black men for White women, both solely in an effort to get as "close" as possible to the colonized, Fanon's (1967a) work gets at the heart of the alienation and "confusion" that results from colonization (see also, Akbar, 1992 [1984]).

Essentially, there are several ways that alienation or estrangement from one's culture that colonization relates to race, crime, and justice. One way alienation manifests itself is in self-hate. This relates both to the individual and the group. For example, hating oneself can result in one not wanting to identify with who they are or, depending on complexion, "passing" so that others see the individual as being a member of the colonizing group. This results in the shedding of one's native identity. But the self-hatred extends beyond the self and includes the group. The alienation can result in attacks against the people that the colonized now hate the most: *themselves.* Of this, Tatum (1994) writes: "Here, the individual hates in others those characteristics he hates most in himself" (p. 38).

Another type of alienation results in racial groups being estranged from each other. This produces racial violence which is often based on a mutual lack of trust that results in paranoia. Cultural alienation typically results in the colonized distancing themselves from their native language and history. And the significance of this is that language and history are at the heart of one's culture (Tatum, 1994; Wilson, 1993; Woodson, 1990 [1933]). So, for example, English and Spanish are not simply languages, they are usually taught in the context of the cultures in which they originated. Thus, in surrendering their language and history, the colonized have all but surrendered to the colonizer. Once this has occurred, what Tatum refers to as alienation against the creative praxis has likely taken hold. Consequently, "The colonized believes that he does not have a measure of choice, influence or control in what happens to him or in what he can make happen. The colonized is full of self-doubt and has a readiness to compromise" (Tatum, 1994, p. 39).

Alienation, though, does not result in solely one response or reaction. In fact, there are three well-known responses that are a product of alienation that results from colonialism. The first reaction is assimilation. Here the colonized simply want to acquiesce and become a fully ascribed citizen of the new colonial society—however delusional that might be considering the premise underpinning colonialism. In short, because White supremacy is often at the heart of colonialism, the colonizer will *never* be considered equal in a colonial society. Thus, for example, if a crime is committed and the two suspects include a colonizer and a "fully assimilated" native person, the suspicion will still fall on the colonized; because, after all, their full assimilation does not remove the badge of being considered the "quintessence of evil."

An additional response to alienation is that some of the colonized will become angry because of their situation, but rather than lash out against the colonizer, the colonized internalizes their feelings. Consequently, the actions result in what has been called "horizontal violence" and related mayhem as opposed to "vertical violence," which would involve attacks against the colonial regime. Pouissant (1972, 1983) and Jeff (1981) also have used such an analysis to explain why there is so much so-called Black-on-Black violence in the African American community. Taking this supposition a bit further, Wilson (1990) has argued that Whites benefit from such violence. In fact, as he sees it, the presence of such self-destructive behavior in Black communities actually serves to further the dominance of Whites. The self-destructive behaviors result in a host of problems that produce elevated levels of "alcoholism, psychiatric disorders, hypertension and crime—particularly homicide—among the oppressed" (Tatum, 1994, p. 40).

Alienation can also result in revolutionary actions against the colonizer. This is when the colonized feels that it is time to "fight back." And, to do so, they have to gain back their identity by reclaiming their history and culture (Tatum, 1994). Lastly, at times, this results in what Tatum describes as "vertical counter violence" or the repression of attacks by the colonizer. Whereas others might stand back and take the often unprovoked attacks by the colonizer, those "radicals," as they are referred to, refuse to take the attacks lying down. In essence, given the means by which the colonizer took rule and maintains its rule (through violence), it is clear, at least to those who respond to alienation this way, that violence must be met with violence and, at times, even greater violence. This, in essence, is the only avenue to true liberation from colonial power.

Another form of colonialism is internal colonialism, which occurs after the initial colonial process. This type of colonialism is described in the next section.

Internal Colonialism

The notion of "internal" colonialism is best understood by first examining "external" colonialism. For the most part, this first part of this chapter outlined external colonialism. Feagin and Feagin (2003) provide us with a clear definition, stating that: "External colonialism [is] the worldwide imperialism of certain capitalist nations, including the United States and European nations" (p. 34). Moreover, Feagin and Feagin (2003) note that it has been estimated that:

> Europe's capitalistic expansion has affected non-European peoples across the globe since the fifteenth century . . . [And] until very recently the greater part of the world's population, not belonging to the white race (if we exclude China and Japan), knew only a status of dependency on one or another of the European colonial powers." (pp. 34–35)

But even after the decline of external colonialism in these countries, neocolonialism or the economic dependence on European powers continued (Feagin & Feagin, 2008). Thus, in practice, internal colonialism is the product of external colonialism. But, in general, internal colonialism "refers to when the control and exploitation of non-European groups in the colonized country passes from whites in the home country to white immigrant groups within the newly independent country" (Feagin & Feagin, 2003, p. 35). One thing remains intact throughout this transition: Whites remain in power.

Internal colonialism has been used to explain the plight of racial and ethnic minorities in America. It has also been used to contextualize race and crime in America (see Blauner, 1969, 1972; Bosworth & Flavin, 2007; Staples, 1974, 1975, 1976a, 1976b). More recently, though, scholars have linked "global colonialism of the past . . . [to] social structures of oppression that persist into the present" (Feagin and Feagin, 2003, p. 35). This is referred to by Ramon Grosfoguel and Chloe Georas as "coloniality" or as (presented in Feagin & Feagin, 2003):

> a situation of cultural, political, and ethnic oppression for subordinated racial and ethnic groups without the existence of an overt colonial administration and its trappings of legal segregation. Official decolonization does not mean an end to coloniality, the colonial hierarchies of racial and ethnic oppression often remain (p. 35).

In their analysis, they point to the subordinate status of African Americans and Puerto Ricans as prime examples of the continuing effects of colonialism.

Within an internal colonial system, this subordinate status manifests itself in three forms: economic subordination, political subordination, and social subordination (Tatum, 1994). Economic subordination can be seen in the slave system that developed in America. This system created a wealth imbalance that has yet to subside (see Anderson, 1994; Shapiro, 2004; Shapiro & Oliver, 1995). Other forms of economic subordination have been experienced by every racial and ethnic group who has arrived in America. Today, this subordination continues to place racial and ethnic minorities (particularly Blacks and Latinos) in those jobs in the secondary labor market that are fraught with low wages and job instability. As such, as Crutchfield (1989) has argued in the past, and more recently along with colleagues (Crutchfield, Matsueda, & Drakulich, 2006), it produces a situation conducive to high levels of social disorder in communities of color.

During the past few centuries, political subordination has been exercised through a variety of means used to restrict minority voter participation in the political process. This has come in the form of poll taxes, literacy tests, voter intimidation, redistricting, etc. In all instances, the aim has been to impede the progress of minorities. But as a consequence of these discriminatory practices, Blacks and other racial and ethnic minorities have had little influence on matters related to crime and justice, which even in contemporary times produces inequities in regard to which groups become the focus of criminal justice

attention and who, in the end, will bear the brunt of punitive "get tough" policies (Beckett & Sasson, 2003; Tonry, 1995).

Social subordination also takes hold during internal colonialism. Here, as
before during external colonialism, Whites—in all aspects of humanity—are
believed to be the superior group, while racial and ethnic minorities are considered inferior. Thus, racial and ethnic groups (particularly indigenous people, Blacks, and Latinos) have been separated from their culture and "have
little knowledge of their cultural heritage, languages, or religions" (Tatum,
1994, p. 47). The one exception here is that "while White ethnic groups often
have to give up their traditional ways in order to assimilate into dominant society, there is no intentional action to destroy their cultural heritage, languages,
religions or traits" (Tatum, 1994, p. 47).

In the end, because of their status in the social order, Whites are less
likely to want to interact with or live near racial or ethnic minorities. This
results in segregation (Massey & Denton, 1993) that has been shown to have
a negative impact on both the level of crime *and* the perception of crime levels (Hurwitz & Peffley, 1997; Krivo, Peterson, & Karafin, 2006; Quillian &
Pager, 2001) in communities of color. Why? The problem is not that crime is
high because racial and ethnic minorities are not living next to Whites. It is
more a product of them being separated from good basic services and
employment opportunities, which, in many cases, have long left inner city
communities (to suburban areas) where large numbers of the most disadvantaged people reside (Wilson, 1987, 1996).

The Current Status of the Colonial Model

On the whole, as evidenced by this review of the perspective, the colonial model has much to offer those seeking to contextualize race and crime.
Even so, the perspective has not fully lived up to its promise, with most
direct tests of its components only showing limited support (Austin, 1983,
1987; Tatum, 2000b). The key problem with these tests, though, is the fact
that colonialism should be considered an antecedent variable. That is, colonialism is the instigator of the problems that are now prevalent in communities of color around the globe (Bosworth & Flavin, 2007; Saleh-Hanna,
2008). Bachman's (1992) conceptual scheme presented in Figure 1.1 best
outlines this. In the figure we see that colonialism precedes other conditions
that are often contextualized using other criminological perspectives such as

Figure 1.1   Theoretical Model for American Indian Homicide.

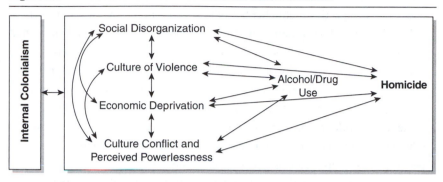

SOURCE: From Bachman, R., *Death and Violence on the Reservation*, Greenwood Publishing Group, Inc., Westport, CT., 1992. Reprinted with permission.

social disorganization, culture conflict, economic deprivation, etc. Thus, in some ways, there will always be considerable limitations when scholars attempt to directly test the colonial perspective (Tatum, 1994). Likewise, other criminological perspectives also will have difficulty fully explaining race, ethnicity, and crime because they exclude measures that attempt to measure colonialism (Gabbidon, 2007).

Besides the difficulty testing the perspective, the colonial model also does not account for why some people who experience one form of alienation may or may not respond differently. In addition, unlike race, class issues are not adequately addressed by the perspective (Tatum, 1994). The perspective also doesn't address how Whites deal with alienation and class issues within a colonial society. So, for example, if a White person becomes alienated in a colonial society because they are on the lower stratum of White society, does this result in deviant behavioral responses? This is simply not addressed by the theory. In line with this limitation, the theory also doesn't address to what extent one's phenotype might play in the colonial order (Tatum, 1994, 2000c). Even with the foregoing limitations, the perspective has much to offer those seeking to contextualize race, ethnicity, and crime.

CONCLUSION

This chapter reviewed the colonial perspective. Though neglected, the perspective provides essential context for understanding the true origins of elevated levels of social problems, including crime, in colonial and post-colonial societies. The perspective highlights both the social and psychological aspects of colonialism and how groups react to the conditions and the alienation that result from exposure to a system that inherently preaches the superiority of the colonizer and the inferiority of the colonized. But to further highlight the direct relevance of the theory to those students of race, ethnicity, crime, and justice, the next five chapters are devoted to countries in which the colonial model has something to offer crime and justice scholars. The next chapter examines race, ethnicity, crime, and justice in Great Britain which, of the countries profiled, became the key instigator of global colonialism. As such, it seems only fitting to first examine how race, crime, and ethnicity has played out in the country that shaped the colonial machinery.

REFERENCES

Agozino, B. (2003). *Counter colonial criminology: A critique of imperialist reason.* London: Pluto Press.

Agozino, B. (2005). Crime, criminology and post-colonial theory: Criminological reflections on West Africa. In J. Sheptycki & A. Wardak (Eds.), *Transnational and comparative criminology* (pp. 117–134). London: Glass House Press.

Akbar, N. (1992). *Chains and images of psychological slavery.* Jersey City, NJ: New Mind Productions. (Originally published in 1984.)

Anderson, C. (1994). *Black labor, white wealth: The search for power and economic justice.* Edgewood, MD: Duncan & Duncan.

Ani, M. (1994). *Yurugu: An African-centered critique of European cultural thought and behavior.* Trenton, NJ: Africa World Press.

Austin, R. L. (1983). The colonial model, subcultural theory and intragroup violence. *Journal of Criminal Justice, 11,* 93–104.

Austin, R. L. (1987). Progress toward racial equality and reduction of black criminal violence. *Journal of Criminal Justice, 15,* 437–459.

Bachman, R. (1992). *Death and violence on the reservation: Homicide, family violence, and suicide in American Indian populations.* New York: Auburn House.

Beckett, K. A., & Sasson, T. (2003). *The politics of injustice: Crime and punishment in America* (2nd ed.). Thousand Oaks, CA: Sage.

Blackwell, J. E. (1971). Race and crime in Tanzania. *Phylon, 32,* 207–214.

Blauner, R. (1969). Internal colonialism and ghetto revolt. *Social Problems, 16,* 393–408.

Blauner, R. (1972). *Racial oppression in America.* New York: Harper & Row.

Bosworth, M. (2004). Theorizing race and imprisonment: Toward a new penalty. *Critical Criminology, 12,* 221–242.

Bosworth, M., & Flavin, J. (Eds.). (2007). *Race, gender, and punishment: From colonialism to the war on terror.* New Brunswick, NJ: Rutgers University Press.

Brewer, R. M., & Heitzeg, N. A. (2008). The racialization of crime and punishment. *American Behavioral Scientist, 51,* 625–644.

Carmichael, S., & Hamilton, C. V. (1967). *Black power: The politics of liberation in America.* New York: Vintage.

Chan, W., & Mirchandani, K. (2001). *Crimes of colour: Racialization and the criminal justice system in Canada.* London: Broadview Press.

Christie, N. (2004). *A suitable amount of crime.* London: Routledge.

Covington, J. (1995). Racial classification in criminology: The reproduction of racialized crime. *Sociological Forum, 10,* 547–568.

Crosby, A.W. (1972). *The Columbian exchange: Biological and cultural consequences of 1492.* Westport, CT: Greenwood Press.

Crutchfield, R. D. (1989). Labor stratification and violent crime. *Social Forces, 68,* 489–512.

Crutchfield, R. D., Matsueda, R. L., & Drakulich, K. (2006). Race, labor markets, and neighborhood violence. In R. D. Peterson, L. J. Krivo, & J. Hagan (Eds.), *The many colors of crime: Inequalities of race, ethnicity, and crime in America* (pp. 199–220). New York: NYU Press.

De Las Casas, B. (1992). *The devastation of the Indies: A brief account.* Baltimore: John Hopkins University Press. (Original work published in 1552.)

Fanon, F. (1963). *The wretched of the earth.* New York: Grove Press.

Fanon, F. (1967a). *Black skin, white masks.* New York: Grove Press.

Fanon, F. (1967b). *A dying colonialism.* New York: Grove Press.

Feagin, J. R., & Feagin, C. B. (2003). *Racial and ethnic relations* (7th ed.). Upper Saddle River, NJ: Prentice Hall.

Gabbidon, S. L. (2007). *Criminological perspectives on race and crime.* New York: Routledge.

Hall, S., Critcher, C., Jefferson, T., Clarke, J., & Roberts, B. (1978). *Policing the crisis: Mugging, the state, and law and order.* London: Macmillan.

Hurwitz, J., & Peffley, M. (1997). Public perceptions of race and crime: The role of racial stereotypes. *American Journal of Political Science, 41,* 374–401.

Jeff, M. F. X. (1981). Why black-on-black homicide? *The Urban League Review, 6,* 25–34.

Killingray, D. (1986). The maintenance of law and order in British colonial Africa. *African Affairs, 85,* 411–437.

Knepper, P. (2008). Rethinking the racialization of crime: Rethinking black first. *Ethnic and Racial Studies, 31,* 503–523.

Krivo, L. J., Peterson, R. D., & Karafin, D. L. (2006). Perceptions of crime and safety in racially and economically distinct neighborhoods. In R. D. Peterson, L. J. Krivo, & J. Hagan (Eds.), *The many colors of crime: Inequalities of race, ethnicity, and crime in America* (pp. 237–255). New York: NYU Press.

Massey, D. S., & Denton, N. A. (1993). *American apartheid: Segregation and the making of the underclass.* Cambridge, MA: Harvard University Press.

Merriam-Webster collegiate dictionary (11th ed.). (2004). Springfield, MA: Merriam–Webster.

Mirande, A. (1987). *Gringo justice.* Notre Dame, IN: University of Notre Dame Press.

Moore, J. W. (1970). Colonialism: The case of the Mexican Americans. *Social Problems, 17*, 463–472.

Onyeozili, E. C. (2004). Gunboat criminology and the colonization of Africa. In A. Kalunta-Crumpton & B. Agozino (Eds.), *Pan-African issues in crime and justice* (pp. 205–227). Aldershot, UK: Ashgate Publishing.

Pouissant, A. F. (1972). *Why blacks kill blacks.* New York: Emerson Hall Publishers.

Pouissant, A. F. (1983). Black-on-black homicide: A psychological–political perspective. *Victimology, 8*, 161–169.

Quillian, L., & Pager, D. (2001). Black neighbors, higher crime? The role of racial stereotypes in evaluation of neighborhood crime. *American Journal of Sociology, 107*, 717–767.

Saleh-Hanna, V. (2008). (Ed.). *Colonial systems of control: Criminal justice in Nigeria.* Ottawa: University of Ottawa Press.

Shapiro, T. M. (2004). *The hidden cost of being African American: How wealth perpetuates inequality.* New York: Oxford University Press.

Shapiro, T. M., & Oliver, M. L. (1995). Black wealth, white wealth: A new perspective on racial inequality. New York: Routledge.

Smolenski, J., & Humphrey, T. J. (2005). (Eds.). *New world orders: Violence, sanction, and authority in the Colonial Americas.* Philadelphia: University of Pennsylvania Press.

Soo-Jin Lee, S. (2005). Racializing drug design: Implications of pharmacogenomics for health disparities. *American Journal of Public Health, 95*, 2133–2138.

Staples, R. (1974). Internal colonialism and black violence. *Black World, 23*, 16–34.

Staples, R. (1975). White racism, black crime and American justice: An application of the colonial model to explain crime and race. *Phylon, 36*, 14–22.

Staples, R. (1976a). *Introduction to black sociology.* New York: McGraw-Hill.

Staples, R. (1976b). Race and family violence: The internal colonialism perspective. In L. E. Gary & L. P. Brown (Eds.), *Crime and its impact on the black community* (pp. 85–96). Washington, DC: Howard University's Institute for Urban Affairs and Research.

Tatum, B. L. (1994). The colonial model as a theoretical explanation of crime and delinquency. In A. T. Sulton (Ed.), *African American perspectives: On crime causation, criminal justice administration and prevention* (pp. 33–52). Englewood, CO: Sulton Books.

Tatum, B. L. (2000a). Toward a neocolonial model of adolescent crime and violence. *Journal of Contemporary Criminal Justice, 16*, 157–170.

Tatum, B. L. (2000b). *Crime, violence and minority youths.* Aldershot, UK: Ashgate.

Tatum, B. L. (2000c). Deconstructing the association of race and crime: The salience of skin color. In M. W. Markowitz & D. Jones-Brown (Eds.), *The system in black and white: Exploring the connections between race, crime, and justice* (pp. 31–46). Westport, CT: Praeger.

Tonry, M. (1995). *Malign neglect: Race, crime, and punishment in America.* New York: Oxford University Press.

Wilson, A. N. (1990). *Black-on-black violence: The psychodynamics of black self-annihilation in service of white domination.* New York: Afrikan World Infosystems.

Wilson, A. N. (1993). *The falsification of Afrikan consciousness: Eurocentric history, psychiatry and the politics of white supremacy.* New York: Afrikan World Infosystems.

Wilson, W. J. (1987). *The truly disadvantaged. The inner city, the underclass and public policy.* Chicago: University of Chicago Press.

Wilson, W. J. (1996). *When work disappears: The world of the new urban poor.* New York: Knopf.

Woodson, C. G. (1990). *The mis-education of the Negro.* Chicago: African World Press. (Originally published in 1933.)

Wright, B. E. (1994). *The psychopathic racial personality and other essays.* Chicago: Third World Press. (Originally published in 1984.)

Figure 2.1   Contemporary Map of the United Kingdom

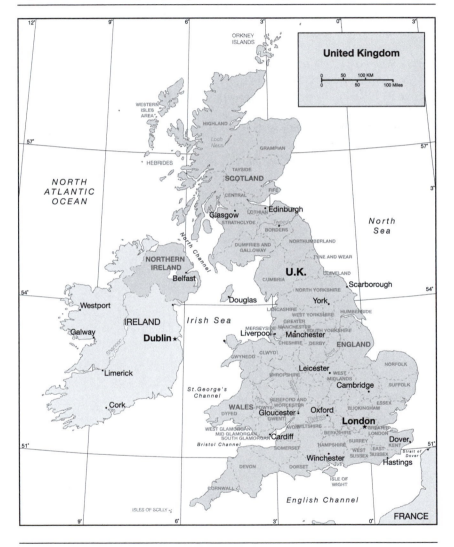

TWO

GREAT BRITAIN

————•◆•————

CHAPTER OVERVIEW

This chapter examines the nature of race, ethnicity, and crime in Great Britain. The chapter begins with an exploration of Britain's vast history. After noting the sparse number of Black people and other ethnic groups in Great Britain prior to World War I, the chapter reviews the experiences of those persons referred to as "new ethnic minorities" who largely immigrated to Great Britain in the first half of the 20th century. Besides their general experience in the country, the chapter also examines how crime intersected with their everyday experience. The chapter closes by examining how racial and ethnic minorities are currently faring in the British criminal justice system.

EARLY HISTORY

Great Britain has a long and, at times, controversial history. Given the vastness of its history, this overview will only provide brief highlights of its early history before turning to a brief review of immigration to England and the more contemporary history which represents the period in which Black and Asian immigrants, who are largely the focus of the later segment on race and crime, began to arrive in the country. Before turning to history, though, we need to be clear about what areas comprise Great Britain. Great Britain (or the United Kingdom) is composed of England, Scotland, and Wales (see Figure 2.1). Therefore, while this chapter will emphasize racial and ethnic issues in England, it is important to understand that there is more to Great Britain than England.

Locating the origins of the first people who lived in Britain has been a difficult challenge for scholars. It is known that people have lived in the area for tens of thousands of years. But determining the earliest inhabitants has been based on speculation since the early inhabitants did not have a written language. At about 3000 B.C., historians seem to agree that the Beaker people inhabited land that is now Great Britain. This assertion is supported by archeologists who have found pottery that is linked to the Beaker culture (Rodrick, 2004). In fact, it is also believed that the well-known Stonehenge structure was constructed around the same period as the existence of the Beaker society. Even so, there is no firm evidence to suggest that they built the massive stone structures. The other group who entered Britain prior to the invasion of the Romans was the Celts, who came from Northern Europe. This is especially notable because the Celts were described as "warlike, courageous, and aggressive" (Rodrick, 2004, p. 14). Such a description would be indicative of the character of Great Britain for centuries to come. On the whole, though, it was not until the invasion of the Roman Empire that there is any consistent historical record of Great Britain.

Before the movement to conquer Great Britain, the Roman Empire, under the direction of Julius Caesar, invaded England during the years 55 B.C. to 54 B.C. Later, from 43 A.D. to 45 A.D., the Romans conquered the British and ruled over the country. Not until the year 409 A.D. did Roman rule come to an end. Over the next millennia the British Empire would become notable through its continuing warring with various groups and also through its unprovoked, aggressive military actions. More to the point, there was the ongoing desire to explore, expand, and control territories across the globe. And the country's success in regard to expansion and colonization has been unmatched. Not only do the contents of the chapters in this book, which profile countries in which there was formerly British rule and/or continues to be British influence, serve as a testament to that fact, but going further there is much truth to the oft-used statement that, at its zenith, "the sun never set on the British Empire" (see Figure 2.2). The breadth and longevity of the British Empire seems to support this notion considering that, by 1900, 25% of the population of the human race still fell under its rule (Daniell, 1998).

In a classic work on immigrants in England, Cunningham (1897) places the Norman Conquest led by William the Conqueror as the beginning of considerable immigration to the country. He writes:

> In each century since the Norman Conquest a considerable number of immigrants have flocked to our country; the stream has never, so far as we can see,

Figure 2.2   The British Empire in 1897

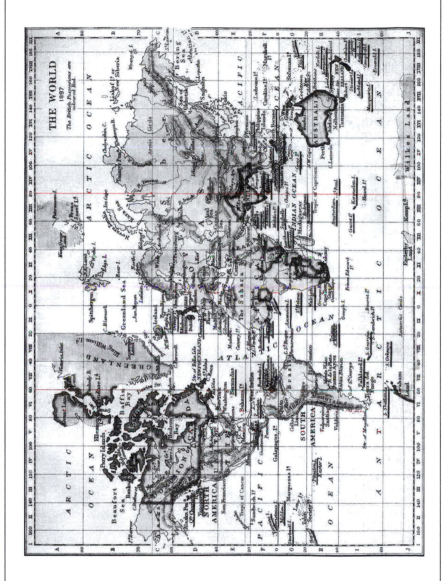

NOTE: Outlining and underlining denote territories under British rule.

entirely ceased to flow; but there have been periods when the ingress has been more frequent and rapid than at other times. (p. 10)

Moreover, based on the contributions in the arts and industrial advancements, those who came after the Norman invasion were considered by Cunningham (1897) to be "by far the most important invasion of Alien immigrants into England" (p. 17).

The next significant phase of immigration outlined by Cunningham took place in the late Middle Ages. During this period, immigrants came from all over Europe and elsewhere. Their biggest influence was in the area of economics. In fact, during this period, immigrants such as Jews and Lombards (of German origin) taught the English about business and finance. Cunningham (1897) writes: "The Jews were our earliest money-lenders. In the twelfth century they formed a widely spread agency for loans throughout the country; the Jewries were to be found in most of the principal towns . . ." (p. 70). Unfortunately, because of their prosperity, and their "foreign" beliefs in a Christian society, Cunningham notes:

> Their status marked them out for the animosity of their neighbours, and served to augment the aversion evoked by racial peculiarities and extortionate dealings; while the evils of their position were aggravated by the zeal of the crusaders, which gave rise to frequent onslaught of Jewish infidels. (p. 70)

As a consequence of this poisonous sentiment, Jews were expelled from England in 1290 A.D. After which, the Lombards carried on the business activities previously dominated by the Jews.

The immigration to England continued in the later Middle Ages and slowed somewhat during the Protestant Reformation because "there was little reason for persons engaging in secular callings to migrate from one country to another on religious grounds; the conditions were so far alike that this motive would hardly come into play" (Cunningham, 1897, p. 137). Over time, though, other immigrants came to England from all over the world. For example, Panayi (1994) notes that, from 1815 to 1945, "The total number of immigrants making their way to Britain . . . surpassed that of all those who had entered the country since the Norman invasion" (p. 23). And even though the presence of Blacks in Britain dates to the Roman occupation (Edwards & Walvin, 1983), there is little substantive discussion of people of African and Asian descent in England until the mid-20th century. So, even though there were slave systems run and profiteered by the English colonial powers (Williams, 1944), very few Africans were integrated into English life until the 1950s. We will examine this more closely below.

"New Ethnic Minorities" in Britain

Allen (1971) provides an early examination of the plight of Asians (Indian and Pakistani descent) and West Indian or "new minorities" in Britain. Prior to World War II, very few people of color lived in Britain. Those who did were comprised primarily of "seamen, servicemen, workers brought to fill labor shortages in the two wars, peddlers, as well as students, businessmen, and professionals" (Allen, 1971, p. 33). And their early tenure in Britain was not without its hardships and encounters with racial violence. While racial violence against Blacks stretches back to the 1870s, Jenkinson (1993) recounts the riots of 1919 that took place in nine British port towns. Though not totally a result of race, Jenkinson notes the racial dimension of the riots was based on the concern that large numbers of West Indian and West African immigrants were competing with Whites for employment opportunities.

Following World War II, many West Indians who served in the war settled in Britain and with their wages purchased homes and/or used the money to secure their education. Pakistanis did the same, but many of them also started restaurants, grocery stores, and lodging houses (Allen, 1971, p. 35). In many instances these groups were segregated into various areas of Britain. By 1958, Bowling (1996) estimates there were 125,000 migrants from the Caribbean in Britain. However, the number of immigrants from the Caribbean and India increased dramatically after this initial wave of immigration. And with this increased immigration, hostility increased from racists who did not welcome colored immigration. Violence against colored people in the Notting Hill area of London in the late 1950s brought increasing attention to race relations. Of this violence, Allen (1971) writes:

> Attacks on colored people and their homes brought counterattacks; as tension mounted, groups of whites, in some cases organized, threatened and manhandled colored passers-by to such an extent that the police advised colored people to keep off the streets, provided protection for those returning home from work at night, and increasing policing of the areas. (p. 39)

The magnitude and details of the Notting Hill "racial riots" was captured in a recent article by Travis (2002). For five nights violence raged in Britain with the "white working class mob out to get the 'niggers'" (Travis, 2002, p. 1). The violence was so brutal that many felt that it was reminiscent of the violence in the American South. While recently released secret files show that officers tried to downplay the racial element of the situation, it was clear that race was a central element of the riots. The notorious White gang, the Teddy

Boys, was at the center of the mayhem. Recent released information from the Metropolitan Police force makes clear that:

> The disturbances were overwhelmingly triggered by 300-to-400-strong "Keep Britain white" mobs, many of them Teddy boys armed with iron bars, butcher's knives and weighted leather belts, who went "nigger hunting" among the West Indian residents of Notting Hill and Notting Dale. The first night left five black men lying unconscious on the pavements of Notting Hill. (Travis, 2002, p. 2)

In the end, the rioting subsided but because many Blacks were also charged with offenses and officials denied the role of race, Blacks lost faith in the Metropolitan police (Travis, 2002; Pilkington, 1996), which, as discussed later, still remains.

Even with the increased sensitivity to race relations, the following year several White youths killed a West Indian carpenter, which continued the concerns regarding the treatment of racial minorities. But, rather than deal with the seed of the problem—racism—the government debated the utility of limiting immigration (Pilkington, 1996). Why? Because it was thought by many that immigrants were the problem. Thus, limiting their immigration into the country would minimize the problem. Such a simplistic and misguided analysis of the problem deflected the attention away from the real issue of the entrenched racism of Britons. Nevertheless, the Commonwealth Immigrants' Act of 1962 was enacted and restricted the immigration of persons from Britain's former colonies. Overall, though, the period leading up to this legislation is summarized best by Bowling (1996) who noted that the attitudes of Whites in Britain was merely the transformation of "colonial racism . . . into indigenous racism" (p. 187).

Given the flawed approach used to handle the racism in Britain, it was no surprise when anti-Black racial disturbances "occurred in the West Midlands towns of Dudley and Smethwick in 1962, in Wolverhampton in 1965 . . . and in Accrington and Leeds in 1964" (Bowling, 1996, p. 192). In the 1960s, Pakistanis were also targeted for racial violence. This racial violence produced more dialogue among politicians. However, the dialogue continued to center on race-based immigration restrictions. By the beginning of the 1970s, the dialogue reached a point where, under the Conservative government, the 1971 Immigration Act was passed, superseding all the other previous legislation. In short, the act made distinctions between those who were "patrials" and those who were "non-patrials." Describing the difference between the two statuses, Bowling (1996) writes that:

> A patrial refers to persons born, adopted, naturalized or registered in the UK, or born of parents one of whom had UK citizenship, or one of

whose grandparents had UK citizenship. Patrials had the right to live in Britain, while non-patrials holding British passports did not . . . . (p. 193)

Ironically, not long after the passage of the Act, Uganda's controversial president Idi Amin expelled 50,000 Asian Indians from his country many of whom were eligible to immigrate to Britain. In total, Britain received 27,000 of the expatriates (Bowling 1996).

As the debate on immigration policies continued with fiery rhetoric coming from figures such as Enoch Powell, a controversial Conservative Party member of Parliament, there also continued to be racial violence against people of color in Britain. Inquiry after inquiry revealed that ethnic minorities were victims of racial violence or racial harassment (Bowling, 1996, pp. 204–208). Reports from the late 1970s also revealed that, because of the discrimination that racial minorities were encountering throughout British society, they had become a disadvantaged population (Smith, 1977). Thus, it was apparent there had been little to no enforcement of earlier legislative enactments aimed at reducing discrimination in British society (Bindman, 2000).

CONTEMPORARY HISTORY

Within the last 30 years, there has continued to be interest in the progress of ethnic minorities in Britain (Jones, 1996). After conducting surveys to assess the progress of racial and ethnic minorities since the mid-1960s (see Brown, 1984; Daniel, 1968; Smith, 1977), the Policy Studies Institute and the Social and Community Planning Research continued the trend in 1994 by conducting the Fourth National Survey of Ethnic Minorities in Britain (Modood, Berthoud, Lakey, Nazroo, Smith, Virdee, & Beishon, 1997). So had things improved for ethnic minorities in Britain by the mid-1990s? Well, this is a crucial question considering that, by the 1990s, the diversity in Britain had expanded. Table 2.1 shows the British population as it was noted in the 1991 census. The largest share of ethnic minorities in Britain remained those classified as Black and Indian, but the British Pakistani population had also grown significantly.

The survey begins with information on the marital status of the British population which revealed that, except for the Caribbean at 39%, 60 to 70%

Table 2.1   Population of Britain, by Ethnicity, 1991

White	51,874,000
Black Caribbean	500,000
Black African	212,000
Black other	178,000
Indian	840,000
Pakistani	477,000
Bangladeshi	163,000
Chinese	157,000
Other Asian	198,000
Other groups	290,000

SOURCE: Modood, T. et al. (1997).

of Whites and other ethnic groups members reported being married (Modood et al., 1997, p. 25). In line with these figures, those of Caribbean origin had, at every age category, the highest rate of persons who were "living as married." Turning to employment-related issues, the survey found that, of all the varying groups of women in British society, Caribbean women were in the workforce at higher levels than women of other groups and that they had higher levels of education and greater fluency in English (see Table 2.2). As for unemployment, women were generally better off than men but, as noted by Tables 2.3 and 2.4, varied in the levels of unemployment by ethnic group.

Unemployment concerns are further highlighted by the unemployment figures in inner cities where a large share of Caribbean and Pakistani/Bangladeshi reside (see Table 2.5). For those males who work, Table 2.6 reveals that in general Whites have higher average weekly wages than ethnic minorities. However, there is some variation among ethnic minorities, with African Asians only averaging a £1 less than Whites. Moreover, the Chinese reported having the same average weekly earnings as Whites. This was a marked increase over the previous survey in which Chinese respondents reported the lowest average weekly earnings (Modood et al., 1997, p. 113).

Table 2.2   Economic Activity Score of Women, by Education and Fluency in English

16- to 59-Year-Olds, Not in Full-Time Education	White	Caribbean	Indian/ African Asian	Pakistani/ Bangladeshi
A-level or degree	65	72	65	(74)
Good English	46	63	55	27
Fair English	n.a.	n.a.	46	14
Poor English	n.a.	n.a.	32	5

SOURCE: Modood, T. et al. (1997).

NOTE: The economic activity score counts full-time work as 1, part-time work or looking for work as ½. Figure in parentheses denote small cell size.

Table 2.3   Rate of Male Unemployment, by Highest British Qualification

	Cell Percentages			
	White	Caribbean	Indian/ African Asian	Pakistani/ Bangladeshi
All Ages				
None	19	42	20	46
O-level or Equivalent	11	31	20	36
A-level or higher	12	23	12	17
Under 35 Years Old				
None	19	61	18	45
O-level or equivalent	13	28	20	43
A-level or higher	15	28	18	15
All Under 35 Years Old	15	34	20	37
Weighted count	*869*	*512*	*721*	*394*
Unweighted count	*778*	*821*	*700*	*641*

SOURCE: Modood, T. et al. (1997).

Table 2.4   Rate of Female Unemployment, by Highest British Qualification

			Cell Percentages	
	White	*Caribbean*	*Indian/ African Asian*	*Pakistani/ Bangladeshi*
All Ages				
None	13	19	13	54
O-level or equivalent	10	16	10	(42)
A-level or higher	7	16	12	(18)
Under 35 Years Old				
None	(36)	(36)	21	(65)
O-level or equivalent	14	16	13	(45)
A-level or higher	8	22	14	(20)
All Under 35 Years Old	13	24	15	43
Weighted count	*716*	*506*	*483*	*116*
Unweighted count	*687*	*390*	*446*	*141*

SOURCE: Modood, T. et al. (1997).

NOTE: Figures in parentheses denote small cell sizes.

The survey also provided insights on neighborhoods and housing issues. One aspect of the survey that specifically highlighted the character of the neighborhoods in which Whites and ethnic groups resided asked respondents to report the various problems within the local area. Table 2.7 reveals that of all the groups Caribbean residents seemed to live in the areas with the most environmental concerns. In terms of home ownership, in general, ethnic groups lived in owner-occupied residences slightly less than Whites (see Table 2.8). However, there was considerable variation among ethnic groups, with ownership ranging from 50% among Caribbean residents to 85% among the Indian population (Modood et al., 1997, p. 199).

Table 2.5   Unemployment in Inner Cities

	Cell Percentages		
	Inner London and Inner Metropolitan	*Outer London and Outer Metropolitan*	*Rest of England and Wales*
Unemployment Rate			
Men			
White	26	14	12
Caribbean	41	30	23
Indian/African Asian	27	15	20
Pakistani/Bangladeshi	47	40	31
Women			
White	12	8	8
Caribbean	18	18	17
Indian/African Asian	14	12	11
Pakistani/Bangladeshi	48	42	31
Percentage of Ethnic Group That Lives in These Areas			
White	11	18	71
Caribbean	41	32	27
Indian/African Asian	11	61	29
Pakistani/Bangladeshi	28	42	30

SOURCE: Modood, T. et al. (1997).

So more than a decade after the work of Modood and his colleagues, how are ethnic minorities doing in Britain? Table 2.9 (from the 2001 census) reveals that ethnic minorities represented 7.9% of the British population; the various Asian groups represented 4% of the population; and Blacks represented 2% of the population. Most of the non-White people in Britain continue to live in large urban areas. For example, "Seventy-eight per cent of Black Africans and 61 per cent of Black Caribbeans lived in London" (*Focus on Ethnicity & Identity,*

(Text continues on page 33)

Table 2.6   Male Employees' Earnings (Base: Male Full-Time Employees)

Column Percentages

	White	Caribbean	Indian	African Asian	Pakistani	Bangladeshi	Chinese	Hindu	Sikh	Muslim	All Ethnic Minorities
Weekly Earnings											
Less than £116	4	1	9	6	13	41	2	6	9	23	7
£116–£192	14	16	22	18	39	29	23	20	24	31	22
£193–£289	33	36	30	34	28	10	24	31	38	24	31
£290–£385	19	28	16	13	9	8	15	15	14	10	18
£386–£500	14	11	13	4	4	4	25	6	10	6	10
More than £500	15	8	10	25	6	8	10	23	5	6	12

	White	Caribbean	Indian	African Asian	Pakistani	Bangladeshi	Chinese	Hindu	Sikh	Muslim	All Ethnic Minorities
Mean Weekly Earnings[1]	£336	£306	£287	£335	£227	£191	(£336)	£338	£249	£223	£296
					Column Percentages						
Weighted count	541	255	154	152	76	42	72	162	84	140	751
Unweighted count	493	179	169	144	113	78	42	154	84	233	726
Refusal/ can't say	6	6	29	16	26	8	3	21	31	18	16

SOURCE: Modood, T. et al. (1997).

NOTE: 1. Means calculated from mid-points of 16 earnings bands.

Table 2.7   Reported Environmental Problems in Local Area

	White	Caribbean	Indian/ African Asian	Pakistani	Bangladeshi	Chinese	All Ethnic Minorities
Percentage Saying Area Has Problems With							
Run-down gardens, run-down open space or vacant properties	23	33	19	24	15	21	24
Graffiti or vandalism	26	33	20	31	26	31	27
Litter/rubbish	24	27	19	34	19	23	24
Dog mess	44	57	33	41	35	34	42
Vermin infestation	5	14	8	13	13	11	11
Condition of paths/roads	35	31	18	20	6	16	21
Street parking	44	41	33	36	27	28	35

SOURCE: Modood, T. et al. (1997).

Table 2.8   Housing Tenure

Column Percentages

	White	Caribbean	Carib/white	S Asian/white	Indian	African Asian	Pakistani	Bangladeshi	Chinese	All Ethnic Minorities
Owner-occupier	67	50	58	70	85	84	79	48	54	66
Council tenant	20	33	29	10	7	10	13	35	19	20
Housing assoc. tenant	3	13	7	3	2	2	2	10	5	6
Private tenant	9	4	6	17	7	5	6	8	22	7
Weighted count	2800	992	230	132	605	408	404	132	184	3245
Unweighted count	2799	751	150	119	628	417	657	311	104	3251

SOURCE: Modood, T. et al. (1997).

Table 2.9   Population, by Ethnic Group, 2001

United Kingdom

	(Numbers)	*Total Population (Percentages)*	*Non-White Population (Percentages)*
White	54,153,898	92.1	
Mixed	677,117	1.2	14.6
Indian	1,053,411	1.8	22.7
Pakistani	747,285	1.3	16.1
Bangladeshi	283,063	0.5	6.1
Other Asian	247,664	0.4	5.3
All Asian or Asian British	2,331,423	4.0	50.3
Black Caribbean	565,876	1.0	12.2
Black African	485,277	0.8	10.5
Black Other	97,585	0.2	2.1
All Black or Black British	1,148,738	2.0	24.8
Chinese	247,403	0.4	5.3
Other ethnic groups	230,615	0.4	5.0
All minority ethnic population	4,635,296	7.9	100.0
All population	58,789,194	100	

SOURCES:
Census, April 1991 and 2001, Office for National Statistics; Census, April 2001, General Register Office for Scotland; Census, April 2001, Northern Ireland Statistics and Research Agency.

NOTES:
Census ethnic group questions: In both 1991 and 2001 respondents were asked to which ethnic group they considered themselves to belong. The question asked in 2001 was more extensive than that asked in 1991, so that people could tick "Mixed" for the first time. This change in answer categories may account for a small part of the observed increase in the minority ethnic population over the period. Different versions of the ethnic group question were asked in England and Wales, in Scotland and in Northern Ireland, to reflect local differences in the requirement for information. However, results are comparable across the UK as a whole. Non-White ethnic group includes all minority ethnic groups but not White Irish or Other White groups.

2005, p. 3). Non-Whites continued to have higher unemployment rates than Whites. Figure 2.3 shows that Bangladeshi men and those with mixed backgrounds had the highest unemployment rates. Blacks (both of African and Caribbean origin) along with Pakistanis also had high levels of unemployment. Of those who were unemployed, the Indian, Chinese, and Whites, in general, were employed in professional occupations at rates higher than other groups. Figure 2.4 illustrates that Blacks, Bangladeshis, and Pakistanis have the lowest number of persons in professional occupations. Turning to health concerns, Asians (Pakistanis and Bangladeshis) "reported the highest rates of 'not good' health in 2001" (*Focus on Ethnicity & Identity,* 2005, p. 11). The Chinese respondents reported the lowest levels of "not good" health (see Figure 2.5).

This brief summary tells us that the transition of Britain to a multi-ethnic society was a difficult one. Once the mass immigration from Britain's colonies began, the society began to fear the worst. And as a result, ethnic and racial minorities were targeted for racial harassment and violence. In the next section, after reviewing some basic crime and justice figures, the chapter examines the crime and justice-related issues pertaining to ethnic minorities in Britain.

CRIME AND JUSTICE IN BRITAIN

In Britain, The Home Office, which "is the government department for leading the national effort to protect the public from terrorism, crime, and anti-social behaviour" (see www.homeoffice.gov.uk/about-us), is also the entity that generates crime-related reports. Before examining the reports related to ethnic minorities, crime, and justice, the general crime trends in Britain are reviewed. In Britain, the two official sources of crime are police records and the British Crime Survey (BCS) that has surveyed residents annually since 1982 regarding their victimization. The BCS is based on interviews "of adults aged 16 and over living in private households in England and Wales" (Nicholas, Kershaw, & Walker, 2007, p. 8). The latest BCS is based on 47,203 face-to-face interviews (Nicholas et al., 2007). The findings from these two sources can be gleaned from the annual *Crime in England and Wales* report released by the Home Office. The most recent report is for 2006/2007.

Tables 2.10 and 2.11 show the details of the results from the BCS and the number of crimes recorded by the police. In 2007, the BCS noted no change in crime, while the data from the police indicated a 2% decrease in crime. Over the last decade, though, according to BCS data, "crime has fallen by 42 per

Figure 2.3   Unemployment Rates: By Ethnic Group and Sex, 2002/2003

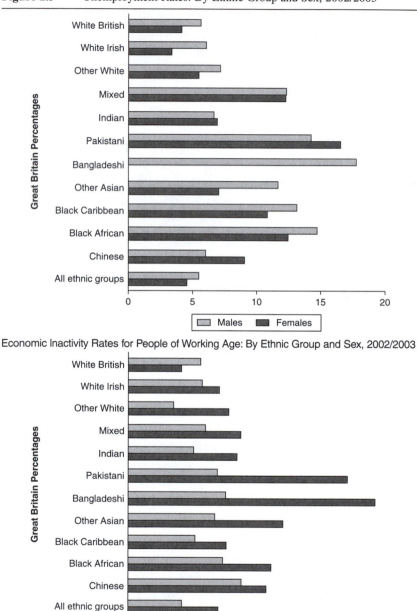

SOURCE: Annual local area Labour Force Survey 2002/2003. Office for National Statistics.

NOTES: The unemployment rate is based on the ILO definition as a percentage of all economically active. Economic inactivity rates are expressed as a proportion of the working age population. Figures are not shown where samples are too small for reliable estimates.

Figure 2.4   People in Professional Occupations as a Percentage of All in
Employment: By Ethnic Group, 2002/2003

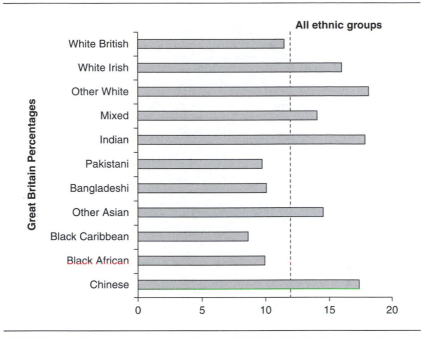

SOURCE: Annual local area Labour Force Survey, 2002/2003. Office for National Statistics.

NOTES: White Irish group has been derived using the annual local area Labour Force Survey
national identity variables.

Self-employment occupation and industry rates are as a proportion of all in employment.

The Other Black group is omitted from the charts as the sample size is too small for reliable
estimates.

cent, representing over eight million fewer crimes, with domestic burglary and
all vehicle thefts falling by over half (59% and 61% respectively) and violent
crime falling by 41 per cent during this period" (Nicholas et al., 2007, p. 11).
A similar long-term trend can be seen in recorded crime (see Figures 2.6 and
2.7). As in most countries, property crimes dominate crime and victimization
statistics in Britain. For the BCS, they represent 78% of the victimization and
73% of police recorded crime (Nicholas et al., 2007, p. 17). As for violent
crimes, they represented 22% of the crimes reported in the BCS and 19% of
the police-recorded crime. Using the figures from police-recorded crime, there
were 755 homicides (inclusive of murder, manslaughter, and infanticide),
13,780 rapes (of women and men), 101,370 robbery offenses, 622,044
burglary offenses, and 765,056 offenses against vehicles, and 194,302 drug
offenses in 2006/07 (Nicholas et al., 2007, pp. 36–39).

Figure 2.5   Age Standardized "Not Good" Health Rates, by Ethnic Group
                     and Sex, April 2001

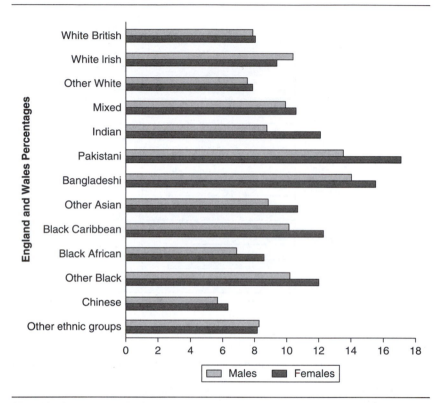

SOURCE: Census, April 2001. Office for National Statistics: Health Survey for England. The
Health of Minority Ethnic Groups 1999, TSO (London 2001).

NOTES: The question in the 2001 Census was "Over the last twelve months would you say your
health has been Good, Fairly Good, or Not Good." Age standardized rates allow comparisons
between populations with different age structure. The method used here is direct standardisation
using the European Standard Population.

While the crime and justice situation in Britain appears "rosy," the next section examines the situation of ethnic minorities. It begins with an overview of
the general history of ethnic minorities and concludes by focusing on the most
pressing contemporary issues related to ethnic minorities, crime, and justice.

ETHNIC MINORITIES, CRIME, AND JUSTICE

From the earlier review of the history of ethnic minorities in Britain, it is obvious
that from the very beginning they were not accepted with open arms. Moreover,

Table 2.10   Number of Crimes and Risk of Being a Victim Based on BCS
Interviews in 2005/06 and 2006/07

	BCS			
	2005/06 Ints	*2006/07 Ints*	*% Change*	*Statistically Significant Change[1]*
Number of Crimes (000s)				
All household crime	6,792	7,101	5	
Vandalism	2,731	2,993	10	★★
Domestic burglary	733	726	−1	
All vehicle thefts	1,731	1,689	−2	
All Household Acquisitive	**4,060**	**4,108**	**1**	
All personal crime	4,120	4,186	2	
Theft from the person	576	574	0	
BCS violence[2]	2,349	2,471	5	
With injury	*1,227*	*1,270*	*3*	
With no injury	*1,121*	*1,201*	*7*	
All Personal Acquisitive	**2,082**	**2,035**	**−2**	
All BCS Crime	10,912	11,287	3	n/a
Percentage Risk of Being a Victim Once or More				
All household crime	18.1	18.9		★★
Vandalism	7.6	7.9		
Domestic burglary	2.4	2.5		
All vehicle thefts[3]	7.5	7.5		
All personal crime	6.4	6.6		
Theft from the person	1.2	1.2		

(Continued)

Table 2.10 (Continued)

	BCS			
	2005/06 Ints	2006/07 Ints	% Change	Statistically Significant Change[1]
BCS violence	3.3	3.6		★
With injury	*1.8*	*2.0*		
With no injury	*1.6*	*1.8*		
All BCS crime	23.5	24.4		★★
Unweighted base	*47,729*	*47,138*		

SOURCE: Nicholas, S., Kershaw, C., & Walker, A. (2007).

NOTES:

1. Statistical significance cannot be calculated for the change in the number of incidents of all BCS crime.
2. All BCS violence includes wounding, robbery, assault with minor injury and assault without injury. Snatch theft is no longer included so the estimates will vary from those previously published. See Glossary for more information about violence categories.
3. Results for 'all vehicle thefts' are based only on households owning, or with regular use of a vehicle. It includes thefts of vehicles, thefts from vehicles and attempts of and from vehicles.
4. A discrepancy may appear between trends in incidence rates (total numbers of offenses) and prevalence rates (the proportion of the population victimized once or more) due to repeat victimization.

not only were they not accepted, they quickly became the targets of racial harassment and violence as evidenced by the riots in the early and mid-20th century. Racism was obviously at the heart of the attacks. Since the 19th century prior to the arrival of any significant numbers of Blacks and Asians, racism, both official (through state agencies such as the police) and unofficial (through negative interactions with citizens or lack thereof), was perpetrated against Irish and Jewish citizens (Payani, 1994, pp. 102–127). Once other immigrants such as West Indians and Indians began to appear in large numbers, they too encountered racism that was often brutal in nature and either carried out under the auspices of the police or through inaction on the part of the police (Payani, 1994). For Blacks, this racism culminated in the 1919 riots and, even more so, with the riots of the 1950s. In both instances, Blacks were not only targeted for racial attacks, but were the ones who bore the brunt of the arrests (Jenkinson, 1993; Travis, 2002); and

Table 2.11   Number of Crimes Recorded by the Police in 2005/06 and 2006/07

Offence Group	Number of Crimes (Thousands)[1]		% Change 2005/06 to 2006/07
	2005/06	2006/07	
Violence against the person (VAP)	1,059.6	1,046.4	−1
Most serious VAP[2]	21.0	19.2	−9
Other violence against the person—with injury[3]	541.3	500.3	−8
Other violence against the person—with no injury[4]	497.3	527.0	6
Sexual offences	62.1	57.5	−7
Most serious sexual crime[5]	47.2	43.7	−7
Other sexual offences	14.9	13.8	−8
Robbery	98.2	101.4	3
Domestic burglary	300.5	292.3	−3
Other burglary	344.6	329.8	−4
Offences against vehicles	792.8	765.1	−4
Other theft offences	1,226.2	1,181.0	−4
Fraud and forgery	232.8	199.8	−14
Criminal damage	1,184.3	1,185.1	0
Total property crime	4,081.2	3,953.0	−3
Drug offences	178.5	194.3	9
Other offences	75.6	75.6	0
Total recorded crime	5,555.2	5,428.3	−2

SOURCE: Nicholas, S., Kershaw, C., & Walker, A. (2007).

NOTES:

1. The figures given in the table are the latest available. Therefore they may differ slightly from figures published in previous bulletins.
2. Most serious violence against the person includes homicide and serious wounding.
3. Other offences against the person—with injury comprises less serious wounding, threats or conspiracy to murder, causing or allowing death of a child or vulnerable person and procuring illegal abortion.
4. Other offences against the person—with no injury includes harassment, endangering railway passengers, possession of weapons, other offences against children, and common assault (where there is no injury).
5. Most serious sexual crime encompass rape, sexual assault, and sexual activity with children.

Figure 2.6   Trends in All BCS Crime, 1981 to 2006/2007

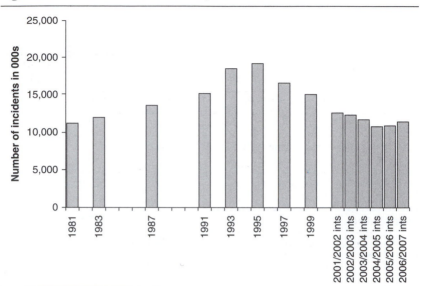

SOURCE: Nicholas, S., Kershaw, C., & Walker, A. (2007).

Figure 2.7   Trends in All BCS Crime, 1981 to 2006/2007

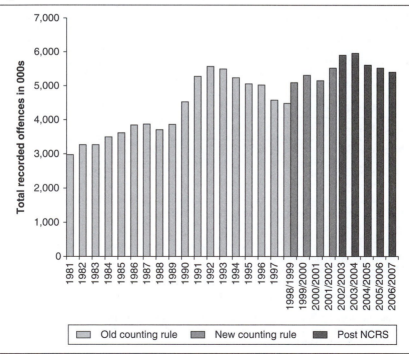

SOURCE: Nicholas, S., Kershaw, C., & Walker, A. (2007).

furthermore, as a testament to the indifference to the brutality encountered by Blacks, "There were few examples of white people coming to the assistance of their black neighbors" (Pilkington, 1996, p. 179).

Since this early history, there has been continuing scholarly emphasis on racial harassment and violence and ethnic minority overrepresentation in crime and justice. Tracing the development of the ethnic minority (focusing on Blacks) and crime literature, Kalunta-Crumpton (2006) argues that the first study to highlight "the disproportionate representation of black people in crime data" (p. 1) was found in Frederick McClintock's work, *Crimes of Violence* (1963). Examining violent crimes in London, his study found that "the number of black people convicted for violent crimes increased from 6.2 percent in 1950 to 13 percent in 1960" (Kalunta-Crumpton, 2006, p. 2).

The 1970s continued to find citizens and scholars concerned about both racial harassment and the overrepresentation of Black people in crime and justice statistics (Smith, 1977, pp. 310–319). But the fact that in the 1970s "the government even rejected the idea that police and other statutory bodies should be covered by the 1976 Race Relations Act because it would slur their good name" (Phillips & Bowling, 2002, p. xv) suggests the government was, at the time, disingenuous about its efforts to crack down on racism. On the heels of the continuing attacks on Blacks and their continuing ascendancy to the role as "the problem" as it related to crime and justice, noted cultural theorist Stuart Hall (for an excellent review of his background, see Jackson & Brown Givens, 2006, pp. 152–171) and his colleagues Chas Critcher, Tony Jefferson, John Clarke, and Brian Roberts produced their classic work, *Policing the Crisis: Mugging, the State, and Law and Order* (1978). The text, which was a comprehensive look not just at the crime of "mugging," but, as the authors themselves note in their introduction:

> We are concerned with "mugging" but as a social phenomenon, rather than as a particular form of street crime. We want to know what the social causes of "mugging" are. But we argue that this is only half—less than half—of the "mugging" story. More important is why British society *reacts to mugging* [italics added] in the extreme way it does . . . . (p. vii)

In general, Hall et al., (1978) were concerned about the "moral panic" concerning robberies in the United Kingdom in the 1970s. To understand their perspective, they provided the following description of moral panics:

> When the official reaction to a person, groups of persons or series of events is *out of all proportion* [italics added] to the actual threat offered, when

"experts," in the form of police chiefs, the judiciary, politicians and editors
perceive [italics added] that threat in all but identical terms, and appear to talk
"with one voice" of rates, diagnoses, "sudden and dramatic" increases (in
numbers or events) and "novelty," above and beyond that which a sober, real-
istic appraisal could sustain, then we believe it is appropriate to speak of the
beginnings of a *moral panic* [italics added]. (p. 16)

Of particular concern was the way in which the press perpetuated the moral
panic and, in the process, how muggings became synonymous with Blacks.
Their analysis discussed how both the media and police, through their actions,
"structured" and "amplified" situations that turned into moral panics. They take
a social constructionist approach arguing that once the media and police start to
believe a problem exists even if there is not one it nonetheless is real to them
and they take action. In the case of "muggings," that action resulted in Blacks
(particularly Black youth) and Asians being vilified as the problem and (bor-
rowing from Tatum's work described in the Introduction) being seen as the
"quintessence of evil." This view resulted in them being the target of police
attention in the form of harassment and other unscrupulous police activities.
And mirroring the United States, the type of crime of most concern (and most
exaggerated in terms of frequency) to White Britons were interracial crimes,
particularly those involving Blacks victimizing Whites (Hall et al., 1978). With
this watershed publication, Hall and his colleagues provided a new way of
thinking about the place of ethnic minorities in British society.

Throughout the 1980s and 1990s, the Home Office continued to produce
reports that highlighted the disproportionate representation of racial and ethnic
minorities in arrest and prison statistics (for an excellent summary, see Kalunta-
Crumpton, 2006). The period also produced more racial conflicts and riots (e.g.,
the 1981 Brixton riot). And, as one might expect, there continued to be commissions and reports produced that called for changes in British society (Bowling &
Phillips, 2002, pp. 9–11). Notably, Section 95 of the Criminal Justice Act of 1991
facilitated the study of race and crime by requiring the following:

(1) The Secretary of State shall in each year publish such information as he
considers expedient for the purpose of: (a) enabling persons engaged in the
administration of justice to become aware of the financial implications of their
decisions; or (b) facilitating the performance of such persons of their duty to
avoid discriminating against any persons on the ground of race or sex or any
other improper ground. (2) Publication of under subsection (1) above shall be
effected in such a manner as the Secretary of State considers appropriate for

the purpose of bringing the information to the attention of the persons concerned. (www.homeoffice.gov.uk/rds/section951.html)

It was likely as a product of the aforementioned legislative mandate that scholars also began to seriously delve into the issue of ethnic minorities, crime, and justice, producing a wide range of publications on racial harassment (Bowling, 1993, 1998; Gordon, 1986; Virdee, 1997), youth crime (Landau, 1981; Landau & Nathan, 1983; Pitts, 1993), and critical overviews of the complexity of the issue (Banks, 1999; Cook & Hudson, 1993; Gilroy, 1987; Gordon, 1988; Holdaway, 1997, Waters, 1990). By no means comprehensive, this selection of scholarship illustrated the diversity of the research that began to appear related to ethnicity and crime in Britain. It set the stage for the scholarship that began to appear in 21st century. Some of this research is discussed below.

Ethnic Minorities and Crime: 2000 and Beyond

Macpherson and Policing Ethnic Minorities

It was fitting that the major issues related to ethnic minorities and crime in the beginning of the 21st century was a problem that plagued Britain for the last 50 years of the 20th century. Racial harassment and violence and the role of the police in curtailing these incidents remained a central focus of the scholarly literature (see generally, Bowling & Phillips, 2003). The central focus of the discourse was the 1993 murder of Stephen Lawrence. Lawrence, an 18-year-old Black student hoping to become an architect, was fatally stabbed while waiting for a bus (Bowling & Phillips, 2002). It is believed that six or seven White youths who shouted "what, what nigger" crossed the road to attack Lawrence and inflict the mortal wounds that severed arteries and resulted in a quick death. The inquest into the death confirmed these facts, but "the police investigation failed to bring the killers to justice and was condemned as 'palpably flawed' and incompetent" (Bowling & Phillips, 2002, p. 15). The outrage produced by the brutal killing made it a symbolic case in the fight against the continuing harassment and violence against ethnic minorities. Because of the public's outrage and the media attention surrounding the incident (see Cottle, 2005), the result was yet another commission, like the one formulated after the 1981 Brixton riots that produced the well-known Scarman Report (Scarman, 1981).

This one had a new name: the Macpherson Report, which was published six years after the murder of Lawrence (Macpherson, 1999). The report notes that while three youths were charges in the murder, they were acquitted because there was no "firm and sustainable evidence" (Macpherson Report, 1999, chap 2, p. 3). Chapter 5 of the report details how Lawrence's friend Duwayne Brooks who also was at the scene was treated as a suspect, not as the traumatized victim that he was. Of this travesty, the commission wrote:

> We are driven to the conclusion that Mr. Brooks was stereotyped as a young black man exhibiting unpleasant hostility and agitation, who could not be expected to help, and whose condition and status simply did not need further examination or understanding. We believe that Mr. Brooks' colour and such stereotyping played their part in the collective failure of those involved to treat him properly and according to their needs. (Macpherson Report, 1999, chap. 5, p. 12)

In all, 70 recommendations made it into the second volume of the report, with the usual things such as diversity training, improved handling of complaints, rooting out institutional racism, and the general improvement of police services being prominently featured in the report. Of the recommendations, "56 . . . were fully accepted, five were accepted in part and seven were referred to the Law Commission to be subjected to further examination" (Bowling & Phillips, 2002, p. 17).

So what has been the progress since the Macpherson Report? Well, shockingly, in 2003, a British Broadcasting Corporation (BBC) documentary suggested that little had changed. The documentary, *The Secret Policeman,* included interviews with police officers undergoing training. Describing the program, Rowe (2004) wrote:

> The programme contained secretly filmed footage of an officer donning a Ku Klux Klan-style white hood, improvised out of a pillowcase, and boasting that he would like to kill Asians and "bury them under the train tracks" if he could get away with it. Another officer boasted that he would issue minority ethnic motorists with fixed penalties in circumstances where he would let white people with an informal caution. A third officer claimed he joined the police service because he knew it was a racist organization and it would allow him to "look after his own." (pp. 1–2)

These disturbing comments were clearly a step in the wrong direction. Police organizations quickly expressed their outrage at the comments. On the other hand, the media quickly took hold of the story and told of instances in which Black and Asian officers had experienced racism. Aside from this unfortunate incident, the main focus has remained how well police agencies are doing in light of the recommendations made in the Macpherson Report.

Based on interviews with 218 persons from major metropolitan police services in England and Wales, Rowe (2004) systematically assessed whether progress had been made following in the release of the Macpherson Report. In terms of recruitment, retention, and promotion of ethnic minorities in police forces, drawing on data from the Home Office, Rowe (2004) found that while there had been slight increases in the number of ethnic minorities in the police service, they remained underrepresented. In general, the belief is that by aggressively recruiting, retaining, and promoting ethnic minorities, there is an increased measure of police legitimacy in ethnic communities. Table 2.12 presents recent Home Office data that shows that the underrepresentation remains a concern. This is despite the fact that they have been a bit more aggressive in their recruitment of ethnic minorities. In addition, there have also been slight increases in the percentage of ethnic minorities in the more senior positions (see Table 2.13). Even with these slight improvements, some scholars have found the experiences of ethnic minority police officers to be rather troubling (Cashmore, 2001).

Table 2.12 Representation by Grade Band of Police Service, 2002

	White	*Minority Ethnic*	*% Minority Ethnic*
Constable	97,616	2,865	2.9
Sergeant	18,474	372	2.0
Inspector	6,195	99	1.6
Chief Inspector	1,584	24	1.5
Superintendent	1,266	23	1.8
Assistant CC	155	2	1.3
Chief Constable	54	1	1.9

SOURCE: Home Office, 2003: 19.

Table 2.13   Minority Ethnic Representation, as Percentage of Each Rank, 1992
                   and 2002

	% Minority Ethnic 1992	*% Minority Ethnic 2002*
Constable	1.43	2.9
Sergeant	0.45	2.0
Inspector	0.30	1.6
Chief Inspector	0.06	1.5
Superintendent	0.20	1.8
Assistant CC	0.00	1.3
Chief Constable	0.00	1.9

SOURCE: ACPO, 1995: 37 and Home Office, 2003: 19.

Cashmore (2001) found continuing racist attitudes among the police service and pointed to police culture as a potential problem in rooting out stereotypical attitudes. But, because of their small numbers on police forces, ethnic
minority officers expressed hesitancy in taking a stand against racism. With
the financial support of the Home Office, following Macpherson, the Black
Police Association also was seen as a positive mechanism to help change the
police service. Even so, Holdaway and O'Neill (2007) outline the frustrations
such organizations had trying to influence change. In terms of training, it was
found that there was suspicion concerning the nature of the training and also
because residents were not involved in the development of the training. This
was an ongoing theme in Rowe's (2004) review of the progress since the
Macpherson Report. In the end, Rowe closed his assessment of post-
Macpherson progress with the following telling passage:

> The continuing racialisation of debates surrounding crime, national identity
> and migration suggest that the transformation of Britain into a society confi-
> dently diverse and securely multi-ethnic and multi-cultural—the kind of soci-
> ety in which racist violence is very much reduced—has yet to be achieved.
> Against such a background it is inevitable that the bold promises of reform
> that greeted the Lawrence Report have yet to be fully realized. (p. 169)

Another key area of concern is stop and searches (Delsol & Shiner, 2006). More specifically, as in other countries, there are concerns about stops and searches of ethnic minorities (often referred to as "profiling"). In Britain, such stops were commonplace prior to the 1980s. Cashmore (2001) describes the results of such stops:

> Much of the manifest hostility of African Caribbean youth towards the police in the 1970s was the result of the late "sus" law that enabled police officers to stop and search persons on mere suspicion; the ordinate number of young black people apprehended suggested that, in practice, this law operated in a racist manner; it was removed. (p. 646)

Following the riots of the 1980s and the release of the Macpherson Report, such stops became the increasing focus of research aimed at determining if ethnic minorities were still being disproportionately stopped by the police (see Norris, Fielding, Kemp, & Fielding, 1992). The year after the publication of the Macpherson Report, the Home Office produced the report, *Profiling Populations Available for Stops and Searches* (Miller, 2000), which examined the critical question of who gets stopped and searched. The report studied hot spots or zones where most of the stop and searches take place. In addition, the researcher sought to "[obtain] profile information of the available pedestrian and vehicle populations within the specified zones using video cameras and observers situated in vehicles driven within the zones" (Miller, 2000, p. vi). The research also captured whether the population of the area aligned with that of those who were stopped and searched. Finally, the research sought to match the type of crimes with the stops and searches, looking for any disparities.

The report concluded there was no "general pattern of bias against people from minority ethnic groups either as a whole or for particular groups" (Miller, 2000, p. vi). Surprisingly, the report found that Whites were stopped at higher rates than their population figures, while Asians were often underrepresented in stops and searches. The data on Blacks showed mixed findings; that is, the data revealed that "sometimes [they were] under-represented in stops and searches and sometimes [they were] over-represented" (Miller, 2000, p. iv). As for the location of the stops, the report noted the following:

> A comparison of the geographic pattern of stops and searches with recorded crime in two sites suggest a fair degree of consistency between the two. However, in both areas, there were some important disparities; there were places where the levels of stops and searches were either higher or lower

than would be expected from local crime levels. On one site where disparities occurred, stops and searches tended to be focused on areas with a particularly high minority ethnic populations [sic]. A small part of the
disproportionality in stops and searches in this area might, therefore, follow
from this mismatch. (p. vii)

In light of these findings, the author concluded that even though the
results appeared promising, the resulting disproportionality is likely a product
of structural factors and inequities that the police cannot address. Thus, in
essence, the police have to deal with the consequences of societal inequities.
In the end, the authors suggest that the police need to redouble their efforts to
"minimise the bad feeling that stop and searches cause, particularly among
those from minority ethnic groups" (Miller, 2000, p. vii). It is important to
note that a recent replication of the Home Office's report in two areas of Great
Britain (Reading and Slough) also found little support for the notion of racial
profiling as being the cause of disproportionate stops of ethnic minorities
(Waddington, Stenson, & Don, 2004). (For more on this emerging perspective,
see Stenson & Waddington, 2007).

One final study is noteworthy here. Moving away from stop and searches
in the streets, Newburn, Shiner, and Hayman (2004) tackle the topic of strip
searches and how suspects are treated in custody. Based on data originally col-
lected in a London police station to examine closed-circuit television (CCTV)
and its impact on police custody, the research shed light on whether ethnic
minorities were disproportionately strip-searched. With nearly 8,000 persons
in their sample, the authors noted the demographic characteristics of those
arrested and found that most were young males, with the largest percentage
being African-Caribbean (42%). The authors also noted the nature of the
offenses in which suspects were arrested. From there they determined the variations in terms of the frequency of strip searches for the various offenses. As
anticipated, those arrested for more serious offenses were more likely to be
strip searched (e.g., drugs, robbery), as were young people and males. In addition, it was found that African-Caribbeans were strip searched nearly twice as
frequently as any other group (17%). But to ensure this finding wasn't just a
product of the nature of the offenses for which they were arrested, the authors
subjected the data to multivariate analyses, which revealed:

On average, being African-Caribbean rather than white European (or Irish)
was associated with a virtual doubling of the probability of being strip

searched. Furthermore, while the differences between white Europeans, Irish, Mediterraneans and Asians were negligible, being Arabic/Oriental rather than white European (or Irish) was associated with a virtual halving of the probability of being strip searched. (Newman et al., 2004, p. 689)

To further support the evidence of discrimination, the authors examined whether strip searches were impacted by the installation of CCTVs. Here, the authors surmised that the addition of CCTV and the "visibility" that it provides would reduce the use of police powers in deciding to conduct strip searches. Overall, the number of strip searches did fall "from 13 to 9 per cent of arrestees" (Newman et al., 2004, p. 689). And in nearly every demographic, the number of strip searches fell. The authors, however, had one lingering and unexplained finding:

> . . . the apparent rule tightening around the use of strip search which appears to have accompanied the introduction of CCTV has, for reasons that we are, at this stage, unable to fully explain, not affected the differential use of this power against African-Caribbean arrestees. (p. 692)

Thus, Newman and his colleagues provide convincing evidence that there still remains some uncharted terrain in the question of institutional racism in British police agencies. The next sections of the chapter explore two other critical areas of the ethnic minorities and crime debate in Britain—courts and corrections.

Ethnic Minorities, Prosecution, and Sentencing in Britain

Bowling and Phillips (2002) note:

> Once a suspect has been charged with an offence at the police station, their case file is sent to the Crown Prosecution Service (CPS) in order that they can make the decision about whether to proceed to court with the case or to terminate the case—in which case the defendant does not have to attend court or face criminal charges. (p. 168)

Such a procedure is fairly standard in most countries; however, there is always the question as to what factors determine what cases move forward and what cases get dismissed. Much of the early research did not reveal any patterns that would lead one to believe that race was a central component of some of the decisions, especially since in many cases the courts do not know the race of the defendants (Bowling & Phillips, 2002). Even so, some research into this question points to high termination rates for Blacks and Asians, which could be a product of the fact that these groups are charged in more cases where there is limited evidence. In addition, of those cases that are moved forward, some suggest that race does matter in prosecution, sentencing (Hood, 1992; Mhlanga, 1997 and legal representation (Banks, 1999).

A recent report from the Home Office continues to reveal the difficulty in determining whether there is bias in the magistrate and Crown Courts (*Statistics on Race and the Criminal Justice System,* 2006). The report notes that improvements in the data collection systems have improved, but the fruits from the improvements might not be seen for a few years. Nevertheless, the report shows that "ethnicity was in only 19% of the magistrates' court data for England and Wales supplied to the Home Office" (p. 53). With such limited data, there is little one can say about the presence of bias in such courts. Keeping this considerable limitation in mind, the data showed the following trends in magistrate courts:

- Blacks (25%), Whites (24%), and Asians (23%) had similar early termination rates (discontinued or withdrawn).
- Whites (59%) had the highest conviction rates followed by Blacks (51%) and Asians (45%).
- The use of custody was similar for Blacks (12%) and Whites (12%) but lower for Asians (8%).
- Blacks (41%) and Asians (40%) were more likely to receive community service than Whites (37%).
- Blacks (17%) and Asians (21%) were less likely to be given a discharge than Whites (25%).
- Asians (27%) were more likely to be given a fine than Blacks (22%) and Whites (21%).
  (*Statistics on Race*, 2006, pp. 53–54)

As for the Crown Courts, the report provides a bit more comprehensive information considering that "ethnicity was reported for 78% of all persons tried before the Crown Court in 2004" (*Statistics on Race,* 2006, p. 58). Some highlights from the Crown Courts are presented below:

- White defendants (75%) were found guilty more often than Blacks (68%) and Asians (66%).

- Blacks (68%) and "others" (68%) received a custodial sentence more often than Whites (61%) and Asians (60%).
- Community sentences were given more often to Whites (30%) than Asians (29%) and Blacks (23%).
- Blacks (80%) were more likely than Asians (74%) and Whites (62%) to receive a custodial sentence for drug offenses.
- Blacks (61%) were more likely than Asians (54%) and Whites (49%) to receive a custodial sentence for fraud and forgery.
- Asians (87%) were more likely than Blacks (83%) and Whites (85%) to receive custodial sentences for robbery.
  (*Statistics on Race*, 2006, p. 58)

On the surface, some of these figures might lead to questions as to whether race might play a role in the outcomes, but in the absence of additional contextual information (prior records, etc.) one is left unsure what to make of the figures. Nevertheless, as the data collection process improves, there will clearly be more evidence to contextualize these raw data.

Ethnic Minorities, Prisons, Probation, and Parole in Britain

In terms of prisons and probation, more data have become available in the last 20 years. It wasn't until 1986 that the Home Office produced the first prison data with ethnic origins (Bowling & Phillips, 2002, p. 192). Since then, the figures have consistently shown the overrepresentation of ethnic minorities in prison populations for both males and females. During a one-day count on June 30, 2005, there were 76,190 persons incarcerated in British prisons. Of these, 25% (or 18,753) was an ethnic minority (*Statistics on Race*, 2006, p. 86). The breakdown for males was as follows: "14% Black, 6% Asian, 3% Mixed, and 1% Chinese and other" (*Statistics on Race*, 2006, p. 86). Ethnic minority females represented 28% of the female prison population. Here, Black women represented 19%, Asian 2%, 5% Mixed, and 2% Chinese and other.

For some time now, many have expressed concerns about the number of Black males and females in the prison population. As is usually the case in discussions to deflect charges of discrimination, the seriousness of the offense is usually pointed to as the likely explanation for the longer sentence and the related overrepresentation of ethnic minorities in correctional populations. Bowling and Phillips (2002) note, however, that overcharging at the police stage of the criminal justice process might account for this. In addition, other socio-economic factors might also help explain these disparities. Whatever the explanation, the increasing use of prisons in Britain during the 1990s clearly paralleled the "get tough" approach in the United States that led to an inflated American prison population.

Moving past simply correctional population figures, not much research has examined the experiences of ethnic minorities once they are incarcerated (Chigwada-Bailey, 1997; McDermott, 1990). However, the Home Office recently conducted studies to examine the views of ethnic minority offenders and the prison staff (Edgar & Martin, 2004) and also to determine ways to improve race relations in prisons (Ellis, Tedstone, & Curry, 2004). Edgar and Martin (2004) interviewed inmates and officers in four British prisons. Of the 237 ethnic minority prisoners who participated in the study, 52% felt they had recently experienced racial discrimination. Some of the inmates also reported incidents in which they were subjected to verbal abuse or some other form of malicious discrimination. Considering the sentiments expressed by the inmates, it was surprising to find that only 2 out of the 53 officers who were interviewed felt that the Prison Service could do more to combat racism. The inmates, however, felt initiatives such as hiring more ethnic minorities and providing White officers with diversity training would help in reducing racism (Edgar & Martin, 2004). Recent research has confirmed the Home Office's findings (see Cheliotis & Liebling, 2006) and, more recently, some have expressed new concern regarding deaths in custody related to lack of care for those Black prisoners with sickle cell anemia (Dyson & Boswell, 2006).

Research on ethnic minorities and probation has been rather scarce. Following early publication on the topic in the late 1960s (Walcott, 1968), Bowling and Phillips (2002) note that not until the 1970s was there any discussion of ethnic minorities and probation. In general, much of the past and more recent emphasis has been on ensuring that ethnic minorities have the appropriate services for their needs and also that White probation officers are sensitive to such needs. The Home Office's most recent report on race and criminal justice shows that the level of probation for all ethnic groups, as one would expect, varies depending on "the ethnic minority composition of the resident population" (*Statistics on Race,* 2006, p. 82). Thus, not very much can be gleaned from a review of the Home Office data. Nevertheless, more recently there have been more thoughtful attempts to determine the needs of ethnic minorities on probation (see Lewis, Raynor, Smith, & Wardak, 2006).

Ethnic minorities and parole has also received scant attention from scholars. Hood and Shute (2000) found that Blacks and Whites were less likely to be granted parole than South Asians and Chinese prisoners. Recent research by Moorthy, Cahalin, and Howard (2004) has confirmed the finding of Hood and Shute. Table 2.14 presents the results from their study of 6,000 parole decisions. Interestingly, the figures reveal that Whites are the ones least likely to receive parole. After subjecting the data to multivariate analyses, the authors concluded that: "This study demonstrated that there was no differential treatment of minority ethnic groups by the Parole Board and that differences in parole release rates between ethnic groups were likely to result from other characteristics associated with release" (Moorthy et al., 2004, p. 6).

The literature on the police and ethnic minorities clearly remains the most abundant. However, other areas of the justice system and how they engage ethnic minorities have increasingly become of more interest to scholars. So while there has been some interesting scholarship examining topics such as the role of minority perspectives (Phillips & Bowling, 2003), creating better systems for capturing the diversity within ethnic communities (Garland, Spalek, & Chakraborti, 2006), and the experiences of ethnic minorities in rural areas (Iganski & Levin, 2004; Jalota, 2004; Robinson & Gardner, 2004), the final section of the chapter closes with a brief note on ethnic minorities, gender, and crime, which is among one of the emerging and most pressing concerns in Britain.

Table 2.14   Prisoners Considered and Released on Parole in 1999/2000 by Ethnic Group

	White	*Black*	*South Asian*	*Chinese/Other*	*Total*
Opt out*	893	113	17	25	1,048
Considered	4,775	1,023	244	166	6,213**
Released	1,879	438	156	88	2,561
Release rate	39%	43%	64%	53%	41%

SOURCE: Moorthy, U., Cahalin, K., & Howard, P. (2004).

NOTE: *Those prisoners who do not want to apply for parole. **Includes five prisoners that have not been categorized in an ethnic group.

Ethnic Minorities, Gender, and Crime

The concern regarding the overrepresentation of female ethnic minorities in the British justice system is not new, especially as it relates to Black and Asian women (Agozino, 1997; Chigwada, 1989; Chigwada-Bailey, 1997). In fact, nearly 20 years ago, Rice (1990) noted the absence of any substantive consideration by feminists of the plight of Black women in the criminal justice system. Now, many of the reports currently produced by the Home Office that take race into consideration consistently find that race and gender are related. Thus, often Blacks, Asians, and foreign national women are overrepresented in some aspect of criminal justice (see Joseph, 2006). Even so, as is often the case in research, the low number of female offenders, in general, tends to steer the dialogue towards the concerns of ethnic minority males.

The recent work of Sudbury (2005a, 2005b, 2005c) has sought to correct the fallacy that because the number of Black women in the justice system pales in comparison to men there is no crisis. Sudbury (2005a) views the expanding female prison populations as being part of the global "prison industrial complex" in which countries in conjunction with private corporations benefit from the increasing prison populations. As others have noted (see Agozino, 2000), the global war on drugs has resulted in Black men *and* women being targeted for criminal justice attention (Sudbury, 2005c). Sudbury observed that after more than 20 Jamaican women were caught smuggling drugs into Britain from Jamaica in 2001, a moral panic ensued that resulted in a connection between the attempted smuggling, the crack trade, and gun violence. This connection turned the nonviolent crime of smuggling into a sensation. During this process, though, Sudbury (2005c) noted not only the problem with this connection, but also told the stories behind the plight of these so-called mules. In short, her interviews illuminated the tough choices facing Caribbean women. Such choices were clearly brought on by socio-economic factors that few of those benefiting from globalization, in general, and the "prison industrial complex" in particular, seem to want to address. Thus, until these issues are addressed, and the unfounded negative stereotypes of ethnic minority women are quelled, concerns regarding race, gender, and crime in Great Britain will likely persist.

SUMMARY AND CONCLUSION

This chapter examined ethnic minorities, crime, and justice in Great Britain. From their earliest encounter with large numbers of ethnic groups, British citizens have been averse to their presence. Such a reception has resulted in persistent ethnic-based antagonisms that, at times, have resulted in racial harassment and violence, which have worsened race relations. The colonial model anticipates such relations between the colonizer and the colonized. Once ethnic groups arrived in the home colony, they were seen as nothing more than colonial migrants. As such, they quickly came to represent the "quintessence of evil." Hence, with most doors of opportunity closed to them, they struggled to survive. This legacy appears to remain present in Great Britain.

Because of the overrepresentation of ethnic minorities throughout the justice system, there have been ongoing efforts to study and ameliorate this growing problem (Bowling & Phillips, 2006). Nonetheless, recent data from the British Crime Survey show that ethnic minorities, more so than Whites, are concerned about crime in their communities. The concerns of ethnic minorities, mixed with the general societal concerns about the mere presence of ethnic minorities (particularly Blacks and Asians), have produced a volatile paradox in Great Britain. That is, even when it seems the government might be making a sincere effort to push for change, the racism that is so deeply ingrained in British society produces tragic incidents such as the Stephen Lawrence murder, which in many ways, on the surface, seems to move the dialogue further along. But in the end, one wonders how much real progress is accomplished? In truth, only time will tell.

REFERENCES

Agozino, B. (1997). *Black women and the criminal justice system: Towards the decolinisation of victimization.* Aldershot, UK: Ashgate.

Agozino, B. (2000). Theorizing otherness, the war on drugs and incarceration. *Theoretical Criminology, 4,* 359–376.

Allen, S. (1971). *New minorities, old conflicts: Asian and West Indian immigrants in Britain.* New York: Random House.

Banks, N. (1999). *White counselors–Black clients: Theory, research, and practice.* Aldershot, UK: Ashgate.

Bindman, G. (2000). Law enforcement or lack of it. In M. Anwar, P. Roach, & R. Sondhi (Eds.), *From legislation to integration? Race relations in Britain* (pp. 40–57). London: Macmillan Press

Bowling, B. (1993). Racial harassment and the process of victimization: Conceptual and methodological implications for the Local Crime Survey. *British Journal of Criminology, 33,* 231–250.

Bowling, B. (1996). The emergence of violent racism as a public issue in Britain, 1945–1981. In P. Panayi (Ed.), *Racial violence in Britain in the nineteenth and twentieth centuries* (pp. 185–220). Leicester, UK: Leicester University Press.

Bowling, B. (1998). *Violent racism: Victimization, policing and social context.* Oxford, UK: Oxford University Press.

Bowling, B., & Phillips, C. (2002). *Racism, crime, and justice.* London: Longman.

Bowling, B., & Phillips, C. (2003). Racist victimization in England and Wales. In D. F. Hawkins (Ed.), *Violent crime: Assessing race and ethnic differences* (pp. 154–170). Cambridge, UK: Cambridge University Press.

Bowling, B., & Phillips, C. (2006). *Young black people and the criminal justice system.* London: Submission to the House of Commons Home Affairs Committee Inquiry.

Brown, C. (1984). *Black and white.* London: Heineman.

Cashmore, E. (2001). The experiences of ethnic minority police officers in Britain: Under-recruitment and racial profiling in a performance culture. *Ethnic and Racial Studies, 24,* 642–659.

Cheliotis, L. K., & Liebling, A. (2006). Race matters in British prisons: Towards a research agenda. *British Journal of Criminology, 46,* 286–317.

Chigwada, R. (1989). The criminalization and imprisonment of black women. *Probation Journal, 36,* 100–105.

Chigwada-Bailey, R. (1997). *Black women's experiences of criminal justice: Discourses on disadvantage.* Winchester, UK: Waterside Press.

Cook, D., & Hudson, B. (Eds.). (1993). *Racism and criminology.* London: Sage.

Cottle, S. (2005). Mediatized public crisis and civil society renewal: The racist murder of Stephen Lawrence. *Crime, Media, and Culture, 1,* 49–71.

Cunningham, W. (1897). *Alien immigrants to England.* London: Swan Sonnenschein & Co.

Daniel, W. W. (1968). *Racial discrimination in England.* London: Penguin.

Daniell, C. (1998). *A traveller's history of England* (4th ed.). New York: Interlink Books.

Delsol, R., & Shiner, M. (2006). Regulating stop and search: A challenge for police and community relations in England and Wales. *Critical Criminology, 14,* 241–263.

Dyson, S. M., & Boswell, G. (2006). Sickle cell anemia and deaths in custody in the UK and the USA. *The Howard Journal, 45,* 14–28.

Edgar, K., & Martin, C. (2004). *Perceptions of race and conflict: Perspectives of minority ethnic prisoners and of prison officers.* London: Home Office.

Edwards, P., & Walvin, J. (1983). *Black personalities in the era of the slave trade.* London: Macmillan.

Ellis, T., Tedstone, C., & Curry, D. (2004). *Improving race relations in prisons: What works?* London: Home Office.

Focus on ethnicity & identity. (2005). Retrieved July 31, 2007, from www.statistics .gov.uk/downloads/theme_compendia/foe2004/Ethnicity.pdf

Garland, J., Spalek, B., & Chakraborti, N. (2006). Hearing lost voices: Issues in researching "hidden" minority ethnic communities. *British Journal of Criminology, 46,* 423–437.

Gilroy, P. (1987). *There ain't no black in Union Jack.* London: Hutchinson.

Gordon, P. (1986). *Racial violence and racial harassment.* London: Runnymede Trust.

Gordon, P. (1988). Black people and the criminal law: Rhetoric and reality. *International Journal of Sociology of Law, 16,* 295–313.

Hall, S., Critcher, C., Jefferson, T., Clarke, J., & Roberts, B. (1978). *Policing the crisis: Mugging, the state, and law and order.* London: Macmillan.

Holdaway, S. (1997). Some recent approaches to the study of race in criminological research. *British Journal of Criminology, 37,* 383–400.

Holdaway, S., & O'Neill, M. (2007). Black police associations and the Lawrence Report. In M. Rowe (Ed.), *Policing beyond Macpherson: Issues in policing, race and society* (pp. 88–106). Devon, UK: Willan Publishing.

Hood, R. (1992). *Race and sentencing.* Oxford, UK: Clarendon Press.

Hood, R., & Shute, S. (2000). *The parole system at work: A study of risk based decision-making.* London: Home Office.

Iganski, P., & Levin, J. (2004). Cultures of hate in the urban and rural: Assessing the impact of extremist organizations. In N. Chakraborti & J. Garland (Eds.), *Rural racism* (pp. 108–121). Devon, UK: Willan Publishing.

Jackson, R. L., & Brown Givens, S. M. (2006). *Black pioneers in communication research.* Thousand Oaks, CA: Sage.

Jalota, S. (2004). Supporting victims of rural racism: Learning lessons from a dedicated racial harassment project. In N. Chakraborti & J. Garland (Eds.), *Rural racism* (pp. 143–160). Devon, UK: Willan Publishing.

Jenkinson, J. (1993). The riots of 1919. In P. Panayi (Ed.), *Racial violence in Britain, 1840–1950* (pp. 92–111). Leicester, UK: Leicester University Press.

Jones, T. (1996). *Britain's ethnic minorities.* London: Policy Studies Institute.

Joseph, J. (2006). Drug offenses, gender, ethnicity, and nationality: Women in prison in England and Wales. *The Prison Journal, 86,* 140–157.

Kalunta-Crumpton, A. (2006). The importance of qualitative research in understanding the disproportionate black presence in crime figures in the United Kingdom. *African Journal of Criminology & Justice Studies, 2,* 1–32.

Landau, S. F. (1981). Juveniles and the police: Who is charged immediately and who is referred to the juvenile bureau? *British Journal of Criminology, 21,* 27–46.

Landau, S. F., & Nathan, G. (1983). Selecting delinquents for cautioning in the London metropolitan area. *British Journal of Criminology, 23,* 128–148.

Lewis, S., Raynor, P., Smith, D., & Wardak, A. (Eds.) (2006). *Race and probation.* Devon, UK: Willan Publishing.

Macpherson, W. (1999). *The Stephen Lawrence inquiry.* London: HMSO.

McClintock, F. (1963). *Crimes of violence: An enquiry by the Cambridge Institute of Criminology into crimes of violence by the person in London.* London: Macmillan.

McDermott, K. (1990). We have no problem: The experience of racism in prison. *New Community, 16,* 213–228.

Mhlanga, B. (1997). *The colour of English justice: A multivariate analysis.* Aldershot: Avebury.

Miller, J. (2000). *Profiling populations for stops and searches (Paper 131).* London: Home Office.

Modood, T., Berthoud, R., Lakey, J., Nazroo, J., Smith, P., Virdee, S., & Beishon, S. (1997). *Ethnic minorities in Britain: Diversity and disadvantage.* London: Policy Studies Institute.

Moorthy, U., Cahalin, K., & Howard, P. (2004). *Ethnicity and parole.* London: Home Office.

Newburn, T., Shiner, M., & Hayman, S. (2004). Race, crime and injustice? Strip search and the treatment of suspects in custody. *British Journal of Criminology, 44,* 677–694.

Nicholas, S., Kershaw, C., & Walker, A. (2007). *Crime in England and Wales 2006/07.* London: Home Office.

Norris, C., Fielding, N., Kemp, C., & Fielding, J. (1992). Black and blue: An analysis of the influence of race on being stopped by the police. *British Journal of Sociology, 43,* 207–224.

Panayi, P. (1994). *Immigration, ethnicity and racism in Britain, 1815–1945.* Manchester, UK: Manchester University Press.

Phillips, C., & Bowling, B. (2003). Race, ethnicity, and criminology: Developing minority perspectives. *British Journal of Criminology, 43,* 269–290.

Pilkington, E. (1996). The West Indian community and the Notting Hill riots of 1958. In P. Panayi (Ed.), *Racial violence in Britain in the nineteenth and twentieth centuries* (pp. 171–184). Leicester, UK: Leicester University Press.

Pitts, J. (1993). Thereotyping: Anti-racism, criminology and black young people. In D. Cook & B. Hudson (Eds.), *Racism & Criminology* (pp. 96–117). London: Sage.

Rice, M. (1990). Challenging orthodoxies in feminist theory: A black feminist critique. In L. Gelsthorpe & A. Morris (Eds.), *Feminist perspectives in criminology* (pp. 57–69). Philadelphia: Open University Press.

Robinson, V., & Gardner, H. (2004). Unraveling a stereotype: The lived experience of black and minority ethnic people in rural Wales. In N. Chakraborti & J. Garland (Eds.), *Rural racism* (pp. 85–107). Devon, UK: Willan Publishing.

Rodrick, A. B. (2004). *The history of Great Britain.* Westport, CT: Greenwood Press.

Rowe, M. (2004). *Policing, race, and racism.* Devon, UK: Willan Publishing.

Scarman, L. (1981). *The Scarman Report.* London: Home Office.

Smith, D. J. (1977). *Racial disadvantage in Britain: The PEP report.* Middlesex, UK: Penguin.

Statistics on race and the criminal justice system–2005. (2006). London: Home Office.

Stenson, K., & Waddington, P. A. J. (2007). Macpherson, police stops and institutionalized racism. In M. Rowe (Ed.), *Policing beyond Macpherson: Issues in policing, race and society* (pp. 128–147). Devon, UK: Willan Publishing.

Sudbury, J. (2005a). Celling black bodies: Black women in the global prison industrial complex. *Feminist Review, 80,* 162–179.

Sudbury, J. (Ed.). (2005b). *Global lockdown: Race, gender, and the prison industrial complex.* New York: Routledge.

Sudbury, J. (2005c). "Mules," "Yardies," and other folk devils: Mapping cross-border imprisonment in Britain. In J. Sudbury (Ed.), *Global lockdown: Race, gender, and the prison industrial complex* (pp. 167–184). New York: Routledge.

Travis, A. (2002, August 24). After 44 years secret papers reveal truth about five nights of violence in Notting Hill. *Guardian.* Retrieved July 31, 2007, from http://arts.guardian .co.uk

Virdee, S. (1997). Racial harrassment. In T. Modood, R. Berthoud, J. Lakey, J. Nazroo, P. Smith, S. Virdee, & S. Beishon. (Eds.), *Ethnic minorities in Britain: Diversity and disadvantage* (pp. 259–289). London: Policy Studies Institute.

Waddington, P. A. J., Stenson, K., & Don, D. (2004). In proportion: Race and police stop and search. *British Journal of Criminology, 44,* 889–914.

Walcott, R. (1968). The West Indian in the British casework setting. *Probation Journal, 39,* 129–132.

Waters, R. (1990). *Ethnic minorities and the criminal justice system.* Aldershot, UK: Avebury.

Williams, E. (1944). *Capitalism and slavery.* London: Andre Deutsch.

Figure 3.1 Contemporary Map of the United States

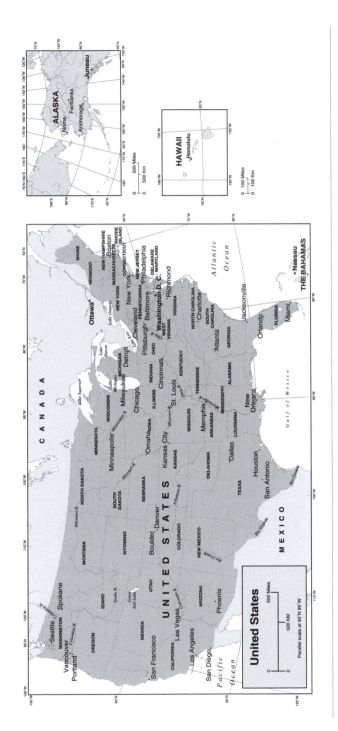

⊰ THREE ⊱

UNITED STATES

—————•◦•————

CHAPTER OVERVIEW

Among the countries profiled in this volume, the United States represents one of the countries that have devoted considerable scholarly attention to the issue of race, ethnicity, and crime. Diverse groups such as Native Americans, African Americans, White ethnic immigrants, Latinos, and Asians, have all, at some point, been the "criminal justice problem" in the country. However, over the last century, no racial minority has received more scholarly attention than African Americans. The chapter begins with a review of the early and contemporary history of the United States, highlighting the experiences of racial and ethnic minorities. This history is rife with connections to Becky Tatum's colonial model. Beginning with Native Americans, colonization left its distinctive and repressive mark on several American racial and ethnic groups. This mark is evidenced by those citizens who are currently overrepresented in the American criminal justice system. The chapter reviews the nature and scope of this overrepresentation.

EARLY HISTORY

The United States is a vast land encompassing 3.5 million miles (see Figure 3.1), which is about the size of Europe and represents 6% of the earth (McInerney 2001, p. 1). Those recounting the early history of the United States typically begin with the arrival of settlers from Europe. However, this is far from the real story of the country's beginnings. While there has been some recent debate about the origins and routes the native people took to get to what is now the United States, recent research has found "that the earliest migrants (from Asia and perhaps from Europe) came by sea, moving along the western or eastern coasts of the Americas over 16,000 years ago" (McInerney, 2001, p.8). Mann (2006) notes that previous theories have suggested:

> Indians came to the Americas through the Bering Strait about thirteen thousand years ago at the tail end of the last Ice Age. Because the sheets of polar ice locked up huge amounts of water, seal levels around the world fell about three hundred feet. The shallow Bering Strait became a wide land bridge between Siberia and Alaska. (p. 17)

And this bridge is the one that Native Americans, as the theory goes, used to simply walk the 55 miles onto American soil.

RACIAL AND ETHNIC GROUPS IN AMERICA

Native Americans

No matter how they got to America, there are records of Paleo-Indians on the continent as far back as 10,000 to 9,000 B.C. From 8,000 to 1,500 B.C., Archaic Indians, the descendants of the Paleo-Indians, set up large settlements and produced a variety of crops to survive. In fact, the development of stable food production also resulted in increased populations. Even so, scholars often point to South America when referring to the most sophisticated societies in the early Americas (most notably the Olmec and Mayan societies). However, some North American Indian societies were rather complex as well. One such society, referred to as the "Mound Builders," was reported to have built structures from the earth that ranged in height "from 20 to 70 feet high, covering acres and, in some instances, several square miles of ground" (McInerney, 2001, p. 9). Other early North American Indian cultures created sophisticated societies that accommodated thousands of people (Mann, 2006).

Native Americans continued to develop their societies with little interruption until the arrival of Europeans. Spaniard Juan Ponce de Leon, in his quest to find the Fountain of Youth, landed on Florida in April of 1513. Eight years later he returned in an attempt to found a permanent colony, first in Tampa, but the Indians succeeded in fighting back this initial colonization effort. After finally fighting off the Indians and later the French, who had also now taken an interest in Florida, the Spanish prevailed and, as a result, "The first permanent [European] settlement in the land destined to become the United States was at St. Augustine (1565)" (Finger, 1959, p. 407). This settlement was, in some ways, the beginning of the end of Indian societies. Why? Because as a consequence of the increasing exploration to the new land, the Indians had increasing interactions with Europeans, which, irrespective of the tenor of those relations, still resulted in the death of millions of Indians. And yes, part of this was the product of the fact that the Europeans were armed with superior weapons, but that alone doesn't tell the whole story. Numerous writers have noted that the most effective means of killing the Indians was European diseases (Crosby, 1972; McInerney, 2001; Meinig, 1986; Polk, 2006). Illustrating the effectiveness of European diseases, McInerney (2001) writes:

> Estimates vary widely, but many historians believe that 50 per cent to 90 per cent of the natives who came in contact with European diseases died as a result of their exposure. Roughly 20 million people lived in Central America in 1519 on the eve of the invasion of Cortez; by 1650, the native population stood at only 2–3 million. The most powerful weapon [that] European colonizers wielded was one they did not even know they possessed. (p. 16)

Hence, even though Indians were known to be fierce fighters (against both other tribes and White colonizers), they found a foe they couldn't defeat. Regardless of whether the decimation of Indians was wholly purposeful or not, the facts remain that there was what amounts to a catastrophic reduction of the Indian population in the Americas.

Africans in America

Eventually, the decimation of Indians in the Americas resulted in the need for additional laborers to carry out the colonizers' work. The well-known Spanish Dominican priest, Bartolomé de las Casas, who accompanied Christopher Columbus to the new world, has been credited with suggesting that Africans be imported to meet the labor needs in the developing colonies (Finger, 1959). The result of this suggestion was the forceful introduction of Africans into the Americas; first in the Caribbean and South America, followed by their appearance in Colonial America. In the latter instance, not long after Colonial America was founded in 1607 by Captain John Smith, under a charter from King James I of England, did Africans start to appear in colonial accounts.

The first Africans appear to have been captors on a pirated slave ship that was originally headed to the West Indies but was likely redirected to Colonial America. That redirection resulted in the slaves being traded for supplies. At this time, though, slaves had similar status as indentured servants in that they could eventually purchase or "work off" their freedom. However, the steady flow of European immigrants caused colonists to rethink their strategy.

The concern was essentially an economic one; in short, the colonists sought to determine a way to extract as much profit out of the new land as possible. To do so, they needed to create a labor system that was profitable. After considering options that included a free labor system, enslaving Indians, enslaving ethnic immigrants, and keeping the prevailing system in place, which was a mix of all of them, they chose to enslave Africans and created a process that produced what is referred to as the Atlantic slave trade. This involved forcibly bringing Africans to them to serve as laborers on the tobacco and cotton plantations primarily in the developing American South (Horton & Horton, 2005).

Though slavery had existed for centuries throughout the world, the slavery that developed in America was thought to be the most brutal. If the enslaved survived the torturous "middle passage" trip between Africa and America, they were then subjected to additional torture on American plantations. Whippings, beatings, amputations, and other inhumane practices were used to control slaves in the American slave system. Given the rising slave population, plantation owners felt a need to discipline their slaves into passivity. To illustrate the growth of the slave population, Franklin and Moss (2000) noted that "in 1790 there had been less than 700,000 slaves. By 1830, there were more than 2 million" (p. 139). Three decades later, in 1860, there were nearly 4 million slaves in America (Franklin & Moss, 2000).

To ensure the survival of the American slave system, the White ruling class (who were slave owners themselves) started to codify the slavery in the late 1600s. This came in the form of slave codes. Russell-Brown (2009) describes the slave codes as a set of laws that dictated the life of African slaves

> from cradle to grave. The codes not only enumerated the applicable law but
> also prescribed the social boundaries for slaves. . . [T]he codes [also] estab-
> lished parameters for the business of slavery, including who could be sold as

slaves, the hours slaves could be made to work, who was responsible when slaves were injured, the punishment for stealing slaves, and the reward for capturing escaped slaves. (p. 35)

To enforce the codes, plantation owners came up with the slave patrol system, which was military in nature and considered a forerunner to modern policing (Gabbidon & Greene, 2009). As Franklin and Moss (2000) describe below, the actual system was quite organized:

Counties [were] . . . usually divided into "beats," or areas of patrol, and free white men were called upon to serve for a stated period of time: one, three, or six months. These patrols were to apprehend slaves out of place and return them to their masters or commit them to jail, to visit slave quarters and search for various kinds of weapons that might be used in an uprising, and to visit assemblies of slaves where disorder might develop or conspiracies might be planned. (p. 143)

Such a system proved effective in minimizing the number of escaped slaves and insurrections. Even so, there were countless minor slave revolts and some major ones (see Aptheker, 1993 [1943]). The most notable and bloodiest revolt was the one by Nat Turner in 1831 that, in a 24-hour period, resulted in the death of 60 Whites (Franklin & Moss, 2000, pp. 164–165). Throughout the slave era, there would be continuous conflicts between slaves and their masters. And when slavery ended with the passage of the Emancipation Proclamation in 1863 and the subsequent passage of the 13th Amendment in 1865, the conflicts did not end. In fact, the Reconstruction period (1863–1877) produced the creation of various hate groups (e.g., Ku Klux Klan) who felt a need to keep the former slaves in their place through ruthless violence that often resulted in the lynching of Blacks who "got out of line." While Blacks benefited from countless advances during this period, by the late 1800s the Supreme Court decision of *Plessey v. Ferguson* of 1896, which legally sanctioned the doctrine of "separate but equal," all but legalized White supremacy (Browne-Marshall, 2007; Higginbotham, 1996).

The 20th century would bring more of the same for Blacks. They would be the targets of racial violence and oppression throughout the 20th century, with civil rights advances coming only after civil rights activists were brutally beaten and killed throughout the last 50 years of the century. Legislative enactments such as the Civil Rights Act of 1964, which outlawed discrimination in entry to public places and in employment, was followed by the passage of the

Voting Rights Act of 1965 that addressed the long-standing efforts of Whites to disenfranchise Black voters, provided clear signs of progress. Since then, additional progress has been made, but many Blacks still remain disadvantaged in America (see Hacker, 2003; Wilson, 1987).

White Ethnics in America

Given the large numbers of Indians who were in America prior to European contact and the number of slaves in the South during the slave era, the obvious question should be: How did Whites become the majority population in the United States? Well, we already know that part of this question can be answered by the fact that, upon arrival, Europeans killed off a substantial number of the native population. An additional reply to the question can quite simply be answered with one word: Immigration. That is, ethnic Whites, for a variety of reasons and in successive waves, have immigrated to the United States en masse since the founding of the colony. Sowell (1981) an observer of this massive immigration has written:

> The peopling of America is one of the great dramas in all of human history. Over the years, a massive stream of humanity—45 million people—crossed every ocean and continent to reach the United States. They came speaking every language and representing every nationality, race, and religion. Today, there are more people of Irish ancestry in the United States than in Ireland, more Jews than in Israel, more blacks than in most African countries. (p. 3)

The long history leading up to Sowell's observations and to the present American makeup is important for our later discussion of race, ethnicity, and crime in America.

At the earliest beginnings of the colony, the nation was quite diverse. There were immigrants from numerous European countries, with most hailing from England. As previously noted, there were also Indians and Africans in the developing colony. Still, there remained a racial hierarchy with the English at the top and everyone else at the bottom. By 1790, Feagin and Feagin (2008) argue that a "Ladder of Dominance" (see Figure 3.2) developed that placed English Americans at the top and African Americans and Native Americans at the bottom. The breakdown of the population figures for Whites in 1790 clearly shows why English-native Whites lay at the top of the ladder. Representing 60% of the White population likely put them at an advantage in all facets of American society. In terms of their population increase, it has been estimated that "by the early eighteenth century, there were approximately 350,000 English and Welsh

Figure 3.2   A Ladder of Dominance: The United States as of 1790

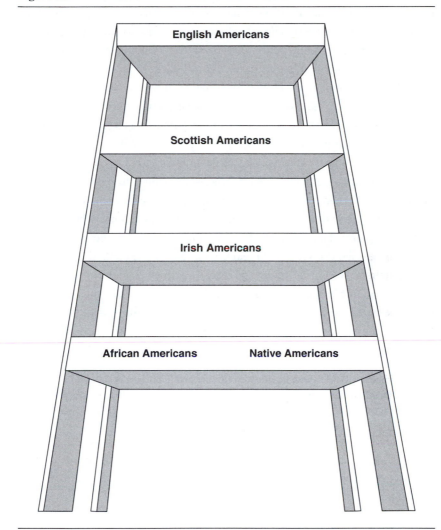

SOURCE: Feagin, R. F. & Feagin, C. B. (2008).

colonists in North America. At the time of the Revolution, this number was approaching 2 million" (Feagin & Feagin, 2008, p. 65).

The wave of White ethnic immigrants from Ireland peaked during the 19th century when they fled the potato famine in Ireland. To demonstrate the magnitude of the immigration during the 1800s from Ireland, it is best to examine the period leading up to the mass immigration. Leading up to 1840, less than a half-million Irish had come to American shores. By contrast, "between 1841 and 1860 ... 1.6 million Irish entered the United States"

(Feagin & Feagin, 2008, p. 83). Another wave of Irish immigrants headed to the United States in the late 1800s. They were joined by immigrants from Italy who, from 1880 to 1920, sent 4 million immigrants to the United States. Likewise, during the same period, a wave of 2.5 million Jewish immigrants fled Europe because of religious persecution (Feagin & Feagin, 2008).

All of these immigrants brought their native cultures and religion to a society that was already known for its intolerance for difference. For example, Catholicism and Judaism were foreign to the primarily Protestant Americans. This led to ostracism and discrimination from the new "natives." Upon arrival, derogatory stereotypes were spewed at the immigrants. Everything from the belief that the Irish were all drunkards who were inclined to fight at a whim, to the notion that Italians were all part of the Mafia, were commonly heard stereotypes. Such stereotypes hardened the resolve of the immigrants who, often out of necessity, formed close-knit ghetto communities in major cities such as New York and Chicago (Sowell, 1981). Even with the diverse cultural backgrounds they brought to America as immigrants, there was one notable commonality that European immigrants could unify around—their color. Feagin and Feagin (2008) note that the "White race" emerged during the 18th and 19th centuries. Whereas each ethnic group arriving in America was considered a separate group, Feagin and Feagin (2008) argue that following the Emancipation Proclamation:

> A white Anglo-Protestant elite developed and circulated the idea of an advanced "white race," in part as a way to provide racial privileges for propertyless British and other European American immigrants and to prevent the latter from bonding with Americans of color. (p. 64)

And while most ethnic groups maintained their ethnic identity upon arrival, over time they too saw the advantage of being subsumed and assimilated into the White populous.

Asians in America

Asians also immigrated to the United States during the late 19th century. For example, Chinese and Japanese immigrants had long been in the United States, working for railroads, mines, and farms. The discrimination they encountered eventually resulted in notorious legislative enactments such as the Chinese Exclusion Act of 1882 that placed quotas on the number of immigrants from China. Such legislation would become the norm for preventing mass immigration from Asian countries. When the U.S. government lifted immigration restrictions nearly 60 years later, Asians from other countries also came to America.

Notably, during the last 20 years of the 20th century, an increasing number of Korean, Vietnamese, and Asian Indians began immigrating to the United States. Like the other immigrants profiled, Asians faced stinging discrimination, but preserved and celebrated their culture within their communities (e.g., Chinatowns) across the country (see generally, Takaki, 1998). In addition, their success in the professions has been notable, with Asians having the highest median household income in America (see Table 3.1).

Table 3.1   Median Household Income in the Past 12 Months by Race and Hispanic Origin: 2006[1]

	Median Household Income (dollars)	
Race and Hispanic origin	*Estimate*	*Margin of Error[2] (±)*
All households	**48,451**	**82**
White alone	51,429	69
White alone, no Hispanic	52,375	73
Black alone	32,372	155
American Indian and Alaska Native alone	33,762	659
Asian alone	63,642	652
Native Hawaiian and other Pacific Islander alone	49,361	2,389
Some other race alone	38,372	349
Two or more races	42,213	443
Hispanic (any race)	38,747	205

SOURCE: U.S. Census Bureau. 2006 American Community, Survey.

1. In 2006 inflation-adjusted dollars. Data are limited to the household population and exclude the population living in institutions, college dormitories, and other group quarters. For information on confidentiality protection, sampling error, nonsampling error, and definitions, see *www.census.gov/acs/www*

2. Data are based on a sample and are subject to sampling variability. The margin of error is a measure of an estimate's variability. The larger the margin of error in relation to the size of the estimate, the less reliable the estimate. The margin of error is the estimated 90-percent confidence interval.

Latinos in America

Currently comprising the largest minority group in the United States, Latinos, or persons of Spanish heritage from the Caribbean and South America, are today a force to be reckoned with. To illustrate the long-standing nature of resistance to people of Latino descent, the focus here is on Mexicans.

Mexicans came to the United States in three waves of immigration. The first wave, occurring prior to and during World War I, involved Mexicans looking for work, which they found in the railroad industry, mining, and agriculture. During this period, the labor shortage caused by the war resulted in a half-million Mexicans arriving in the United States. However, once the depression set in, Mexican workers were considered "undesirables." The second wave occurred during the Second World War because of a severe labor shortage. At this time, Mexicans were again afforded an opportunity to enter the United States to work. The Bracero Program allowed Mexicans to enter the country as guest workers. When the program ended in 1964, some 5 million Mexicans had participated. The third wave of Mexican immigration involved the immigration of Mexicans to the United States, up to the present. This period continues to see the push for restrictive legislation regarding immigration, border control, and immigrant rights. Even with their continuing willingness to fill labor shortages in the United States, Latinos, particularly Mexican immigrants, have been saddled with stereotypical status. This has also been the case for other Latino immigrants, most notably, Puerto Ricans, Cubans, and those from South American countries (Feagin & Feagin, 2008).

CONTEMPORARY HISTORY

The last 30 years in America have been defined by the conservatism that swept over the nation. Beginning with the election of Ronald Reagan in 1980, the conservative philosophies related to economics, education, national security, and crime have all shaped the current American landscape. While race relations in America had made notable strides since the groundbreaking legislation of the 1960s, the Republican approach called for the movement away from policies such as affirmative action and the use of race as a consideration in employment and college admissions. The buildup of arms also was seen as a key strategy for ensuring American superiority across the globe. In terms of crime, Reagan took a punitive and "get tough" approach which resulted in a "war on drugs" that produced unprecedented levels of incarceration.

After the Reagan administration, the one term served by his former vice president, George H. W. Bush, was a continuation of Reagan's policies. During the next 8 years, William Clinton, a Democrat, would seek to move away from some of the conservative polices, but in the end, at least as it related to crime, very little changed, with the crime bill of 1994 being one of the most punitive such bills in history. With the election of George W. Bush in 2000, conservatism again swept the nation, but this time it was supported by Republican control of Congress and a conservative-dominated Supreme Court. This dominance of the political landscape led to the rollback of numerous programs aimed at diversifying workplaces and also continued the punitive criminal justice policies that, as will be discussed later, left many racial and ethnic minorities disproportionately entangled in the criminal justice system.

The story of the last decade is one of sweeping diversification of the American populous. Immigrants, both legal and illegal, have continued to see America as a place where opportunities abound. As such, more than 300 million citizens now live in the United States. Of these citizens, more than 100 million of them are racial and ethnic minorities. Data from the U.S. Census Bureau, presented in Table 3.2, shows that Whites still predominate the American population, with people of Latino heritage being the largest minority group in America. The increasing Latino population has been one of the most significant issues in contemporary America. By 2004, more than 40 million people of Latino descent resided in the United States, with nearly 65% of them being of Mexican origin. Notably, an illustration of the changing diversity among the Latino population shows that, whereas Puerto Ricans formerly represented a large segment of the Latino population, in 2004 more than 5 million Latinos identified their origin as being from either Central or South America, while only 3.8 million identified Puerto Rico as their place of ancestry (U.S. Census Bureau, 2004).

To add to the increasingly volatile national discussion on immigration, the terrorist acts of September 11, 2001, dramatically changed the dialogue on immigration issues in America. Thus, while there have always been concerns in America about "crazed" immigrants entering the country and wreaking havoc, this tragic day revisited this image in the minds of Americans by revealing the "worst case scenario." Consequently, immigration laws that had been previously overlooked were now being rigorously enforced. Further, immigration which had taken a back seat to other national policy issues was now front and center, where it remains. In recent years, to stem the tide of illegal immigration from Mexico, "Congress . . . authorized $1.2 billion for about 700 miles of fencing, including about 330 miles of a so-called virtual fence—a network of cameras, high-tech sensors, radar and other technology" (Caldwell, 2007, p. A10). Such measures have reduced (Carl, 2007) but not stopped attempts by Mexicans to cross into the United States somewhere along the 2,100 mile border.

Much of the early and contemporary history provides a clear foundation to better understand the nature of race, ethnicity, crime, and justice in the United States. To begin that discussion, the next section provides an overview of crime and justice statistics in America.

Table 3.2   Estimates of Population by Race/Ethnicity, 2006

Race/Ethnicity	Population
White	198,744,494
Hispanic	44,321,038
Black/African American	40,240,898
Asian	14,907,198
American Indian/Alaskan Native	4,497,895
Native Hawaiian/Pacific Islander	1,007,644

SOURCE: U.S. Census Bureau (2007).

CRIME AND JUSTICE IN AMERICA

For those interested in exploring crime and justice statistics in America, two data sources are typically used to gauge the level and nature of crime and victimization: The Uniform Crime Reports (UCR) and the National Crime Victimization Survey (NCVS). The UCR, which is currently distributed by the Federal Bureau of Investigation (FBI), has been around since the 1930s. The UCR tabulates crime statistics from local police departments. Both crimes reported to the police and arrest statistics form the basis of the report. The document is separated into Part I and Part II offenses. Part I offenses (or index offenses) are considered the more serious crimes, such as murder and non-negligent manslaughter, forcible rape, robbery, aggravated assault, burglary, larceny–theft, motor vehicle theft, and arson. Part II offenses cover just about everything else.

Before presenting recent figures from the UCR, it is important to understand that the report is composed of data that are voluntarily submitted to the FBI; the report only captures those crimes that are reported or in which an arrest is made; and the report provides mostly aggregate data. As such, the figures should be viewed with caution.

In 2006, there were more than 10 million arrests for criminal offenses in the United States. The racial breakdown of these figures is presented in Table 3.3. The table reveals that close to 70% of the arrests in the United States are of White people, with Blacks representing 28% of the arrests and the remainder of the arrests being for persons of American Indian or Asian/Pacific Islander backgrounds. So where are the arrest figures for Latinos? That is a good question! In short, because Latinos in the United States are considered an ethnic group not a racial group, sometimes they are lumped into White arrests, while in other instances they might be clumped into Black arrests. Keeping this in mind, there still remain some notable patterns in the arrest figures. The most telling observation made by most observers of the Part I or more serious offenses is that Blacks are considerably overrepresented in all of them but particularly so in the murder/non-negligent homicide and robbery categories.

In Part II offenses, some of this overrepresentation also was pronounced in offense categories such as gambling (72%), weapons-related offenses

(Text continues on page 78)

Table 3.3   Arrests by Race, 2006

Offense Charged	Total Arrests					Percent Distribution[1]				
	Total	White	Black	American Indian or Alaskan Native	Asian or Pacific Islander	Total	White	Black	American Indian or Alaskan Native	Asian or Pacific Islander
Total	**10,437,620**	**7,270,214**	**2,924,724**	**130,589**	**112,093**	**100.0**	**69.7**	**28.0**	**1.3**	**1.1**
Murder and non-negligent manslaughter	9,801	4,595	4,990	110	106	100.0	46.9	50.9	1.1	1.1
Forcible rape	17,042	11,122	5,536	195	189	100.0	65.3	32.5	1.1	1.1
Robbery	93,393	39,419	52,541	611	822	100.0	42.2	56.3	0.7	0.9
Aggravated assault	326,721	206,417	112,645	3,949	3,710	100.0	63.2	34.5	1.2	1.1
Burglary	221,732	152,965	64,655	2,123	1,989	100.0	69.0	29.2	1.0	0.9
Larceny-theft	798,983	548,057	230,980	9,377	10,569	100.0	68.6	28.9	1.2	1.3
Motor vehicle theft	100,612	63,090	35,116	978	1,428	100.0	62.7	34.9	1.0	1.4
Arson	11,972	9,101	2,591	116	164	100.0	76.0	21.6	1.0	1.4

Offense Charged	Total Arrests					Percent Distribution[1]				
	Total	White	Black	American Indian or Alaskan Native	Asian or Pacific Islander	Total	White	Black	American Indian or Alaskan Native	Asian or Pacific Islander
Violent crime[2]	446,957	261,553	175,712	4,865	4,827	100.0	58.5	39.3	1.1	1.1
Property crime[2]	1,133,299	773,213	333,342	12,594	14,150	100.0	68.2	29.4	1.1	1.2
Other assaults	949,940	619,825	306,078	13,097	10,940	100.0	65.2	32.2	1.4	1.2
Forgery and counterfeiting	79,258	55,562	22,337	433	926	100.0	70.1	28.2	0.5	1.2
Fraud	196,930	135,329	59,087	1,213	1,301	100.0	68.7	30.0	0.6	0.7
Embezzlement	14,705	9,668	4,741	82	214	100.0	65.7	32.2	0.6	1.5
Stolen property; buying, receiving, possessing	89,850	58,066	30,267	670	847	100.0	64.6	33.7	0.7	0.9
Vandalism	219,652	165,518	48,781	2,987	2,366	100.0	75.4	22.2	1.4	1.1
Weapons; carrying, possessing, etc.	147,312	84,929	59,863	1,134	1,386	100.0	57.7	40.6	0.8	0.9

(Continued)

Table 3.3 (Continued)

Offense Charged	Total Arrests					Percent Distribution[1]				
	Total	White	Black	American Indian or Alaskan Native	Asian or Pacific Islander	Total	White	Black	American Indian or Alaskan Native	Asian or Pacific Islander
Prostitution and commercialized vice	59,616	33,827	23,612	569	1,608	100.0	56.7	39.6	1.0	2.7
Sex offenses (except forcible rape and prostitution)	63,048	46,194	15,465	640	749	100.0	73.3	24.5	1.0	1.2
Drug abuse violations	1,376,792	875,101	483,886	8,198	9,607	100.0	63.6	35.1	0.6	0.7
Gambling	9,001	2,358	6,467	12	164	100.0	26.2	71.8	0.1	1.8
Offenses against the family and children	91,618	61,278	28,086	1,678	576	100.0	66.9	30.7	1.8	0.6
Driving under the influence	1,034,651	914,226	95,260	13,484	11,681	100.0	88.4	9.2	1.3	1.1
Liquor laws	466,323	398,068	50,035	12,831	5,389	100.0	85.4	10.7	2.8	1.2

Offense Charged	Total Arrests					Percent Distribution[1]				
	Total	White	Black	American Indian or Alaskan Native	Asian or Pacific Islander	Total	White	Black	American Indian or Alaskan Native	Asian or Pacific Islander
Drunkenness	408,439	344,155	54,113	7,884	2,287	100.0	84.3	13.2	1.9	0.6
Disorderly conduct	517,264	325,991	179,733	7,606	3,934	100.0	63.0	34.7	1.5	0.8
Vagrancy	27,016	15,308	11,238	333	137	100.0	56.7	41.6	1.2	0.5
All other offenses (except traffic)	2,906,311	1,962,017	872,571	37,935	33,788	100.0	67.5	30.0	1.3	1.2
Suspicion	1,723	1,011	658	41	13	100.0	58.7	38.2	2.4	0.8
Curfew and loitering law violations	114,166	69,624	42,496	814	1,232	100.0	61.0	37.2	0.7	1.1
Runaways	83,749	57,393	20,896	1,489	3,971	100.0	68.5	25.0	1.8	4.7

SOURCE: Uniform Crime Reports, 2007 (Federal Bureau of Investigation) .

NOTE: 11,249 agencies; 2006 estimated population 216,685,152.

1. Because of rounding, the percentages may not add to 100.0.

2. Violent crimes are offenses of murder and non-negligent manslaughter, forcible rape, robbery, and aggravated assault. Property crimes are offenses of burglary, larceny-theft, motor vehicle theft, and arson.

(42%), and vagrancy offenses (38%). Whites, too, were noticeably overrepresented in alcohol-related offenses such as driving under the influence (88.4%), liquor law violations (85.4%), and drunkenness (84.3%).

Separating out the arrests for those under 18 years of age, the UCR figures reveal similar overall patterns, except in some offenses the overrepresentation of Black and White youth is more pronounced. Table 3.4 shows that Black youth were overrepresented in arrests for violent crimes. This was even more pronounced for murder/non-negligent manslaughter (59.2%) and robbery (67.4%). Whites, again, dominated the arrests for alcohol-related offenses, which considering the legal drinking age in the United States is 21 also speaks to the level of underage drinking among White youth. Illustrative of the drinking problem among White youth is the fact that they represented 93.7% of the arrests for driving under the influence and 91.3% of the arrests for liquor law violations.

So far nothing has been said about arrests of Native Americans and Asian/Pacific Islanders. Why? Well, it is usually the case that when a group has low arrest figures, scholars tend to pay less attention to them. For example, prior to the 1970s, this was the case with scholarships pertaining to women and crime in the United States. Breaking from this trend, a perusal of the arrest figures for American Indians reveals that they align fairly well with their corresponding population figures. In some of the alcohol-related categories (e.g., liquor law violations and drunkenness), there was noticeable overrepresentation. As for Asian/Pacific Islanders, they were notably *under*represented in just about every offense category. Only in the case of prostitution (and commercialized vice) (2.7%) and gambling (2.1%) was there any offense approaching their representation in the population. This general trend held true with the data for juveniles as well. But here, only their arrests for runaways approached their overall population figures.

Given the considerable limitations of the UCR data, in the early 1970s the National Crime Survey (NCS) or what is now know as the National Crime Victimization Survey (NCVS) was created to capture some of the "dark figure" or unreported/unknown crime that the UCR does not capture. This data source is based on surveys to the citizenry that queries them on their recent victimization. The most recent results from the survey are based on data from more than 76,000 households and 135,300 persons 12 years of age and older (Rand & Catalano, 2007). Since random sampling procedures are used to select participants, estimates of victimization for the entire American populous

(Text continues on page 84)

Table 3.4   Arrests by Race, 2006

Offense Charged	Arrests Under 18					Percent Distribution[1]				
	Total	White	Black	American Indian or Alaskan Native	Asian or Pacific Islander	Total	White	Black	American Indian or Alaskan Native	Asian or Pacific Islander
Total	**1,621,167**	**1,088,376**	**490,838**	**18,592**	**23,361**	**100.0**	**67.1**	**30.3**	**1.1**	**1.4**
Murder and non-negligent manslaughter	956	374	566	6	10	100.0	39.1	59.2	0.6	1.0
Forcible rape	2,507	1,592	863	30	22	100.0	63.5	34.4	1.2	0.9
Robbery	26,060	8,074	17,569	116	301	100.0	31.0	67.4	0.4	1.2
Aggravated assault	44,314	24,697	18,652	439	526	100.0	55.7	42.1	1.0	1.2
Burglary	60,987	40,426	19,221	657	683	100.0	66.3	31.5	1.1	1.1
Larceny-theft	205,201	138,577	60,545	2,275	3,804	100.0	67.5	29.5	1.1	1.9

(Continued)

Table 3.4 (Continued)

Offense Charged	Arrests Under 18					Percent Distribution[1]				
	Total	White	Black	American Indian or Alaskan Native	Asian or Pacific Islander	Total	White	Black	American Indian or Alaskan Native	Asian or Pacific Islander
Motor vehicle theft	25,285	13,576	10,965	265	479	100.0	53.7	43.4	1.0	1.9
Arson	5,868	4,646	1,075	49	98	100.0	79.2	18.3	0.8	1.7
Violent crime[2]	73,837	34,737	37,650	591	859	100.0	47.0	51.0	0.8	1.2
Property crime[2]	297,341	97,225	91,806	3,246	5,064	100.0	66.3	30.9	1.1	1.7
Other assaults	181,288	106,785	70,639	1,899	1,965	100.0	58.9	39.0	1.0	1.1
Forgery and counterfeiting	2,568	1,892	617	21	38	100.0	73.7	24.0	0.8	1.5
Fraud	5,656	3,623	1,938	34	61	100.0	64.1	34.3	0.6	1.1
Embezzlement	1,036	624	391	6	15	100.0	60.2	37.7	0.6	1.4
Stolen property; buying, receiving, possessing	15,574	8,750	6,522	123	179	100.0	56.2	41.9	0.8	1.1

Offense Charged	Arrests Under 18					Percent Distribution[1]				
	Total	White	Black	American Indian or Alaskan Native	Asian or Pacific Islander	Total	White	Black	American Indian or Alaskan Native	Asian or Pacific Islander
Vandalism	85,850	67,487	16,417	854	1,092	100.0	78.6	19.1	1.0	1.3
Weapons; carrying, possessing, etc.	34,611	21,142	12,745	285	439	100.0	61.1	36.8	0.8	1.3
Prostitution and commercialized vice	1,207	533	651	10	13	100.0	44.2	53.9	0.8	1.1
Sex offenses (except forcible rape and prostitution)	11,465	8,185	3,086	80	114	100.0	71.4	26.9	0.7	1.0
Drug abuse violations	143,267	97,800	43,080	1,126	1,261	100.0	68.3	30.1	0.8	0.9
Gambling	1,620	140	1,471	1	8	100.0	8.6	90.8	0.1	0.5

(Continued)

Table 3.4 (Continued)

Offense Charged	Arrests Under 18					Percent Distribution[1]				
	Total	White	Black	American Indian or Alaskan Native	Asian or Pacific Islander	Total	White	Black	American Indian or Alaskan Native	Asian or Pacific Islander
Offenses against the family and children	3,621	2,737	823	26	35	100.0	75.6	22.7	0.7	1.0
Driving under the influence	14,225	13,328	506	232	159	100.0	93.7	3.6	1.6	1.1
Liquor laws	102,230	93,368	4,987	2,635	1,240	100.0	91.3	4.9	2.6	1.2
Drunkenness	12,035	10,764	977	200	94	100.0	89.4	8.1	1.7	0.8
Disorderly conduct	152,869	88,420	61,438	1,799	1,212	100.0	57.8	40.2	1.2	0.8
Vagrancy	3,734	2,872	823	17	22	100.0	76.9	22.0	0.5	0.6
All other offenses (except traffic)	278,902	200,742	70,771	3,104	4,285	100.0	72.0	25.4	1.1	1.5

Offense Charged	Arrests Under 18					Percent Distribution[1]				
	Total	White	Black	American Indian or Alaskan Native	Asian or Pacific Islander	Total	White	Black	American Indian or Alaskan Native	Asian or Pacific Islander
Suspicion	316	205	108	0	3	100.0	64.9	34.2	0.0	0.9
Curfew and loitering law violations	114,166	69,624	42,496	814	1,232	100.0	61.0	37.2	0.7	1.1
Runaways	83,749	57,393	20,896	1,489	3,971	100.0	68.5	25.0	1.8	4.7

SOURCE: Uniform Crime Reports, 2007 (Federal Bureau of Investigation) .

NOTE: 11,249 Agencies; 2006 Estimated Population 216,685,152.

1. Because of rounding, the percentages may not add to 100.0.
2. Violent crimes are offenses of murder and non-negligent manslaughter, forcible rape, robbery, and aggravated assault. Property crimes are offenses of burglary, larceny-theft, motor vehicle theft, and arson.

are calculated using the victimization figures provided by the respondents. In 2006, there were an estimated 18.8 million property crimes and 5.2 million violent crimes (see Table 3.5). Thus, in contrast to the UCR, the NCVS estimated that there were more than 25 million criminal victimizations in the United States. Such figures clearly illuminate the disparities between the two data sources. However, the NCVS also has its problems. Respondents could forget a victimization incident and not report it, while others for unknown reasons could choose to lie about their victimization experience. Nonetheless, it is likely that the crime rate in the United States stands somewhere between both sources.

The NCVS data also yields useful information on the state of race, crime, and justice. After a precipitous drop in Black violent victimization rates from 1993 to 2001, the rate leveled off from 2001 to 2005. But by 2005, the figures according to Harrell (2007) were still of concern considering that:

> Blacks were victims of an estimated 805,000 nonfatal violent crimes and of about 8,000 homicides in 2005. While blacks accounted for 13% of the U.S. population in 2005, they were victims in 15% of all nonfatal violent crimes and nearly half of all homicides. (p. 1)

Table 3.6 presents figures revealing that American Indians actually have the highest violent victimization rates at 56.8 per 1,000 persons aged 12 and over (Harrell, 2007). (For a recent examination of this problem, see Abril, 2007). The rate for Latinos was 24.3, which was between that of Whites (22.8) and Blacks (28.7). A year later, though, the rates for Blacks had increased 5 points to 32.7 (see Table 3.7). Furthermore, irrespective of race or ethnicity, the figures reveal that males are victimized at higher rates than females; younger people (16+) are victimized more than older people (50+); married men are victimized less than those who have never been married; those with lower incomes are victimized more than those with higher incomes; and those in urban areas are more likely to be victimized than those in suburban areas or rural areas (Harrell, 2007, p. 10).

So what do all these figures mean? At least since the last century, this is the question scholars have been seeking to answer. During that period, just about every major criminological perspective, with varying results, has been applied to the issue of racial disparities in crime and victimization statistics (Gabbidon, 2007). Unfortunately, many of those scholars examining this question have been shortsighted and only felt a need to examine the topic with data

Table 3.5   Criminal Victimization, Numbers and Rates, 2006

Type of Crime	Number	Rate[a]
All crimes	25,077,700	
Violent crimes[b]	6,094,720	24.6
Rape/sexual assault	272,350	1.1
Robbery	711,570	2.9
Assault	5,110,810	20.7
Aggravated	1,354,750	5.5
Simple	3,756,060	15.2
Personal theft	174,150	0.7
Property crimes	18,808,820	159.5
Household burglary	3,539,760	30.0
Motor vehicle theft	993,910	8.4
Theft	14,275,150	121.0

SOURCE: Rand, M., & Catalano, S. M. (2007).

NOTE: Detail may not add total shown because of rounding. The total population age 12 or older was 247,290,210 in 2006. The total number of households was 117,952,450 in 2006.

a. Victimization rates are per 1,000 persons age 12 or older or per 1,000 households.
b. Excludes murder because the NCVS is based on interviews with victims and therefore cannot measure murder.

from their time period or shortly before. In so doing, they failed to realize that from the very beginnings of American society, diversity or difference has been synonymous with perceived criminality. Consequently, when one examines the early court records, laws, correctional figures, and the other criminal justice figures dating back to Colonial America, it quickly becomes apparent that race and ethnicity mattered even then (see Gabbidon & Greene, 2009). Today, researchers focusing on the United States have produced an enormous body of scholarship on the question of race, ethnicity, and crime, some of which is reviewed in the next section.

Table 3.6   Average Annual Violent Victimization Rate by Race/Hispanic Origin and Type of Crime, 2001–2005

| Race/Hispanic Origin | Rate per 1,000 Persons Age 12 or Older | | | | |
| | Total Violent Crime | Rape/ Sexual Assault | Robbery | Assault | |
				Aggravated	Simple
Black/African American[a]	28.7	1.7	4.3	7.7	14.9
White[a]	22.8	0.9	2.0	4.2	15.7
American Indian/Alaska Native[a]	56.8	0.9[b]	4.8[b]	11.6	39.5
Asian/Pacific Islander[a]	10.6	0.5[b]	2.3	1.7	6.2
Hispanic/Latino	24.3	0.8	3.6	5.3	14.5

SOURCE: Harrell, E. (2007).

NOTE:

a. Not Hispanic or Latino.
b. Based on 10 or fewer sample cases.

Table 3.7   Violent and Property Victimizations, by Race of Victim or Race of Head of Household, 2006

| Race of Victim | Violent | | | Property | | |
	Population	Number	Rate[a]	Households	Number	Rate[a]
White only	201,524,080	4,682,980	23.2	96,382,970	15,016,110	155.8
Black only	29,980,370	980,400	32.7	14,819,970	2,721,330	183.6
Other race[b]	12,849,300	240,740	18.7	5,506,430	759,650	138.0
Two or more races[c]	2,936,460	190,590	64.9	1,243,070	311,720	250.8

SOURCE: Rand, M., & Catalano, S. M. (2007).

NOTE:

a. Victimization rates are per 1,000 persons age 12 or older or per 1,000 households.
b. Includes American Indians, Eskimo, Asian Pacific Islander if only one of these races is given.
c. Includes all persons of any race, indicating two or more races.

SCHOLARSHIP ON RACE, ETHNICITY, CRIME, AND JUSTICE

Race/Ethnicity and Policing

Over the years, policing agencies in America have received considerable scholarly attention when considering race, ethnicity, and crime. In fact, entire books have examined topics such as their effectiveness in minority communities (Barlow & Barlow, 2000), the experiences of Blacks in the policing profession (Bolton & Feagin, 2004), and racial profiling (del Carmen, 2008; Harris, 2002; Herbert & Rose, 2004; Withrow, 2006). While some observers believe that the police unfairly bear the brunt of racial frustrations within the criminal justice system (see Wilbanks, 1987; MacDonald, 2003, 2008).

As one can imagine, the concerns regarding the police are rather complex. On the one hand, often times racial and ethnic minority communities do have higher rates of street crime (e.g., drugs, robbery) than other communities. As such, they often become the focus of police attention. This leads to additional police attention that, as was seen in the UCR figures, produces disparities in arrest figures. While, on the other hand, there is the belief that the police use excessive force in their efforts to reduce crime in minority communities, as evidenced by the level of brutality incidents in such communities (Cooper, 2003; Greene, 1994), targeting them for unnecessary stops and searches (Higgins, Vito, & Walsh, 2008).

Inevitably, the discussion gets reduced to the question as to whether the disparities in arrests are a result of discrimination or something else, such as Blacks or Hispanics simply engaging in more crimes (Mann, 1993; Wilbanks, 1987). There are even names for those who adhere to one of these two competing perspectives. Those who adhere to the notion that the criminal justice system is racist are in line with the *discrimination thesis* (DT), and those who feel that the disparities are "naturally" occurring for other reasons are in line with the *no discrimination thesis* (NDT). Since these terms were constructed in the late 1980s, other scholars have suggested that the poles of these two perspectives are inadequate to contextualize the nature of criminal justice (Walker, Spohn, & DeLone, 2007). Walker and his colleagues argue that, within these poles, the criminal justice system can be characterized by institutional discrimination (where discrimination largely exists within specific institutions that may result in a discriminatory outcome). Further, they present the notion that the system can be characterized by contextual discrimination in which discrimination can be found, for example, in the South, a particular courtroom, police department, or in some other isolated context. They also suggest that, in some instances, it might be that the level of discrimination has been reduced to a point where only individual criminal justice officials engage in discrimination (Walker et al., 2007). To examine some of these notions, the next section examines the issue of racial profiling.

Racial Profiling in America

While racial and ethnic minorities have long claimed that they were profiled by police officers, only within the last decade has this supposition been seriously considered. As a consequence of lawsuits across the nation, that alleged African Americans were being disproportionately stopped on roadways in Florida, Maryland, and New Jersey, researchers began to take note of data regarding traffic stops (Harris, 1999, 2002). Harriet (2004) aptly notes that for some time scholars seemed to have little interest in the topic, as evidenced by the paucity of scholarship on the topic in major criminology and criminal justice journals from 1995 to 1999. Over time, the allegations were supported, and researchers began to investigate traffic stops and additional aspects of racial profiling (Del Carmen, 2008; Milovanovic & Russell, 2001). Some of these additional aspects have been captured in Withrow's (2006) recent summary of the racial profiling scholarship published up to 2004. After reviewing numerous studies on racial profiling, Withrow (2006) noted the following:

- Blacks and Hispanic were stopped more frequently than other groups.
- Overall, all races were stopped for the same reasons.
- Racial and ethnic minorities were more likely to be searched than Whites.
- Stops involving minorities tended to be more punitive.
- Racial and ethnic minorities were not detained longer than Whites,
- Stops with racial and ethnic minorities were more likely to have instances of physical resistance and confrontation.
- Officer characteristics did not matter (e.g., officers race or ethnicity did not matter).

Since 2004, scholars have continued to investigate racial profiling or bias-based policing, as it is also now described. For example, the literature has diversified showing that Latinos also are being disproportionately stopped (Rice, Reitzel, & Piquero, 2005; Ruiz & Woessner, 2006; Weitzer & Tuch, 2005). Other literature, however, has revealed either minimal or no profiling (Gaines, 2006; Grogger & Ridgeway, 2006; Lange, Johnson, & Voas, 2005; Schafer, Carter, Katz-Bannister, & Wells, 2006), while other recent scholarship has pointed to continuing methodological challenges in the way in which states are collecting traffic-stop data (Liederbach, Trulson, Fritsch, Caeti, & Taylor, 2007).

Public opinion poll data has also been assessed to determine how the American public feels about profiling. A 2001 *New York Times* poll found that New Yorkers who felt that the New York City Police Department (NYPD) was doing a good job did not feel profiling was widespread. On the other hand, those New Yorkers who had negative encounters with the NYPD were more likely to believe that profiling was prevalent (Reitzel & Piquero, 2006). A more recent Gallup poll of randomly selected residents from across the country found that 52.64% of the respondents believed that racial profiling was widespread on roads and highways (Gallup Organization, 2004).

Notably, the racial profiling literature also began to produce numerous studies on consumer racial profiling that examine the way racial and ethnic minorities are treated in retail establishments (Gabbidon, 2003; Gabbidon, Craig, Okafo, Marzette, & Peterson, 2008; Gabbidon & Higgins, 2007; Higgins & Gabbidon, 2009). Such studies have shown that while racial and ethnic minorities might be profiled as suspected shoplifters more than Whites, they are no more likely to actually steal (Dabney, Hollinger, & Dugan, 2004; Dabney, Dugan, Topalli, & Hollinger, 2006). Another recent study found that Blacks were 10 times more likely than non-Blacks to feel they had been profiled in a retail setting (Gabbidon & Higgins, 2007). In addition, the aforementioned Gallup poll also found that 49.06% of the respondents felt that consumer racial profiling was widespread (Gallup Organization, 2004). In sum, though neglected, consumer racial profiling remains a vastly understudied but viable area of racial profiling research.

This brief overview reveals that "no matter how you slice it," the treatment of racial and ethnic profiling by American police agencies (Alpert, Dunham, & Smith, 2007; Brunson, 2007; Jones-Brown, 2007; Stewart, 2007) *and* retail store personnel remains a serious concern. The next section examines race/ethnicity and the courts.

Race/Ethnicity, Courts, and Sentencing

Following an arrest for an offense, depending on the nature of the crime, offenders are processed through either the federal, state, or local court systems. Here, too, an established body of literature argues that racial/ethnic discrimination has played a role in the distribution of justice. First, with Native Americans, the historical record shows that in the 1630s, the courts enforced doctrines that supported the English takeover of land previously occupied by Native Americans. Once such legislation was enacted, they were treated with severity by the court system, with many of them using enslavement or banishment as punishments (Higginbotham, 1978). White ethnics, especially the Irish, were also dealt with differently than English immigrants. As for African Americans, as you can imagine, they fared no better in the early court system in Colonial America.

After slavery was legally sanctioned in the 1660s, the laws increasingly allowed the courts to turn over the fate of African American criminals and those who tried to escape the ravages of slavery to the slave masters (Higginbotham, 1978). Furthermore, comprehensive analyses of court cases from the earliest decisions involving African Americans show clear instances of disparate treatment (Gabbidon & Greene, 2009). Such disparities also were found in the courts as Mexicans and Asian Americans headed to American shores.

The mass immigration to America in the 19th and 20th centuries produced similar outcomes for the ethnic immigrants, but as has been suggested elsewhere, once they assimilated into white America, they became less entangled in the criminal justice system because of their European ethnic background, which over time became a unifying characteristic; however, it was their skin color that provided the most visible and unifying attribute that separated them from African American migrants from the South and immigrants from the Caribbean and African countries (Feagin & Feagin, 2008; Gabbidon & Greene, 2009).

Long after their arrival in America, African Americans and Latinos are still receiving discriminatory treatment in the courts. As an example, Free (2002) conducted a detailed analysis of multivariate studies examining presentencing, which dated to the 1970s. The review found that race and gender did matter in the majority of the studies. In some studies, lower-class Blacks were found to be at a greater disadvantage than lower-class Whites. More specifically, Blacks were more likely to have to post higher cash or surety bonds than Whites (Free, 2002). Other research has found that racial and ethnic minority defendants are more likely to be disadvantaged and have to depend on public defense systems for counsel. Under normal circumstances this would be fine, but in far too many instances such systems are grossly underfunded. One study of the public defense system in Pennsylvania, for example, found that in some instances hiring one expert witness could deplete the entire defense budget (Pennsylvania Supreme Court, 2003). Another study found that Whites received better plea bargains than Blacks (Donzinger, 1996).

Jury selection is yet another area of the courts where the cards are stacked against racial and ethnic minorities. Here, there has been a nationwide concern regarding the lack of racial and ethnic minorities serving on juries. As such, there have been yeomen efforts to get more diverse representation on juries. Some states have resorted to providing child-care services, transportation, and increased stipends to increase diversity. Unfortunately, though, legal strategists for the defense and prosecution, in the end, often seek to strike racial and ethnic minority jurors—even after the outcry over their limited jury service (Cole, 1999; Gabbidon, Kowal, Jordan, Roberts, & Vincenzi, 2008).

If a case proceeds to the sentencing stage, this represents another stage of the American criminal justice system where disparities can occur. Higginbotham (1978) has clearly shown that early colonial sentencing decisions discriminated against African Americans and Native Americans. By poring through a substantial number of early cases throughout the Colonial period and the Colony, the legal decisions show a clear pattern of judicial injustice, with Whites receiving the more lenient treatment, and more brutal sentences, such as beatings, mutilations, castrations, and executions, largely reserved for Native Americans, African Americans, and poor White ethnics (Gabbidon & Greene, 2009).

The reality is that, today, such disparities still exist in sentencing. During the last 30 years, there was a swift and dramatic shift from the "rehabilitative ideal" to the "get tough" approach. These contrasting approaches have significant repercussions for sentencing. When rehabilitation prevailed, the sentences were more indeterminate and flexible; but when they turned more punitive, the sentences became more stringent and inflexible. So, while the names of the sentencing approaches changed (e.g., sentencing guidelines, mandatory minimums, truth-in-sentencing laws), the impact remained the same—i.e., longer sentences being disproportionately handed down to racial and ethnic minorities (Tonry, 1995; Gabbidon & Greene, 2009).

During this period, the so-called war on drugs magnified the sentencing disparities because the enforcement of drug laws in communities heavily populated by racial and ethnic minorities who were disproportionately exposed to aggressive police tactics (Miller, 1996). Consequently, because of these tactics, racial and ethnic minorities became the unfortunate beneficiaries of draconian sentences under such laws. Of particular note by scholars and citizens was the fact that the crack cocaine and powder cocaine laws called for those arrested with 500 grams of cocaine and 5 grams of crack cocaine to receive the same punishment (Russell-Brown, 2004). This differential, which started with unilateral support from Blacks and White politicians alike (see Kennedy, 1997), became, after the laws were found to have a disparate impact on racial and ethnic minorities, the rallying cry for a change in drug laws. Thus, even though the U.S. Sentencing Commission, the agency that makes recommendations for sentencing penalties to Congress, advised equalizing the penalties, not surprisingly no politician was willing to take up the cause of arguing to reduce crack penalties! This inaction, however, speaks to the way in which the long-standing devaluation of racial and ethnic minority lives plays out in American sentencing policy (see Hawkins, 1983). Hence, in this instance, there is no cause for alarm among the White-dominated Congress when significant numbers of ethnic and racial minorities waste away in correctional institutions because of irrational and racist sentencing policies.

The Death Penalty

The death penalty represents the ultimate sentence. America remains one of the few industrialized or "advanced" societies that still use the death penalty. Banner (2002) points to the fact that in the 18th century, early in American history, there were "swelling numbers of capital statutes applicable only to Blacks" (p. 8). Furthermore, statistics from 1880 to 1960 show that 3,442 Blacks were lynched throughout the country. Lynchings were vigilante-type justice that often occurred in the South, particularly when Blacks were felt to be "getting out of control" or they were alleged to have attacked a White woman (Cox, 1945). Most of these incidents (95%) occurred between 1880 and 1920 (Cahalan & Parsons, 1986). But, there are two things of note here. First, these were the documented incidents of lynching. Many went unrecorded during an era when racist White aggression against Blacks and other "undesirable" groups was implicitly sanctioned by local, state, and federal government (Katz, 1986). Second, once the number of lynchings was reduced, some scholars have argued that America then turned to legalized lynching to handle "troublesome" racial and ethnic minorities (Clarke, 1998; Zimring, 2003). This came in the form of the increased use of state-sanctioned executions. Recent scholarship has traced the decline of lynching and the rise of capital punishment and found that the level and nature of the two strikingly parallel one another (Clarke, 1998; Zimring, 2003).

So what about the death penalty today? In short, very little has changed. The most recent death penalty statistics by race reveals that at the end of 2005, 56% (1,805) of those on death row were White, while 42% (1,372) were Black (Snell, 2006). In terms of ethnicity, 13% (362) of the inmates were identified as Hispanic. Since 1977, the year after the United States Supreme Court's decision in *Gregg v. Georgia* (1976), which effectively reinstituted the use of the death penalty in America, 3,005 Blacks have been under the sentence of death, while 3,573 Whites have been under a similar sentence (Snell, 2006). These figures reveal the gross overrepresentation of Blacks in those under death sentences. Numerous scholars have sought to contextualize these figures to determine if the disparity that exists is the product of the nature of Black homicides or the presence of discrimination in the administration of the death penalty. Classic research by Paternoster (1983) and Baldus, Woodworth, and Pulaski (1990) found clear indications that the race of the victim was a significant predictor of whether a Black person was likely to receive the death penalty. Following this early pioneering research, more recent death penalty scholarship has continued to find that the race and gender of the victim matter in capital sentencing outcomes (Keil & Vito, 2006; Stauffer, Smith, Cochran, Fogel, & Bjerregaard, 2006; Williams & Holcomb, 2004).

Whereas most of the previous death penalty literature has centered on the experience of Blacks in capital sentencing, for obvious reasons, Hispanics have increasingly become the focus similar research. Lee (2007), for example, examined capital sentencing cases in San Joaquin County, California, from 1977 to 1986, to determine whether Hispanics were treated more like Blacks or Whites in capital sentencing cases. The results of Lee's multivariate analysis of 122 cases revealed that "defendants in White victim cases (and perhaps to some extent Asian American victim cases) faced much greater odds of being charged with a death-eligible offense than defendants in Black victim cases" (Lee, 2007, p. 22). Lee also found that cases with White victims were more likely to result in the defendant being charged with capital homicide "than defendants in Hispanic victim cases" (p. 22). Moreover, after controlling for the victim–offender relationship, weapon(s) used and prior record, the research still revealed a gender effect in that "killing a woman versus a man increased a defendant's odds of facing a capital homicide charge" (Lee, 2007, pp. 22–23). While limited to one jurisdiction, the results of this study suggest that race and death penalty research must be extended to focus on race, ethnicity, and gender. Below, the chapter provides a glimpse of race/ethnicity and corrections.

Race/Ethnicity and Corrections

With the increasing punitive nature of American sentencing, correctional systems and budgets have grown exponentially in the last three decades. It was foreseeable that there would need to be an expansion of prison capacity around the country to accommodate the seemingly endless influx of new inmates. It should have been also foreseeable that racial and ethnic minorities would be the ones filling correctional systems. Why? Again, history tells us that mass incarceration has been reserved for such populations (Wacquant, 2000). For example, prior to the Emancipation Proclamation, Whites primarily populated the prisons in the South, but following this period Whites came up with the convict–lease system to control Blacks who were no longer slaves. The system allowed for states to lease convicts to farmers facing a labor shortage as a result of the end of slavery. Unfortunately, the system led to the targeting of Blacks and poor Whites through the use of Black codes or laws that criminalized everything from vagrancy to not being employed (Du Bois, 1901; Myers, 1998; Oshinsky, 1996). Across other segments of the United States, the population of institutions remained largely White, but in the 20th century Blacks and other ethnic minorities started to become a slight majority of the correctional population. Today, according to the Bureau of Justice Statistics, Blacks and Hispanics represent 60% of state and federal inmates (Harrison & Beck, 2006). Moreover, these striking figures are further pronounced by the fact that "8.1% of Black males age 25 to 29 were in prison on December 31, 2005, compared to 2.6% of Hispanic males and about 1.1% of white males in the same age group" (Harrison & Beck, 2006, p. 8).

So what explains these troubling figures? In the early 1980s, Blumstein (1982) examined this question by analyzing state-level correctional data which showed that "80% of actual racial disproportionality in incarceration is accounted for by differential involvement in arrest" (pp. 1267–1268). The remaining 20% was unexplained and could have been the result of discrimination. More than a decade later, Blumstein (1993) did the study again and noted that things had gotten worse, with 24% of the disproportionality now being unexplained. Here, Blumstein pointed to the likelihood that drug offenses were the source of the increased unexplained numbers. Other scholars have simply pointed to the fact that the so-called prison industrial complex or the massive financial investments in corrections, both public and private (see Hallett, 2006; Price, 2006), and the related industries had spurred the need for increased inmate populations (Davis, 2003; Dyer, 2000; Huling, 2002; Lotke, 1996).

As a consequence of bearing the brunt of these increasing prison populations, racial and ethnic minorities have suffered a variety of collateral consequences.

Recent research has focused on their loss of voting rights. Many states preclude for-mer inmates from voting either for a certain period after their release or perma-nently (Preuhs, 2001; The Sentencing Project, 2008). Researchers have found that this disenfranchisement has serious ramifications for the electoral process and harms the democracy (Manza & Uggen, 2006). In recent years, there has been a successful movement to repeal some of the laws that disenfranchised offenders. One recent report noted that more than 750,000 ex-offenders have regained the right to vote (King, 2008). In addition to disenfranchisement, another crucial collateral consequence of incarceration is the difficulty that released inmates have securing employment. Given that 600,000 inmates are being released each year (Petersilia, 2003), securing employment remains critical to their success. Research by Pager (2007) has revealed that those inmates seeking employment will have a hard time finding jobs—especially considering that in her experimental studies Whites with criminal records were more likely to get jobs than Blacks without criminal back-grounds. Such findings suggest that the collateral consequences of being incarcer-ated, at least for racial and ethnic minorities, leads to a continuing cycle of inequality and continuing incarceration (Clear, 2007; Western, 2006). In the end, not surprisingly, this cycle continues to fuel the "prison industrial complex."

SUMMARY AND CONCLUSION

After a detailed overview of American history, this chapter examined race/ethnicity and justice in America. After completing this survey of the literature, one can only agree with professors Daniel Georges-Abeyie and Delores Jones-Brown who, in recent years when examining race-related issues in criminal jus-tice, have both declared: "The more things change, the more things remain the same" (Georges-Abeyie, 2001; Jones-Brown, 2007). This statement captures the essence of race/ethnicity and crime in America. Put another way, while hundreds of years have passed since the colonization of Native Americans and the slave era, numerous legislative enactments have been passed, and criminal justice agencies have become more diverse, racial and ethnic minorities more often than not still face significant challenges related to fairness in the American criminal justice system. Therefore, while traffic-stop data are starting to align with racial populations, significant questions still remain about profiling in retail settings. As for courts and sentencing, the data continue to show cause for concern. Yes, racial and ethnic minorities who commit crimes and should be punished; but, over the past few centuries, they have consistently received the more serious punishments. So even today, when one sifts through the mounds of research studies on race/ethnicity and crime, study after study finds that even when controlling for numerous critical variables, the incarceration rates of racial and ethnic minorities far exceeds that of Whites.

This chapter has only scratched the surface of issues related to race/ethnicity and crime in America. It is no secret that the American scholarship in this area is expansive. Even so, new areas of exploration are emerging. For example, the increasing immigration of Latinos to the United States has spurred a renewal of interest in ethnicity, immigration, and crime (Martinez & Valenzuela, 2006). Thus, given the volatile nature of immigration discussions taking place in American politics, it is likely that this will become a whole new segment of the race/ethnicity and crime literature.

In closing, as discussed in Chapter 1 and further evidenced by the contents of this chapter, the American experience of racial and ethnic groups can clearly be contextualized by the colonial model. The Native American experience best illustrates the full impact of colonization. Beginning with genocidal attacks, Native Americans have endured both cultural denigration and cultural imposition (continued attempts to assimilate them to European ways). In addition, they have been victims of social, economic, and political subordination. This experience has contributed to disorganized communities that have produced the highest criminal victimization rates in the United States. The experiences of African Americans and Latinos also points to the applicability of the colonial model. In the case of African Americans, after being forcibly brought here, their early experience mirrored that of a colonial situation. Here again, this colonial experience placed them in a position of disadvantage they have not fully overcome. Latinos freely came to American seeking work, but after a period of time they encountered conditions and circumstances that produced disadvantage, which is characteristic of colonialism. In all of these instances, at some point the colonial model's anticipation of the creation of a caste system based on race and class came to fruition.

REFERENCES

Abril, J. C. (2007). Native American Indian identity and violent victimization. *International Perspectives in Victimology, 3,* 1–7.

Alpert, G. P., Dunham, R. G., Smith, M. R. (2007). Investigating racial profiling by the Miami–Dade police department: A multimethod approach. *Criminology & Public Policy, 6,* 25–56.

Aptheker, H. (1993). *American Negro slave revolts.* New York: International Publishers. (Originally published in 1943).

Baldus, D. C., Woodworth, G., & Pulaski, C. A. (1990). *Equal justice and the death penalty: A legal and empirical analysis.* Boston: Northeastern University Press.

Banner, S. (2002). *The death penalty: An American history.* Cambridge, MA: Harvard University Press.

Barlow, D. E., & Barlow, M. H. (2000). *Police in a multicultural society: An American story.* Prospect Heights, IL: Waveland Press.

Blumstein, A. (1982). On the racial disproportionality of U.S. prison populations. *Journal of Criminal Law & Criminology, 73,* 1259–1281.

Blumstein, A. (1993). Racial disproportionality of U.S. prison populations revisited. *University of Colorado Law Review, 64,* 743–760.

Bolton, K., & Feagin, J. R. (2004). *Black in blue: African-American police officers and racism.* New York: Routledge.

Browne-Marshall, G. (2007). *Race, law and American Society, 1607 to present.* New York: Routledge.

Brunson, R. K. (2007). "Police don't like black people": African-American young men's accumulated police experiences. *Criminology & Public Policy, 6,* 71–102.

Cahalan, M., & Parsons, L. (1986). *Historical corrections in the United States, 1850–1984.* Washington, DC: Bureau of Justice Statistics.

Caldwell, A. A. (2007, August 12). Mending fences: Plugging holes along border never ends for agents. *The Patriot-News,* p. A10.

Carl, T. (2007, August 12). Illegal migrations drop along U.S. border. *The Patriot-News,* p. A10.

Clarke, J. W. (1998). Without fear or shame: Lynching, capital punishment, and the subculture of violence in the American South. *British Journal of Political Science, 28,* 269–289.

Clear, T. R. (2007). *Imprisoning communities: How mass incarceration makes disadvantaged neighborhoods worse.* New York: Oxford University Press.

Cole, D. (1999). *No equal justice.* New York: New Press.

Cooper, C. (2003). Prosecuting police officers for police brutality: From a minority perspective. In D. D. Jones-Brown & K. J. Terry (Eds.), *Policing and minority communities: Bridging the gap* (pp. 115–159). Upper Saddle River, NJ: Prentice-Hall.

Cox, O. C. (1945). Lynching and the status quo. *Journal of Negro Education, 14,* 576–588.

Crosby, A. W. (1972). *The Columbian exchange: Biological and cultural consequences of 1492.* Westport, CT. Greenwood Press.

Dabney, D. A., Dugan, L., Topalli, V., & Hollinger, R. C. (2006). The impact of implicit stereotyping on offender profiling: Unexpected results from an observational study of shoplifting. *Criminal Justice and Behavior, 33,* 646–674.

Dabney, D. A., Hollinger, R. C., & Dugan, L. (2004). Who actually steals? A study of covertly observed shoplifters. *Justice Quarterly, 21,* 693–728.

Davis, A. Y. (2003). *Are prisons obsolete?* New York: Seven Stories Press.

Del Carmen, A. (2008). *Racial profiling in America.* Upper Saddle River, NJ: Prentice-Hall/Pearson.

Donzinger, S. R. (1996). *The real war on crime.* New York: Harper Perennial.

Du Bois, W. E. B. (1901). The spawn of slavery: The convict lease system in the South. *Missionary Review of the World, 14,* 737–745.

Dyer, J. (2000). *The perpetual prisoner machine: How America profits from crime.* Boulder, CO. Westview Press.

Feagin, R. F., & Feagin, C. B. (2008). *Racial and ethnic relations* (8th ed.). Upper Saddle River, NJ: Prentice Hall.

Felon disenfranchisement laws in the United States. (2008). Washington, DC: The Sentencing Project.

Finger, B. (1959). *Concise world history.* New York: Philosophical Library.

Franklin, J. H., & Moss, A. A. (2000). *From slavery to freedom: A history of African Americans* (8th ed.). New York: McGraw-Hill.

Free, M. D. (2002). Racial bias and the American criminal justice system: Race and presentencing revisited. *Critical Criminology, 10,* 195–223.

Gabbidon, S. L. (2003). Racial profiling by store clerks and security personnel in retail establishments: An exploration of "shopping while black." *Journal of Contemporary Criminal Justice, 19,* 345–364.

Gabbidon, S. L. (2007). *Criminological perspectives on race and crime.* New York: Routledge.

Gabbidon, S. L., Craig, R., Okafo, N., & Marzette, L., & Peterson, S. A. (2008). The consumer racial profiling experiences of Black students at historically Black colleges and universities: An exploratory study." *Journal of Criminal Justice, 36,* 354–361.

Gabbidon, S. L., & Greene, H. T. (2009). *Race and crime* (2nd ed.). Thousand Oaks, CA: Sage.

Gabbidon, S. L., & Higgins, G. E. (2007). Consumer racial profiling and perceived victimization: A phone survey of Philadelphia area residents. *American Journal of Criminal Justice, 32,* 1–11.

Gabbidon, S. L., Kowal, L., Jordan, K., Roberts, J., & Vincenzi, N. (2008). Race-based peremptory challenges: An empirical analysis of litigation from the U.S. Court of Appeals, 2002–2006. *American Journal of Criminal Justice 3,* 59–68.

Gaines, L. K. (2006). An analysis of traffic stop data in Riverside, California. *Police Quarterly, 9,* 210–233.

Gallup Organization. (2004). Minority rights and relations; Black and social audit poll. Retrieved September 24, 2006, from Gallup Brain database, www.gallup.com

Georges-Abeyie, D. (2001). Petit apartheid in criminal justice: The more things change, the more things stay the same. In D. Milovanovic & K. K. Russell (Eds.), *Petit apartheid in the U.S. criminal justice system: The dark figure of racism* (pp. ix–xiv). Durham, NC: Carolina Academic Press.

Greene, H. T. (1994). Black perspectives on police brutality. In A. T. Sulton (Ed.), *African-American perspectives on: Crime causation, criminal justice administration, and crime prevention* (pp. 139–148). Englewood, CO: Sulton Books.

Gregg v. Georgia. (1976). *The Oyez project* (428 U.S. 153). Available at www.oyez.org

Grogger, J., & Ridgeway, G. (2006). Testing for racial profiling in traffic stops from behind a veil of darkness. *Journal of the American Statistical Association, 101,* 878–887.

Hacker, A. (2003). *Two nations: Black and white, separate, hostile, unequal* (Rev. ed.). New York: Scribner.

Hallett, M. A. (2006). *Private prisons in America: A critical race perspective.* Urbana, IL: University of Illinois Press.

Harrell, E. (2007). *Black victims of violent crime.* Washington, DC: Bureau of Justice Statistics.

Harriet, A. (2004). Presumed criminality, racial profiling, and policing in America—with special attention to the Diallo case. In D. D. Jones-Brown & K. J. Terry (Eds.), *Policing and minority communities: Bridging the gap* (pp. 22–35). Upper Saddle River, NJ: Prentice-Hall.

Harris, D. A. (1999). *Driving while black: Racial profiling on our nation's highways.* Retrieved January 23, 2001, from www.aclu.org/index/html

Harris, D. (2002). *Profiles in injustice: Why racial profiling cannot work.* New York: The New Press.

Harrison, P. M., & Beck, A. (2006). *Prisoners in 2005.* Washington, DC: Bureau of Justice Statistics.

Hawkins, D. F. (1983). Black and white homicide differentials: Alternatives to an inadequate theory. *Criminal Justice and Behavior, 10,* 407–440.

Herbert, S., & Rose, L. (2004). *The color of guilt and innocence: Racial profiling and police practices in America.* San Ramon, CA: Page Marque Press.

Higginbotham, A. L. (1978). *In the matter of color: Race and the American legal process: The colonial period.* New York: Oxford University Press.

Higginbotham, A. L. (1996). *Shades of freedom: Racial politics and the presumptions of the American legal process.* New York: Oxford University Press.

Higgins, G. E., & Gabbidon, S. L. (2009). Perceptions of consumer racial profiling and negative emotions: An exploratory study. *Criminal Justice and Behavior, 36,* 77–88.

Higgins, G. E., Vito, G. F., & Walsh, W. F. (2008). Searches: An understudied area of racial profiling. *Journal of Ethnicity in Criminal Justice, 6,* 23–40.

Horton, J. O., & Horton, L. E. (2005). *Slavery and the making of America.* New York: Oxford University Press.

Huling, T. (2002). Building a prison economy in rural America. In M. Mauer & M. Chesney-Lind (Eds.), *Invisible punishment: The collateral consequences of mass imprisonment* (pp. 197–213). New York: New Press.

Lotke, E. (1996). *The prison-industrial complex.* Baltimore: National Center on Institutions and Alternatives.

Jones-Brown, D. (2007). Forever the symbolic assailant: The more things change the more things stay the same. *Criminology & Public Policy, 6,* 103–122.

Katz, W. L. (1986). *The invisible empire: The Ku Klux Klan impact on history.* Seattle: Open Hand Publishing.

Kcil, T. J., & Vito, G. F. (2006). Capriciousness or fairness? Race and prosecutorial decisions to seek the death penalty in Kentucky. *Journal of Ethnicity in Criminal Justice, 4,* 27–49.

Kennedy, R. (1997). *Race, crime, and the law.* New York: Pantheon.

King, R. S. (2008). *Expanding the vote: State felony disenfranchisement reform, 1997–2008.* Washington, DC: The Sentencing Project.

Lange, J. E., Johnson, M. B., & Voas, R. B. (2005). Testing the racial profiling hypothesis for seemingly disparate traffic stops on the New Jersey Turnpike. *Justice Quarterly, 22,* 193–223.

Lee, C. (2007). Hispanics and the death penalty: Discriminatory charging practices in San Joaquin County, California. *Journal of Criminal Justice, 35,* 17–27.

Liederbach, J., Trulson, C. R., Fritsch, E. J., Caeti, T. J., Taylor, R. W. (2007). Racial profiling and the political demand for data: A pilot study designed to improve methodologies in Texas. *Criminal Justice Review, 32,* 101–120.

Mac Donald, H. (2003). *Are cops racist? How the war against the police harms black Americans.* Chicago: Ivan R. Dee.

MacDonald, H. (2008, Spring). Is the criminal justice system racist? No: The high percentage of blacks behind bars reflects crime rates, not bigotry. *City Journal.* Retrieved May 6, 2008, from www.city-journal.org

Mann, C. C. (2006). *1491: New revelations of the Americas before Columbus.* New York: Vintage Books.

Mann, C. R. (1993). *Unequal justice: A question of color?* Bloomington, IN: Indiana University Press.

Manza, J., & Uggen, C. (2006). *Locked out: Felon disenfranchisement and American democracy.* New York: Oxford University Press.

Martinez, R., & Valenzuela, A. (Eds.). (2006). *Immigration and crime: Race, ethnicity, and violence.* New York: NY University Press.

McInerney, D. J. (2001). *A traveller's history of the USA.* New York: Interlink Books.

Meinig, D. W. (1986). *The shaping of America: A geographical perspective on 500 years of history.* New Haven, CT: Yale University Press.

Miller, J. G. (1996). *Search and destroy: African American males in the criminal justice system.* Cambridge, UK: Cambridge University Press.

Milovanovic, D., & Russell, K. K. (Eds.). (2001). *Petit apartheid in the U.S. criminal justice system: The dark figure of racism.* Durham, NC: Carolina Academic Press.

Myers, M. A. (1998). *Race, labor, and punishment in the new south.* Columbus, OH: Ohio State University Press.

Oshinsky, D. M. (1996). *Worse than slavery: Parchman farm and the ordeal of Jim Crow justice.* New York: Free Press.

Pager, D. (2007). *Marked: Race, crime, and finding work in an era of mass incarceration.* Chicago: University of Chicago Press.

Paternoster, R. (1983). Race of victim and location of crime: The decision to seek the death penalty in South Carolina. *Journal of Criminal Law and Criminology, 74,* 701–731.

Pennsylvania Supreme Court. (2003). *Pennsylvania Supreme Court Committee on racial and gender bias in the justice system.* Retrieved January 1, 2004, from www.courts.state.pa.us

Petersilia, J. (2003). *When prisoners come home: Parole and prisoner reentry.* New York: Oxford University Press.

Polk, W. R. (2006). *The birth of America: From Columbus to the revolution.* New York: HarperCollins.

Preuhs, R. R. (2001). State felon disenfranchisement policy. *Social Science Quarterly, 82,* 733–748.

Price, B. E. (2006). *Merchandizing prisoners: Who really pays for prison privatization?* Westport, CT: Praeger.

Rand, M., & Catalano, S. M. (2007). *Criminal victimization, 2006.* Washington, DC: Bureau of Justice Statistics.

Reitzel, J., & Piquero, A. R. (2006). Does it exist? Studying citizens' attitudes of racial profiling. *Police Quarterly, 9,* 161–183.

Rice, S. K., Reitzel, J. D., & Piquero, A. R. (2005). Shades of brown: Perception of racial profiling and the intra-ethnic differential. *Journal of Ethnicity in Criminal Justice, 3,* 47–70.

Ruiz, J. R., & Woessner, M. (2006). Profiling, Cajun style: Racial profiling and demographic profiling in Louisiana's war on drugs. *International Journal of Police Science & Management, 8,* 176–197.

Russell, K. K. (1998). *The color of crime: Racial hoaxes, white fear, black protectionism, police harassment, and other macroaggressions.* New York: NY University Press.

Russell-Brown, K. K. (2004). *Underground codes: Race, crime, and related fires.* New York: NY University Press.

Russell-Brown, K. K. (2009). *The color of crime (2nd edition).* New York: New York University Press.

Schafer, J. A., Carter, D. L., Katz-Bannister, A., & Wells, W. M. (2006). Decision making in traffic stop encounters: A multivariate analysis of police behavior. *Police Quarterly, 9,* 184–209.

Snell, T. L. (2006). *Capital punishment, 2005.* Washington, DC: Bureau of Justice Statistics.

Sowell, T. (1981). *Ethnic America: A history.* New York: Basic Books.

Stauffer, A. R., Smith, M. D., Cochran, J. K., Fogel, S. J., & Bjerregaard, B. (2006). The interaction between victim race and gender on outcomes in capital murder trials: A further exploration. *Homicide Studies, 10,* 98–117.

Stewart, E. A. (2007). Either they don't know or they don't care: Black males and negative police experiences. *Criminology & Public Policy, 6,* 133–130.

Takaki, R. (1998). *Strangers from a different shore: A history of Asian Americans.* Boston: Little, Brown and Company.

Tonry, M. (1995). *Malign neglect.* New York: Oxford University Press.

United States Census Bureau. (2004). *Current population survey.* Retrieved August 12, 2007, from www.census.gov

Wacquant, L. (2000). The new "peculiar institution": On the prison as surrogate ghetto. *Theoretical Criminology, 4,* 377–389.

Walker, S., Spohn, C., & DeLone, M. (2007). *The color of justice: Race, ethnicity, and crime in America* (4th ed.). Belmont, CA: Thomson Learning.

Weitzer, R. & Tuch, S. A. (2002). Perceptions of racial profiling: Race, class, and personal experience. *Criminology, 40,* 435–456.

Western, B. (2006). *Punishment and inequality in America.* New York: Russell Sage Foundation.

Wilbanks, W. (1987). *The myth of a racist criminal justice system.* Belmont, CA: Brooks/Cole.

Williams, M. R., & Holcomb, J. E. (2004). The interactive effects of victim race and gender on death sentence disparity findings. *Homicide Studies, 8,* 350–376.

Wilson, W. J. (1987). *The truly disadvantaged: The inner city, the underclass, and public policy.* Chicago: University of Chicago Press.

Withrow, B. L. (2006). *Racial profiling: From rhetoric to reason.* Upper Saddle River, NJ: Prentice-Hall.

Zimring, F. (2003). *The contradictions of American capital punishment.* New York: Oxford University Press.

Figure 4.1 Contemporary Map of Canada

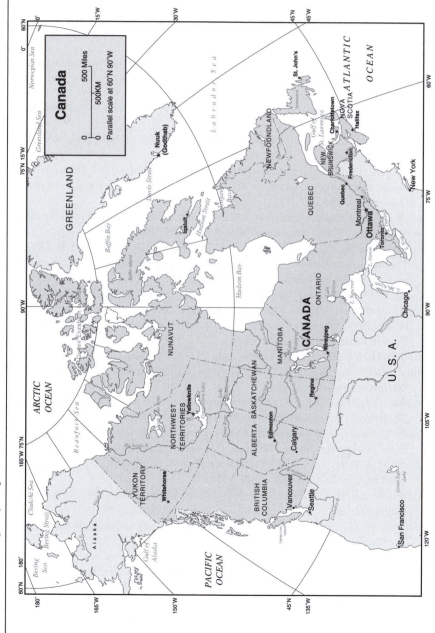

◄ FOUR ►

CANADA

——◆•◆•◆——

CHAPTER OVERVIEW

This chapter begins with a review of the history and development of Canada. This history illuminates the early European colonization of the Aboriginal people. In the Canadian context, the colonization involved both the British and French; however, the result was the same: the decimation of the Aboriginal people. The chapter then explores the nature and scope of crime in Canada, with an emphasis on the plight of the Aboriginal people and residents that Canadians refer to as "visible minorities" or persons who are non-Caucasian in race or non-White in color (not including Aboriginals).

EARLY HISTORY

Canada is the second largest country in the world (see Figure 4.1). It is surrounded by the Pacific, Atlantic, and Arctic oceans. It was originally populated by indigenous persons (referred to as Amerindians) who, it is believed, between 12,000 to 20,000 years ago made their way from northern Asia, with some possibly having origins in Manchuria and Mongolia (See, 2001, p. 23). In addition, from A.D. 700 to 1000, the Inuit people from Arctic regions migrated to Canada. The native people were well-adjusted to cold climates and created survival methods, the diversity of which, is highlighted by Morton (1997a):

> Whether it was the light snow shoes of the Algonquins, the hunting organi-
> zation of the Blackfoot and Crees, or the Arctic clothing, kayaks, and igloos

of the Innu. All had unique artistic and decorative skills, sophisticated myths and legends to explain their world to themselves and others, and religious beliefs that sustained the human qualities needed for survival. (p. 23)

While Norsemen likely were among the first Europeans to settle in North America, John Cabot is credited with the first major settlement in Canada, having founded and claimed Newfoundland for Britain, in 1497 (Ray, 1997, pp. 20–21). And though Cabot had originally set out, like other European explorers, to find a quicker route to the riches in the Far East, he settled for the discovery of cod, which was heavily sought after in Europe (Ray, 1997). On the other hand, when Jacques Cartier claimed North America for France in 1534, his mission had been made clear in his commission from the King of France: "[Discover] certain isles and countries where it is said there must be great quantities of gold and other riches" (Ray, 1997, p. 22). In the end, no gold was found and because of the religious wars in France from 1560 to 1590, "the French had little time to spend on speculative trips across the Atlantic, and none at all for cold and disappointing Canada" (Bothwell, 2002, p. 13). In the early 1600s, the French returned to what they referred to as New France, and Pierre du Gua de Monts and Samuel de Champaign made modern-day Quebec the center of their new colony because of its strategic location. It became the center of the lucrative fur trade, which had a strong market in Europe.

Approximately 500,000 to 1 million native people lived in Canada when the Europeans arrived. However, as in other places, disease, weapons (guns and knives), attempts at religious conversion, and the introduction of alcohol into native life, resulted in the decimation of the native population (see Daunton & Halpern, 1999; Dickason, 2006; and more generally, Crosby, 1972). In some instances, the Europeans sided with certain tribes in wars with rival tribes. By doing so, they disrupted the natural order of tribal development and growth. For example, Champaign assisted the Huron tribe in fighting the Iroquois; however over time, the Iroquois eventually defeated the Huron and other tribes. Thus, by 1850, Bothwell (2002) reports that there were only 100,000 native people remaining.

Again, mirroring other colonial situations, as the native population decreased, the colonial population increased. With other settlements in strategic locations, such as Montreal, the French population increased from 20,000 in 1710 to 55,000 by 1754. However, this increase paled in comparison to the rising British population. In 1710, the British settlements had more than 400,000 persons, and by 1755 this figure had increased to 1.5 million (Bothwell, 2002). Drawn to British settlements by better weather than the French colonies and more land and freedom (Bothwell, 2002), such numbers proved to be a decisive advantage when the French and British intermittently warred, from 1689 to 1763, over control of Canada. However, it was the Seven Years' War, from 1756 to 1763, that resulted in the defeat of the French. Signed in 1763, the Treaty of Paris ended the war (See, 2001, p. 54). The treaty also included concessions for indigenous territories; however in the same year comes this from Pontiac, the chief of the Ottawa: "In a last ditch effort to hold back European expansion . . . mounted a series of bloody, terrifying raids on interior trading post . . . which . . . killed more than two thousand people" (Wynn, 1997, p. 194). Thus, while "Indian Territory" was initially listed on the revised map, a little more than a decade later, it was removed (Wynn, 1997, p. 194).

Even with Britain's decisive victory over the French, another major war was on the horizon. A few decades after the defeat of the British in the American Revolutionary War, the Americans felt the time was ripe to take Canada from the British. Because the British were engulfed in military actions overseas, the Americans, who considerably outnumbered the Canadians, decided to try and take Canada, which they anticipated would result in a swift victory. However, the War of 1812 proved to be more protracted than the Americans had anticipated. Bothwell (2002) notes that, while the Canadians and the British army were, in fact, outnumbered, the American military was too fractured to mount a serious campaign against them. As a result, the undermanned British and colonial forces were victorious. With the signing of the Treaty of Ghent in 1814, the war officially ended.

After years of debate and hostilities, the various Canadian provinces moved to form a united nation and after some thought, in 1867 organized the Kingdom of Canada, which was later renamed the Dominion of Canada. The new government included a governor–general, who was a representative of the British government, and the Canadian federal Parliament, which included a House of Commons and a Senate. Cabinets were headed by the Prime Minister, but "were selected from among the majority in the House of Commons" (Bothwell, 2002, p. 55). Having taken notice of how the weak central government in America fell apart during the Civil War, the Canadians created a political structure with a strong central government. So, even though there were several provinces (Nova Scotia, New Brunswick, Quebec, and Ontario), they had limited powers other than handling local affairs (Bothwell,

2002, p. 56). Even so, Manitoba became a province in 1870 and in 1871, with the promise of building a transcontinental railway, British Columbia joined the Dominion of Canada. Moreover, Prince Edward Island became a province in 1873 and in 1905, Saskatchewan and Alberta became provinces as well.

Even with these "unifying" developments, in the first decade of the 20th century, Canadians were still struggling with issues pertaining to language, schools, and indigenous people. In fact, Cook (1997) describes the way "outsiders" were handled in the early 20th-century Canada:

> Native people were hived off on reservations; blacks, with the exception of small communities in Nova Scotia, Montreal, and Southern Ontario, were excluded; while entry of Chinese, Japanese, and even fellow members of the British Empire who came from India were severely restricted. (p. 391)

The general approach with the indigenous people was one of isolation. However, there was the hope they would assimilate into the mainstream of Canadian society. To expedite this process, the Indian Affairs branch of the Department of the Interior had as its major goal "the assimilation of native peoples into white society—when they were ready" (Cook, 1997, p. 435). The government worked in conjunction with missionaries to "modernize" them by altering their culture and religious beliefs. Moreover, as in other colonies, "children were separated from their families and sent off to a mission school in utterly unfamiliar surroundings" (Cook, 1997, p. 436). Cook notes that the fate of indigenous adults was equally destitute:

> Men were pressed to give up trapping and hunting in favour of farming, which many native groups viewed as women's work. Demoralization and alienation followed. Those who drifted off the reserves into the cities rarely escaped the traps of alcohol and prostitution. (p. 436)

However, the onset of World War I gave the country another focus. During the war, Canada sent 425,000 soldiers, with more than 60,000 of them lost in battle (Bothwell, 2002, p. 77). Oddly enough, the war was good for Canada; it jump-started the Canadian economy. Nevertheless, the prosperity that followed the end of the war only lasted about a decade; at which time Canada, as in the United States, headed into a depression. Brought on largely by a drought and reduced exports of grain, pulp and paper, minerals, and other goods, the Canadian economy resulted in dramatic income declines and increasing unemployment

(Cook, 1997, p. 444). It would take another world war to jump-start the Canadian economy.

The breakout of World War II meant that Canada would be involved in yet another war. Even so, they understood the necessity of their participation in a war to stop Hitler's aggression near their former mother country. Consequently, more than 1 million Canadians served in World War II, with more than 100,000 casualties (See, 2001, p. 133). While there was initially some heavy debate about the need for conscription, eventually, as in other countries, Canadians rallied around the cause. At home, where necessary, women filled in, in place of men. Unfortunately, though, when Japan entered the war, Canada also followed the practice of isolating persons of Japanese descent. Describing this practice, Cook (1997) wrote that:

> Early in 1942, when Japan had joined the war, the Canadian government moved to dispossess and relocate all British Columbians of Japanese origin, even those who were Canadian citizens; families were split up and whatever property they could not carry was disposed of by the government. This was the culmination of decades of anti-Asiatic feeling on the Pacific coast. (p. 460)

During the war, Canada had enjoyed full employment and a steady stream of income (Morton, 1997b, p. 469). But despite concerns from the Canadian government and the populace, Canada's prosperity was sustained and did not result in a depression, as it had a decade after World War I. In fact, their prosperity was so good that in 1948 Newfoundland, hoping to also reap some benefits from the prosperity, entered the confederation and became a province of Canada (Morton, 1997b, p. 474).

With continued prosperity, the 1950s and 1960s saw the development of suburbs in Canada. Along with that, the Canadian baby boom caused a shortage of schools. During this period, Canadians also became increasingly concerned about the "American influence." American culture was being imported through television programs which after some concern became widely accepted by Canadian society. Besides American culture, there was increasing concern regarding increasing immigration to Canada. To illustrate the magnitude of the immigration "problem," Morton indicates that, from 1947 to 1967, 3 million people immigrated to Canada (Morton, 1997b, p. 482). This increasing immigration changed the nature of Canada and continued its long history of struggles with difference.

CONTEMPORARY HISTORY

The 1970s saw Canadian Prime Minister Pierre Trudeau try to institute social policies that contributed to social justice. His program involved reforms that included "regional economic development, unemployment insurance, Medicare, and education subsidies" (Bothwell, 2002, p. 140). Moreover, during the period, because of agreements made with the United States in the 1960s, the auto industry boomed in Canada. Regardless of the positives of the period, there was still concern that a constitutional change would be necessary to quell threats from separatists in Quebec. In Quebec, some were concerned about the Multiculturalism Act that encouraged immigrants to be themselves. In passing the Act, the government was responding to the wave of immigrants from Europe, Asia, the Caribbean, and African countries. However, the separatists felt that the Act would leave their culture in jeopardy.

In addition, things in general were changing in Canada; the once puritanical society now struggled with similar problems as in other industrialized countries. Born out of "dogmas based on conservative selfishness," Morton (1997b) described the result of the adherence to such a philosophy:

> Between 1971 and 1978, the abortion rate in Canada doubled. So did murder convictions. Urban parents, once terrified by the drug culture, now worried that their offspring would be swept into exotic religious cults . . . More than a third of all marriages now ended in divorce and the advance of feminism coincided with the spread of pornography and sexual assault. (p. 300)

The situation was further exasperated by increasing poverty rates in the 1980s and 1990s. Kazemipur and Halli (1999) observed that during most of the 1980s the poverty rate in Canada remained fairly stable and actually declined by 1990. However, by 1991, the rate had risen to 15.8%, up from 12.1% a year earlier. These rates were attributed to the declining income of the middle class, and the rising wealth of the upper class. Many also believed that slower economic growth in Canada and around the world contributed to this new poverty. Describing this new poverty, Kazemipur and Halli (1999) wrote:

> The new wave of poverty is different from the earlier ones, not only in size but also in the comparison of its victims. The poverty rates of different groups in Canada show that, in 1996, female-headed, lone-parent families with children, women, unattached individuals, common-law families, young adults 18–24, and the elderly were over-represented among the poor. (p. 8)

The authors argue that the "feminization of poverty" (Kazemipur & Halli, 1999, p. 8) caused by the high divorce rates, cut into their family incomes. The divorce rate, combined with the fact that females were typically in low-paying, part-time jobs, likely also contributed to their poverty levels. As for the elderly, as in most countries, increasing longevity contributed to their increasing poverty rates. As for racial/ethnic groups, it was believed that they were also affected by the new poverty, but there was a lack of interest in the ethnicization of poverty (Kazemipur & Halli, 1999, p. 10). This was particularly problematic considering that ethnic minorities were clustered in many of the poorer neighborhoods where crime has traditionally flourished.

Even with these poverty-related issues, by the late 1990s, Canada consistently rated high among the United Nations as one of the "most fortunate places to live on earth" (Bothwell, 2002, p. 159). So while the government went through some changes during the 1990s, with the first female Prime Minister, Kim Campbell, replacing the retired Brian Mulroney, the country remained fairly stable. And in 2006, Stephen Harper became the Prime Minister of Canada.

CANADA: A BRIEF OVERVIEW OF SOCIO-DEMOGRAPHICS

In 2001, the Canadian census counted approximately 30 million people residing in Canada. By January 2008, the Canadian population had risen to more than 33 million people. Table 4.1 clearly illustrates the diversity of the Canadian population. More than 5 million visible minorities live in the country. Like the United States, Canada is truly a nation of immigrants. And when one examines where ethnic minorities reside in Canada, it is clear they are fairly integrated throughout the land, but in some provinces, such as Ontario, there tends to be even more diversity. This is, in large part, due to the presence of the city of Toronto in Ontario.

The 2006 census figures also reveal that the largest "visible minority" in Canada are people of South Asian descent (see Table 4.2). Chinese and Blacks have the second and third highest representation of "visible minorities," respectively. Thus, while the largest share of immigrants arriving in Canada from 2002 to 2004 were from Asia, between 1998 to 2004 the number of African immigrants "accepted in Canada as permanent residents has practically doubled since 1998, from 14,500 to 27,600 in 2004" (Belanger, 2006, p. 3). As for the Aboriginal population, the 2006 census counted 1,172,785 residents.

(Text continues on page 116)

Table 4.1   Population of Canada

Visible Minority Groups (15)	Total-Immigrant Status and Period of Immigration	Non-Immigrants[1]	Immigrants[2]	Before 1991	1991 to 2000	1991 to 1995	1996 to 2000	2001 to 2006[3]	Non-Permanent Residents[4]
Total population by visible minority groups	31,241,030	24,788,720	6,186,950	3,408,415	1,668,550	823,925	844,625	1,109,980	265,355
Total visible minority population[5]	5,068,095	1,528,345	3,362,150	1,295,475	1,234,010	611,145	622,860	832,665	177,595
Chinese	1,216,570	310,085	870,955	340,345	348,320	172,325	175,995	182,285	35,525
South Asian[6]	1,262,865	370,535	867,450	295,180	330,020	147,330	182,690	242,250	24,875

Visible Minority Groups (15)	Total-Immigrant Status and Period of Immigration	Non-Immigrants[1]	Immigrants[2]	Before 1991	1991 to 2000	1991 to 1995	1996 to 2000	2001 to 2006[3]	Non-Permanent Residents[4]
Black	783,795	346,950	411,840	195,165	125,800	67,815	57,985	90,875	25,010
Filipino	410,695	105,205	289,365	101,185	112,710	62,175	50,535	75,465	16,120
Latin American	304,245	64,070	218,155	91,040	67,600	40,720	26,880	59,515	22,025
Southeast Asian[7]	239,935	74,940	159,530	96,160	44,985	30,010	14,970	18,385	5,465
Arab	265,550	71,795	182,550	52,580	70,495	33,595	36,895	59,480	11,205
West Asian[8]	156,700	23,240	129,060	27,865	57,225	22,110	35,115	43,970	4,400
Korean	141,895	21,260	99,695	26,655	37,025	13,350	23,670	36,020	20,940
Japanese	81,305	51,355	21,615	9,640	6,470	2,570	3,895	5,505	8,330
Visible minority, n.i.e.[9]	71,420	24,335	45,530	23,530	14,725	8,665	6,060	7,270	1,550

(Continued)

Table 4.1 (Continued)

Visible Minority Groups (15)	Total- Immigrant Status and Period of Immigration	Non- Immigrants[1]	Immigrants[2]	Before 1991	1991 to 2000	1991 to 1995	1996 to 2000	2001 to 2006[3]	Non- Permanent Residents[4]
Multiple visible minority[10]	133,120	64,570	66,405	36,120	18,635	10,470	8,165	11,650	2,145
Not a visible minority[11]	26,172,940	23,260,375	2,824,805	2,112,940	434,540	212,775	221,765	277,320	87,765

SOURCE: Statistics Canada, 2008. Visible Minority Groups (15), Immigrant Status and Period of Immigration (9), Age Groups (10) and Sex (3) for the Population of Canada, Provinces, Territories, Census Divisions and Census Subdivisions, 2006 Census - 20% Sample Data (table). Topic-based tabulation. 2006 Census of Population

NOTES:

1. Non-immigrants
   Non-immigrants are persons who are Canadian citizens by birth. Although most Canadian citizens by birth were born in Canada, a small number were born outside Canada to Canadian parents.
2. Immigrants
   Immigrants are persons who are, or have ever been, landed immigrants in Canada. A landed immigrant is a person who has been granted the right to live in Canada permanently by immigration authorities. Some immigrants have resided in Canada for a number of years, while others are recent arrivals. Most immigrants are born outside Canada, but a small number were born in Canada. Includes immigrants who landed in Canada prior to Census Day, May 16, 2006.
3. 2001 to 2006
   Includes immigrants who landed in Canada prior to Census Day, May 16, 2006.
4. Non-permanent residents
   Non-permanent residents are persons from another country who, at the time of the census, held a Work or Study Permit or who were refugee claimants, as well as family members living with them in Canada.

5. Total visible minority population

   The Employment Equity Act defines visible minorities as "persons, other than Aboriginal peoples, who are non-Caucasian in race or non-white in colour".

6. South Asian

   For example, "East Indian," "Pakistani," "Sri Lankan," etc.

7. Southeast Asian

   For example, "Vietnamese," "Cambodian," "Malaysian," "Laotian," etc.

8. West Asian

   For example, "Iranian," "Afghan," etc.

9. Visible minority, n.i.e.

   The abbreviation "n.i.e." means "not included elsewhere". Includes respondents who reported a write-in response such as "Guyanese," "West Indian," "Kurd," "Tibetan," "Polynesian," "Pacific Islander," etc.

10. Multiple visible minority

    Includes respondents who reported more than one visible minority group by checking two or more mark-in circles, e.g., "Black" and "South Asian".

11. Not a visible minority

    Includes respondents who reported "Yes" to the Aboriginal identity question (Question 18) as well as respondents who were not considered to be members of a visible minority group.

△ Data quality note(s)

- Excludes census data for one or more incompletely enumerated Indian reserves or Indian settlements.

Table 4.2 Aboriginal Identity Population by Age Groups, Median Age and Sex, 2006 Counts, for Canada, Provinces and Territories — 20% Sample Data

Geographic Name	Total Population	Aboriginal Identity Population[1]	North American Indian	Métis	Inuit	Non-aboriginal Identity Population
Canada[1]	31,241,030	1,172,785	698,025	389,780	50,480	30,068,240
Newfoundland and Labrador	500,610	23,455	7,765	6,470	4,715	477,160
Prince Edward Island	134,205	1,730	1,225	385	30	132,475
Nova Scotia[1]	903,090	24,175	15,240	7,680	325	878,920
New Brunswick	719,650	17,650	12,385	4,270	185	701,995
Quebec[1]	7,435,905	108,425	65,085	27,980	10,950	7,327,475
Ontario[1]	12,028,895	242,495	158,395	73,605	2,035	11,786,405
Manitoba[1]	1,133,515	175,395	100,640	71,805	565	958,115
Saskatchewan[1]	953,850	141,890	91,400	48,120	215	811,960
Alberta[1]	3,256,355	188,365	97,275	85,495	1,610	3,067,990

Geographic Name	Total Population	Aboriginal Identity Population[1]	North American Indian	Métis	Inuit	Non-Aboriginal Identity Population
British Columbia[1]	4,074,385	196,075	129,580	59,445	795	3,878,310
Yukon Territory[1]	30,190	7,580	6,280	800	255	22,615
Northwest Territories	41,060	20,635	12,640	3,580	4,160	20,420
Nunavut[1]	29,325	24,915	100	130	24,635	4,405

SOURCE: Statistics Canada, 2008. *Aboriginal identity population by age groups, median age and sex, 2006 counts, for Canada, provinces and territories - 20% sample data* (table) and *Aboriginal Peoples Highlight Tables*. 2006 Census. Statistics Canada Catalogue no. 97-558-XWE2006002. Ottawa. Released January 15, 2008. http://www12.statcan.ca/english/census06/data/highlights/aboriginal/index.cfm?Lang=E (accessed June 21, 2008).

NOTE:

1. The total Aboriginal identity population includes the Aboriginal groups (North American Indian, Métis and Inuit), multiple Aboriginal responses and Aboriginal responses not included elsewhere.

Other recent figures of interest include those showing that in 2004, the median total income for families with a couple living together was $64,800, while lone-parent families had median incomes of $29,500. In addition, Canada has one of the longest life expectancies in the world, with men living until age 77 and women surviving to age 82 (Belanger, 2006, p. 2).

CRIME AND JUSTICE STATISTICS

As in most countries, Canada keeps records of national crime statistics. Since the early 1960s, police-reported crime data have provided information on "actual criminal incidents that have come to the attention of police, as well as those that have been detected through criminal investigation" (Gannon, 2006, p. 2). Almost identical in name to the United States, the system is referred to as the Uniform Crime Reporting (UCR) survey. In 2006, the news was good. Crime had dropped by 3% (Silver, 2007). Excluding drug offenses, traffic offenses, and other federal statute violations, there were 2,452,787 federal incidents reported to the police (see Table 4.3). Figure 4.2 reveals that crime peaked in 1991, and has steadily gone down. Even so, across Canada crime varies considerably by province (see Figure 4.3).

Like elsewhere in the world, crime statistics in Canada are delineated by categories such as violent and property offenses. Violent crime includes the following crimes: homicide, attempted murder, assault, sexual assault, other assault, other sexual assault, abduction, and robbery. There were 310,307 violent offenses in 2006, most of which were assaults. While the number of homicides rose in Canada from 2004 to 2005 (Gannon, 2006), it went down 10% in 2006 to a total of 605. As seen in Table 4.4, Canada has one of the lower homicide rates when compared to other countries. In Canada, like the United States, firearms are often used in homicides. In 2006, 31.4% of Canadian homicides were labeled as firearms-related. The remaining homicides were the result of stabbings (34.7%), beatings (19.3%), strangulation (7.9%), or some other cause (see Table 4.5) (Li, 2007). The nature in which homicide victims were killed mirrored global victim–offender trends, with 49% being killed by someone they knew, 17.3% involving spousal homicides, and another 17.2% being gang-related. For the latter category of homicides, gang-related included incidents that were confirmed and suspected as being gang-related (Li, 2007, p. 15).

(Text continues on page 129)

Table 4.3 Federal Statute Incidents Reported to Police, by Most Serious Offence, Canada, 2002 to 2006[1]

	2002		2003		2004		2005[r]		2006		Percent Change 2005 to 2006	Percent Change 1996 to 2006
	Number	Rate	Number	Rate	Number	Rate	Number	Rate	Number	Rate	Rate	Rate
Population	**31,372,587**		**31,676,077**		**31,989,454**		**32,299,496**		**32,623,490**			
Homicide[2]	582	1.9	549	1.7	624	2.0	663	2.1	605	1.9	−10	−14
Attempted murder	678	2.2	707	2.2	671	2.1	822	2.5	852	2.6	3	−12
Assault—total	**235,710**	**751**	**236,802**	**748**	**234,259**	**732**	**236,682**	**733**	**239,702**	**735**	**0**	**−1**
Level 1	189,185	603	188,667	596	184,883	578	183,231	567	183,504	562	−1	−8
Level 2-Weapon	43,793	140	45,222	143	46,643	146	50,356	156	52,910	162	4	35
Level 3-aggravated	2,732	9	2,913	9	2,733	9	3,095	10	3,288	10	5	9
Other assaults	12,454	40	12,534	40	12,811	40	12,845	40	12,981	40	0	−3
Sexual assault—total	**24,499**	**78**	**23,514**	**74**	**23,036**	**72**	**23,521**	**73**	**22,136**	**68**	**−7**	**−26**
Level 1	23,973	76	22,983	73	22,449	70	22,956	71	21,572	66	−7	−25

(Continued)

Table 4.3 (Continued)

	2002		2003		2004		2005^{r}		2006		Percent Change 2005 to 2006	Percent Change 1996 to 2006
	Number	Rate	Number	Rate	Number	Rate	Number	Rate	Number	Rate	Rate	Rate
Level 2-weapon	373	1	359	1	397	1	389	1	381	1	−3	−47
Level 3-aggravated	153	0	172	1	190	1	176	1	183	1	3	−44
Other sexual offences	2,756	9	2,565	8	2,614	8	2,777	9	2,789	9	−1	−24
Abduction	605	2	559	2	637	2	579	2	535	2	−9	−50
Robbery—total	**26,662**	**85**	**28,437**	**90**	**27,495**	**86**	**28,798**	**89**	**30,707**	**94**	**6**	**−12**
Firearms	3,483	11	3,856	12	3,645	11	3,508	11	3,671	11	4	−51
Other weapons	10,104	32	10,057	32	8,362	26	8,566	27	8,775	27	1	−24
No weapons	13,075	42	14,524	46	15,488	48	16,724	52	18,261	56	8	14
Violent crime—total	**303,946**	**969**	**305,667**	**965**	**302,147**	**945**	**306,687**	**950**	**310,307**	**951**	**0**	**−5**
Breaking and entering—total	**275,573**	**878**	**284,925**	**899**	**275,869**	**862**	**261,362**	**809**	**250,467**	**768**	**−5**	**−43**

	2002		2003		2004		2005ʳ		2006		Percent Change 2005 to 2006	Percent Change 1996 to 2006
	Number	Rate	Number	Rate	Number	Rate	Number	Rate	Number	Rate	Rate	Rate
Residential	163,156	520	161,494	510	153,223	479	150,500	466	147,002	451	–3	–45
Business	81,162	259	86,842	274	86,226	270	80,317	249	79,042	242	–3	–35
Other	31,255	100	36,589	116	36,420	114	30,545	95	24,423	75	–21	–50
Motor vehicle theft	161,912	516	174,208	550	169,977	531	160,014	495	158,944	487	–2	–20
Theft over $5,000	19,816	63	19,416	61	16,968	53	17,201	53	17,060	52	–2	–43
Theft $5,000 and under	667,312	2,127	700,605	2,212	673,999	2,107	638,684	1,977	616,194	1,889	–4	–32
Possession of stolen goods	30,056	96	33,151	105	35,743	112	34,466	107	35,134	108	1	0
Fraud	91,812	293	92,924	293	97,443	305	95,377	295	92,599	284	–4	–18
Total Property crime	**1,246,481**	**3,973**	**1,305,229**	**4,121**	**1,269,999**	**3,970**	**1,207,104**	**3,737**	**1,170,398**	**3,588**	**–4**	**–32**

(Continued)

Table 4.3 (Continued)

	2002		2003		2004		2005ʳ		2006		Percent Change 2005 to 2006	Percent Change 1996 to 2006
	Number	Rate	Number	Rate	Number	Rate	Number	Rate	Number	Rate	Rate	Rate
Mischief	333,334	1,063	357,568	1,129	353,518	1,105	354,651	1,098	378,311	1,160	6	–6
Counterfeiting currency	79,970	255	139,267	440	201,108	629	165,014	511	117,987	362	–29	426
Bail violations	96,206	307	101,095	319	106,664	333	101,773	315	106,699	327	4	40
Disturbing the peace[3]	89,354	285	102,909	325	117,389	367	122,095	378	117,023	359	–5	95
Offensive weapons	15,930	51	17,621	56	18,202	57	19,907	62	19,234	59	–4	6
Prostitution	5,770	18	5,688	18	6,452	20	5,787	18	5,701	17	–2	–19
Arson	13,131	42	13,875	44	13,150	41	13,356	41	13,504	41	0	–4
Kidnapping/forcible confinement	3,095	10	3,250	10	3,483	11	3,918	12	4,449	14	12	108
Other	230,227	734	227,003	717	218,859	684	210,169	651	209,174	641	–1	–21

	2002		2003		2004		2005[r]		2006		Percent Change 2005 to 2006	Percent Change 1996 to 2006
	Number	Rate	Number	Rate	Number	Rate	Number	Rate	Number	Rate	Rate	Rate
Other Criminal Code offences—total	**867,017**	**2,764**	**968,276**	**3,057**	**1,038,825**	**3,247**	**996,670**	**3,086**	**972,082**	**2,980**	**–3**	**–12**
Criminal Code—total (excluding traffic)—crime rate	**2,417,444**	**7,706**	**2,579,172**	**8,142**	**2,610,971**	**8,162**	**2,510,461**	**7,772**	**2,452,787**	**7,518**	**–3**	**–16**
Impaired driving[4]	80,045	255	77,645	245	80,339	251	78,370	243	74,331	228	–6	–30
Fail to stop/remain	22,040	70	23,336	74	24,022	75	26,974	84	29,078	89	7	–47
Dangerous operation of a motor vehicle/boat/aircraft	9,194	29	9,795	31	9,887	31	10,286	32	10,197	31	–2	39
Driving motor vehicle while prohibited	6,292	20	6,389	20	5,882	18	5,958	18	6,357	19	6	–40

(Continued)

Table 4.3 (Continued)

	2002		2003		2004		2005[r]		2006		Percent Change 2005 to 2006	Percent Change 1996 to 2006
	Number	Rate	Number	Rate	Number	Rate	Number	Rate	Number	Rate	Rate	Rate
Criminal Code traffic—total	**117,571**	**375**	**117,119**	**370**	**120,637**	**377**	**121,588**	**376**	**119,963**	**368**	**–2**	**–33**
Criminal Code—total (incl. traffic)	**2,535,015**	**8,080**	**2,696,291**	**8,512**	**2,731,608**	**8,539**	**2,632,049**	**8,149**	**2,572,750**	**7,886**	**–3**	**–17**
Drugs—total	**92,781**	**296**	**86,791**	**370**	**97,630**	**305**	**93,664**	**290**	**96,164**	**295**	**2**	**33**
Cannabis possession	49,647	158	41,295	130	47,957	150	43,208	134	43,634	134	0	19
Other cannabis[5]	20,040	64	19,792	62	19,938	62	17,284	54	15,244	47	–13	–1
Cocaine	12,737	41	14,225	45	16,974	53	19,270	60	22,074	68	13	75
Other drugs[6]	10,357	41	11,479	36	12,761	40	13,902	43	15,212	47	8	97

	2002		2003		2004		2005[r]		2006		Percent Change 2005 to 2006	Percent Change 1996 to 2006
	Number	*Rate*	*Number*	*Rate*	*Number*	*Rate*	*Number*	*Rate*	*Number*	*Rate*	*Rate*	*Rate*
Other federal statutes	40,122	128	36,264	114	34,017	106	31,167	96	28,733	88	–9	–24
Total federal statutes (incl. C.C.)	2,667,918	8,504	2,819,346	8,901	2,863,255	8,951	2,756,880	8,535	2,697,647	8,269	–3	–16

SOURCE: Statistics Canada. Canadian Centre for Justice Statistics, Uniform Crime Reporting Survey.

NOTES: Rates are calculated on the basis of 100,000 population. The population estimates come from Statistics Canada. Demography Division. Populations as of July 1st final postcensal estimates for 2002 and 2003; updated postcensal estimates for 2004 and 2005; and preliminary postcensal estimates for 2006.

0 true zero or a value rounded to zero

r revised

1. Percent change based on unrounded rates.
2. As a result of ongoing investigations in Port Coquitlam, B.C. there were 15 homicides in 2002, 7 homicides in 2003 and 5 homicides in 2004 that occurred in previous years. Homicide are counted according to the year in which police file the report.
3. Note that for minor offences such as disturb the peace, some police services choose to clear these offences under a municipal by-law or provincial statute offence rather than under the *Criminal Code.*
4. Includes impaired operation of a vehicle causing death, causing bodily harm, alcohol rate over 80mg, failure/refusal to provide a breath/blood sample. Previous to 2004, Vancouver Police only reported incidents of impaired driving when a charge had been laid. As of 2004, their data also include incidents where the driver was tested to be over .08 and received a road-side suspension. This resulted in 1,900 more impaired driving incidents being reported in 2004 than 2003.
5. Other cannabis includes trafficking, importation, and production.
6. Other drugs include the categories heroin, "restricted drugs," "controlled drugs" and "other" drugs.

Figure 4.2   Crime Rates, Canada, 1962 to 2006

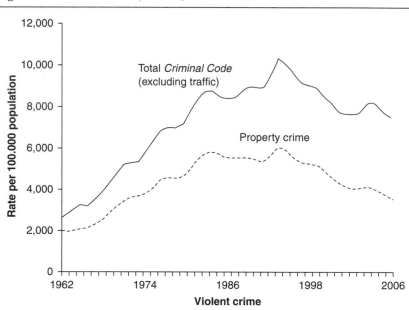

SOURCE: Statistics Canada, Canadian Centre for Justice Statistics, Uniform Crime Reporting Survey.

Figure 4.3   Crime Rates by Province, 2006

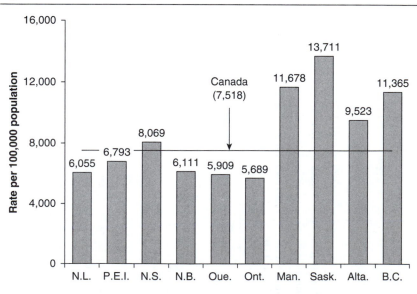

SOURCE: Statistics Canada, Canadian Centre for Justice Statistics, Uniform Crime Reporting Survey.

Table 4.4   Homicide Rates for Selected Countries, 2006

Country	Rate per 100,000 population
Turkey[1]	6.23
United States	5.69
Germany[1]	2.90
Switzerland[1]	2.73
Sweden[1]	2.64
New Zealand	2.37
Finland	2.12
Canada	**1.85**
Scotland[2]	1.83
Hungary[1]	1.64
England and Wales[3]	1.41
France	1.39
Northern Ireland[3]	1.32
Australia	1.06
Denmark	0.90
Japan[1]	0.64
Hong Kong	0.51
Singapore	0.38

SOURCE: National Central Bureau, Interpol Ottawa and National Statistical Office websites.

NOTES:

1. Figures reflect 2005 data.
2. Figures reflect 2005/2006 data.
3. Figures reflect 2006/2007 data.

Table 4.5   Methods Used to Commit Homicide, Canada, 1996 to 2006

Year	Shooting		Stabbing		Beating		Strangulation/ Suffocation		Shaken Baby Syndrome[1]		Fire (Smoke Inhalation, Burns)	
	Number of Victims	Percent	Number of Victims	Percent	Number of Victims	Percent	Number of Victims	Percent	Number of Victims	Percent	Number of Victims	Percent
1996	212	33.4	195	30.7	132	20.8	59	9.3	. . .	. . .	8	1.3
1997	193	32.9	168	28.7	115	19.6	53	9.0	6	1.0	30	5.1
1998	151	27.1	186	33.3	125	22.4	61	10.9	6	1.1	12	2.2
1999	165	30.7	143	26.6	125	23.2	55	10.2	7	1.3	11	2.0
2000	184	33.7	149	27.3	128	23.4	40	7.3	13	2.4	5	0.9
2001	171	30.9	171	30.9	122	22.1	47	8.5	8	1.4	8	1.4
2002	152	26.1	182	31.3	126	21.6	67	11.5	8	1.4	9	1.5
2003	161	29.3	142	25.9	121	22.0	64	11.7	8	1.5	12	2.2
2004	173	27.7	205	32.9	136	21.8	63	10.1	6	1.0	13	2.1
2005ʳ	223	33.6	197	29.7	144	21.7	47	7.1	12	1.8	10	1.5
2006	190	31.4	210	34.7	117	19.3	48	7.9	3	0.5	12	2.0

	Poisoning		Vehicle[1]		Other[2]		Unknown		Total	
	Number of Victims	Percent	Number of Victims	Percent	Number of Victims	Percent	Number of Victims	Percent	Number of Victims	Percent
1996	6	0.9	. . .	. . .	12	1.9	11	1.7	635	100.0
1997	8	1.4	6	1.0	2	0.3	5	0.9	586	100.0
1998	6	1.1	3	0.5	2	0.4	6	1.1	558	100.0
1999	5	0.9	13	2.4	4	0.7	10	1.9	538	100.0
2000	4	0.7	14	2.6	1	0.2	8	1.5	546	100.0
2001	8	1.4	5	0.9	5	0.9	8	1.4	553	100.0
2002	3	0.5	7	1.2	6	1.0	22	3.8	582	100.0
2003	6	1.1	6	1.1	7	1.3	22	4.0	549	100.0
2004	8	1.3	6	1.0	1	0.2	13	2.1	624	100.0

(Continued)

Table 4.5 (Continued)

	Poisoning		Vehicle[1]		Other[2]		Unknown		Total	
	Number of Victims	Percent	Number of Victims	Percent	Number of Victims	Percent	Number of Victims	Percent	Number of Victims	Percent
2005r	7	1.1	4	0.6	3	0.5	16	2.4	663	100.0
2006	1	0.2	9	1.5	1	0.2	14	2.3	605	100.0

SOURCE: Statistics Canada, Canadian Centre for Justice Statistics. Homicide Survey.

NOTE: Percentages may not add up to 100% due to rounding.

1. Data became available in 1997.
2. Other includes exposure/hypothermia, starvation/dehydration and, prior to 1997, Shaken Baby Syndrome and deaths caused by vehicles.

The general characteristics of homicides revealed nothing new to students of homicide. For example, the rates of homicide were highest for young adult males (ages 18 to 24). Among youths younger than 18, there were 84 homicides, the highest figure since 1961 and an increase of 19 homicides over 2005. Here it was also noted that a higher percentage of youth homicides involved victims who were strangers (30% compared to 16% for adults) (Li, 2007, p. 6). Finally, other "precipitating factors" identified as being related to homicides in Canada included drug and alcohol consumption and the fact that the homicide occurred during the commission of another offense. As for other offenses, robberies rose slightly in 2006, sexual assaults slightly declined, while general assaults rose (Silver, 2007, p. 14). Property crimes decreased in 2006, with 1.17 million property crimes reported that year. Below we review some victimization data.

Victimization Data

Following other nations, in 1988 Canada began conducting victimization surveys as a way to grasp the so-called "dark figure of crime" or unreported crime. The last one was conducted in 2004 and included "about 24,000 people, aged 15 years and older living in the 10 provinces" (Gannon & Mihorean, 2005, p. 2). Based on the replies from participants, the survey found "that 28% of Canadians aged 15 years and over reported that they were victimized one or more times in the 12 months preceding the survey. This represents a slight increase from 1999 (26%)" (Gannon & Mihorean, 2005, p. 4). The most frequent type of victimization was that occurring in the household (34%). In addition, nearly 30% of the respondents reported that they were victims of violent crime, with 25% stating they had been victims of thefts of personal property (p. 4).

Considering that violent crime remained stable over the 5-year period, the residents reported feeling safer in 2004 than they did in 1999. This was despite the fact that both household victimization (14%) and personal property theft (24%) increased (see Figure 4.4). Additional findings regarding violent victimization as noted by Gannon and Mihorean (2005) include:

- Men and women have similar violent victimization levels.
- Young people have higher victimization levels.
- Participating in evening activities elevates one's risk for victimization.
- Marital status was linked to violent victimization (single people are at greater risk for victimization).
- Unemployed and students have higher rates of victimization.
- Poor and urban residents have higher rates of victimization.
- Being gay or lesbian elevates one's risk of violent victimization.

Figure 4.4   Rates of Household Property Theft and Vandalism Continue to Increase

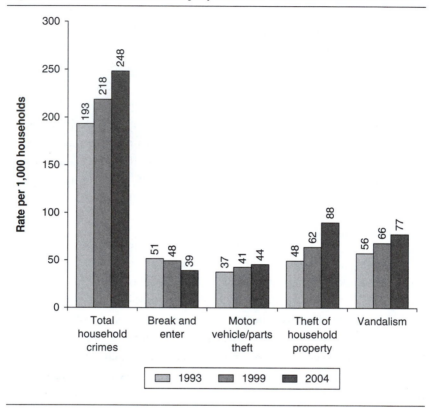

SOURCE: Statistics Canada, General Social Survey, 1993, 1999, and 2004.

Another important aspect of crime and justice statistics is correctional data. The next section examines data on both the youth and adult correctional systems in Canada.

Adult and Youth Corrections in Canada

In Canada, those sentenced to 2 years or less and to community-based sanctions are handled in the provinces and territories. Those offenders sentenced to more than 2 years head to the federal penitentiary system, which is administered by the Correction Service of Canada (CSC) (Landry & Sinha, 2008 p. 2). In 2005/2006, "adult correctional services in Canada processed 232,810 admissions to custody and 109,539 intakes into community supervision" (Landry & Sinha, 2008, p. 2). Table 4.6 reveals some

Table 4.6 Composition of the Adult Correctional Admissions

Correctional Services	1996/1997			2001/2002			2005/2006			From 2001/2002 to 2005/2006	From 1996/1997 to 2005/2006
	Number			Number			Number			% Change in Adjusted Admissions	
	Admissions	Adjusted Admissions[1]	% of Total[1] %	Admissions	Adjusted Admissions[1]	% of Total[1] %	Admissions	Adjusted Admissions[1]	% of Total[1] %	%	%
Custodial supervision											
Provincial/territorial custody, sentenced	108,003	107,136	32.0	83,155	81,726	24.6	78,081	77,394	22.8	−5.3	−27.8
Remand[2]	107,911	107,783	32.2	120,512	119,843	36.1	131,620	131,095	38.6	9.4	21.6
Other temporary detention, provincial/territorial	12,468	12,468	3.7	26,197	12,822	3.9	15,521	15,520	4.6	21.0	24.5
Total provincial/ territorial custody	228,382	227,387	68.0	229,864	214,391	64.6	225,222	224,009	66.0	4.5	−1.5
Federal custody, sentenced	7,422	7,422	2.2	7,381	7,381	2.2	8,285	8,285	2.4	12.2	11.6

(Continued)

Table 4.6 (Continued)

Correctional Services	1996/1997			2001/2002			2005/2006			% Change in Adjusted Admissions	
	Number		% of Total[1]	Number		% of Total[1]	Number		% of Total[1]	From 2001/2002 to 2005/2006	From 1996/1997 to 2005/2006
	Admissions	Adjusted Admissions[1]	%	Admissions	Adjusted Admissions[1]	%	Admissions	Adjusted Admissions[1]	%	%	%
Total custodial supervision	**235,804**	**234,809**	**70.2**	**237,245**	**221,772**	**66.8**	**233,507**	**232,294**	**68.5**	**4.7**	**–1.1**
Community Supervision											
Probation	80,599	79,908	23.9	84,549	83,185	25.1	81,430	80,330	23.7	–3.4	0.5
Provincial parole	4,847	4,847	1.4	2,301	2,301	0.7	1,875	1,875	0.6	–18.5	–61.3
Conditional sentences	7,673	7,669	…	18,604	17,600	5.3	18,580	17,133	5.0	–2.7	…
Total provincial community supervision	93,119	92,424	27.6	105,454	103,086	31.0	101,885	99,338	29.3	–3.6	7.5
Community releases (CSC[3])	6,987	7,389	2.2	7,162	7,162	2.2	7,654	7,654	2.3	6.9	3.6

| | 1996/1997 | | | 2001/2002 | | | 2005/2006 | | | % Change in Adjusted Admissions | |
	Admissions	Adjusted Admissions[1]	% of Total[1]	Admissions	Adjusted Admissions[1]	% of Total[1]	Admissions	Adjusted Admissions[1]	% of Total[1]	From 2001/2002 to 2005/2006	From 1996/1997 to 2005/2006
	Number		%	Number		%	Number		%		
Total community supervision	100,106	99,813	29.8	112,616	110,248	33.2	109,539	106,992	31.5	–3.0	7.2
Total correctional services	335,910	334,622	100.0	349,861	332,020	100.0	343,046	339,286	100.0	2.2	1.4

SOURCE: Statistics Canada, Canadian Centre for Justice Statistics, Adult Correctional Services Survey.

NOTE: Percentages may not add to 100 due to rounding.

1. Because of missing data for some years, all data from Prince Edward Island, Northwest Territories and Nunavut, and other temporary detention data from British Columbia and conditional sentences from Manitoba, have been excluded from "Adjusted admissions" in order to make comparisons between years. The percentages of total statistics are based upon adjusted admissions.

2. Figures for remand may include admissions for other temporary detention.

3. This category represents movement from custody to federal conditional release and includes provincial/territorial and federal offenders on day parole and full parole and federal offenders on statutory release. Offenders released on warrant expiry and other release types are excluded. CSC denotes the Correctional Service of Canada.

minor fluctuations in custodial and community supervision. For example, from 1996/1997 to 2005/2006 custodial supervision decreased 1.1%, while from 2001/2002 to 2005/2006 there was an increase of 4.7%. For community supervision, in the short-term comparison (2001/2002 to 2005/2006), the number of persons decreased by 3.0%, but the longer term comparison (1996/1997 to 2005/2006) produced a 7.2% increase. The increase in custodial supervision is believed to be tied to legislation that approved the increasing use of detention prior to cases to ensure justice, but in other legislative enactments the increased discretion to detain people was done to protect victims and witnesses. It is believed that the increase in community supervision can likely be attributed to the adjustment in the Canadian criminal codes in the late 1990s, which approved the use of conditional sentences (Landry & Sinha, 2008, p. 4).

The handling and institutionalization of Canadian youth also has been a national concern. During the past 100 years, Canadian youth have been dealt with under the guise of three different policies. First, in 1906, the Juvenile Delinquents Act (JDA) guided their treatment. Imitating the approach used by the American juvenile court, the act "promoted the child welfare of young offenders. This perspective required judges to treat children not as criminals, but as misdirected and misguided youth . . . The aim of the JDA was to permit social intervention in order to 'save' misdirected children" (Calverley, 2006, p. 4). By the 1960s, many officials were expressing concern about the need for a balance between child welfare and juvenile rights. Their concern culminated with the passage of the Youth Offenders Act (YOA) in 1984, which provided juveniles with more legal rights and again mirrored American policies: "It brought regulations into force for every stage of the judicial process. Moreover, the YOA placed greater emphasis on the protection of society and accountability, resulting in an increase in the punitive nature of sentences" (Calverley, 2006, p. 4). Finally in 2003, the Youth Criminal Justice Act (YCJA) was passed, which moved away from some the practices of the YOA and called for more thoughtful sentencing approaches and the increased use of diversion.

So what has been the result of the latest change in the philosophy of the Canadian juvenile justice system? Simply put, the reductions to the custodial admissions of Canadian youth have been dramatic. Table 4.7 shows that the overall reduction was 25% between 2002/2003 to 2003/2004, with some classifications of custody dropping as much as 46% (Calverley, 2006, p. 4). In addition to being entangled in the system less for those who are formally processed, the sentences for youth have been considerably shortened, with most being for 6 months or less (Calverley, 2006, p. 5). The reductions, though less dramatic, continued from 2003/2004 to 2004/2005, with an overall decline of 11.8% for both custodial and community supervision (Calverley, 2007; see Table 4.8).

Though many of the figures reviewed in this section on crime and justice appear positive, we now turn to crime and justice figures related to the Aboriginal population and to the limited sources that mention visible minorities. This is followed by a review of some of the early and more current scholarship on race, crime, and justice in Canada.

Table 4.7   Number of Young Persons Admitted to Custodial Services, 2002/2003 to 2003/2004

	2002/2003		*2003/2004*		
	Total Admissions	*% of Total Custodial Admissions*	*Total Admissions*	*% of Total Custodial Admissions*	*% Change From 2002/03 to 2003/04*
Total custodial admissions	**22,743**	**100**	**17,113**	**100**	**−25**
Remand	14,387	63	12,462	73	−13
Sentenced custody	8,356	37	4,651	27	−44
Secure custody	4,335	19	2,483	15	−43
Open custody	4,021	18	2,168	13	−46

SOURCE: Youth Custody and Community Services Survey. Canadian Centre for Justice Statistics. Statistics Canada.

NOTE: Excludes New Brunswick, Ontario 12 to 15 year olds, and Saskatchewan.

Table 4.8   Composition of Admissions to Youth Correctional Services,
                     2003/2004 and 2004/2005

	2003/2004		2004/2005		*Percentage Change from 2003/2004*
	Number	*Percentage of Total*	*Number*	*Percentage of Total*	
Custodial supervision					
Sentenced custody	4,771	13.3	4,439	14.0	−7.0
Secure custody	2,548	7.1	2,245	7.1	−11.9
Open custody	2,223	6.2	2,194	6.9	−1.3
Remand	12,303	34.2	11,505	36.2	−6.5
Total custodial supervision	**17,074**	**47.4**	**15,944**	**50.2**	**−6.6**
Community supervision					
Probation	16,146	44.9	12,877	40.6	−20.2
YCJA sentences[1]	2,767	7.7	2,925	9.2	5.7
Total community supervision	**18,913**	**52.6**	**15,802**	**49.8**	**−16.4**
Total correctional services	**35,987**	**100**	**31,746**	**100**	**−11.8**

SOURCES: Statistics Canada. Canadian Centre for Justice Statistics, Youth Custody and Community Services Survey, Integrated Correctional Services Survey.

NOTE: Excludes Prince Edward Island, Ontario 12 to 15 year olds, Saskatchewan, Yukon, the Northwest Territoires and Nunavut.

1. YCJA sentences include the community portion of a custody and supervision order and deferred custody and supervision.

CRIME AND JUSTICE ISSUES AMONG THE ABORIGINAL POPULATION AND VISIBLE MINORITIES

In general, the news has not been good for Aboriginals and visible minorities in Canada in terms of criminal justice. In 2004, 40% of Aboriginals (age 15 and up) reported being crime victims (Brzozowski, Taylor-Butts, & Johnson, 2006, p. 4). This was in contrast to the 28% figure for the general Canadian population. In terms of violent victimization against Aboriginal people, Figure 4.5 shows that their rates for such victimization far exceed those of non-Aboriginals. Moreover, those most likely to be victimized were females and young people. As with the general victimization data, the Aboriginal

Figure 4.5 Aboriginal People More Likely to Be Victims of Violent Crime, 2004[1, 2]

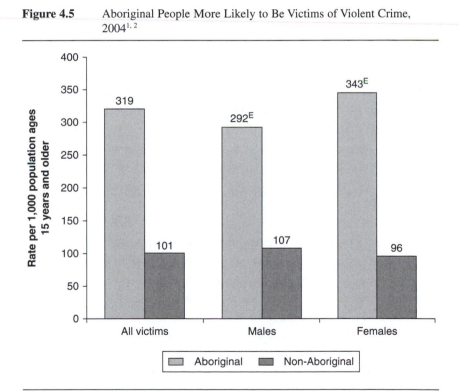

SOURCE: Statistics Canada, General Social Survey, 2004.

NOTES:

E. Use with caution

1. Includes incidents of spousal physical and sexual assault.

2. Includes sexual assault, assault and robbery.

victims knew their perpetrators. Other findings from the data suggest that many violent incidents among Aboriginal people go unreported; many of the incidents occur in the homes of Aboriginals; weapons use and injuries were not common in violent incidents; and alcohol or drug use was related to the violence (Brzozowski et al., 2006, p. 6).

Spousal abuse data showed that while the level of spousal violence remained unchanged from 1999 to 2004, incidents involving Aboriginals were more severe than those involving non-Aboriginal people. Of this situation, Brzozowski et al., (2006) wrote:

> Aboriginal victims of spousal violence were much more likely than non-Aboriginal victims to suffer the most severe forms of spousal violence, such as being beaten, choked, threatened with or had a gun or knife used against them, or sexually assaulted (41% versus 27%). (p. 6)

As a consequence of this more severe spousal abuse, Aboriginal people were more likely to sustain injuries during such encounters (43% versus 31%).

Homicide victimization was another area where the news was bad. Representing 3% of the Canadian population, Aboriginal people accounted for 17% of the victims of homicide (Brzozowski et al., 2006, p. 7). Figure 4.6 shows the high rate of homicide victimization for Aboriginal and non-Aboriginal males and females. In line with these figures, Figure 4.7 shows that from 1997 to 2000 Aboriginal people were overrepresented as the persons likely to be accused of homicide.

Crime on reserves represents another place where Aboriginal crime can be examined. Nearly 90% of those living on reserved lands are Aboriginal people. And on these lands there were 93,000 Criminal Code violations. Figure 4.8 reveals the different patterns that emerge when one compares on-reserve offenses to those committed by the general Canadian population off the reserves. For example, there tends to be more violent crime among adults and youth who live on reserves. In addition, there are fewer property crimes, but more "Other Criminal Code offenses" such as mischief and disturbing the peace (Brzozowski et al., 2006, p. 10). In general, though, "the rate of youth crime on reserves was three times higher than the rate of youth crime through-out the rest of Canada" (Brzozowski et al., 2006, p. 11).

Aboriginal people also tend to have contact with the police for more seri-ous reasons than other Canadians. For instance, "Aboriginal people were more likely to come into contact with police as victims (13% compared to 7%),

Figure 4.6 Rates of Homicide Much Higher for Aboriginal Victims, 1997–2000 [1,2,3]

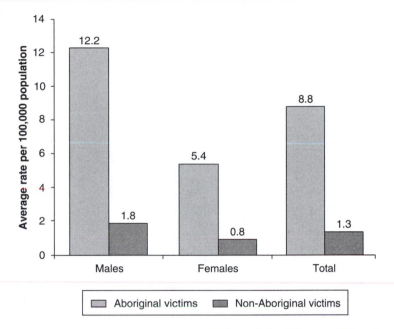

SOURCE: Statistics Canada, Canadian Centre for Justice Statistics. Homicide Survey.

NOTES:

1. Rates are calculated per 100,000 population and are based on the average number of homicides per year, between 1997 and 2000.

2. Excludes homicides where the Aboriginal status of the victim was unknown.

3. Population estimates were derived from 2001 postcensal estimates and 1996 Census counts, provided by Statistics Canada, Census and Demographic Statistics, Demography Division.

witness to a crime (11% compared to 6%) and by being arrested (5% compared to 1%)" (Brzozowski et al., 2006, p. 12). Predictably then, when Aboriginal and non-Aboriginals were surveyed regarding their satisfaction with the performance of the police, the responses from Aboriginal people were lower in every category (e.g., treating people fairly, enforcing the laws, responding promptly). It is also likely that the satisfaction levels were lower because Aboriginal people were twice (31% versus 14%) as likely as non-Aboriginals to report that they were the victims of racial discrimination. And on the streets where they were most likely to encounter the police, they were also more likely to report experiencing discrimination (14% compared to 4%) (Brzozowski et al., 2006, p. 11).

Figure 4.7   Aboriginal People More Likely to Be Accused of Homicide, 1997–2000[1,2,3]

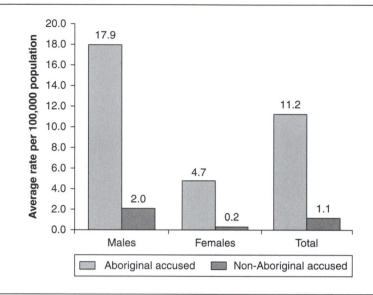

SOURCE: Statistics Canada, Statistics Canada. Canadian Centre for Justice Statistics, Homicide Survey.
NOTES:

1. Rates are calculated per 100,000 population and are based on the average number of homicides per year, between 1997 and 2000.

2. Excludes homicides where the Aboriginal status of the accused was unknown.

3. Population estimates were derived from 2001 postcensal estimates and 1996 Census counts, provided by Statistics Canada, Census and Demographic Statistics. Demography Division.

Canada also maintains information on Aboriginal people and corrections. As in other areas of criminal justice, there are serious concerns about their representation. Thus, while they represent a small part of the Canadian populous, in 2003/2004 they "accounted for 21% of admissions to provincial/territorial sentenced custody, 19% to conditional sentence, 18% to remand and 16% to probation . . . They also represented 18% of all admissions to federal custody" (Brzozowski et al., 2006, p. 12). Gender appears to also be a salient variable when examining figures related to admissions. Aboriginal females actually have higher levels of proportional representation in admissions than males. That is, Aboriginal females represented 25% to 29% of female admissions to sentenced custody between 1994/1995 to 2003/2004, while during the same period Aboriginal males represented 15% to 18%. This trend held true for remand situations as well. Other important findings showed that Aboriginal

Figure 4.8   Violent Crimes Most Common for Adults Charged On-Reserve, Least
Common for Youth, 2004

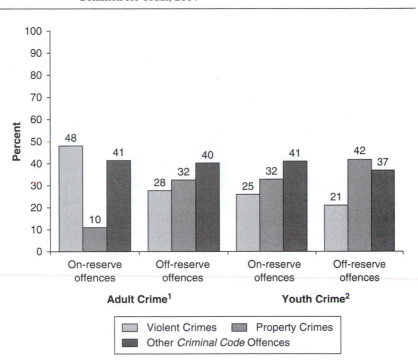

SOURCE: Statistics Canada, Canadian Centre for Justice Statistics. On-reserve and off-reserve
police-reported crime database.

1. Includes adults aged 18 and over charged with a *Criminal Code* offense.

2. Includes youth aged 12 to 17 accused of a *Criminal Code* offense.

adults in correctional facilities are "younger, less educated, [and] more likely
to be unemployed" (Brzozowski et al., 2006, p. 13). Aboriginal youth represented 1 in 5 of those who were admitted to sentenced custody. Figure 4.9
shows the diversity of admissions for Aboriginal youth in custody.

Collectively, these figures show the long reach of the justice system into
the lives of Aboriginal people. However, the figures do not provide any insight
into how visible minorities are faring in the Canadian justice system. This is
where the available official data falls short. Very few reports have been solely
devoted to the plight of visible minorities and crime and justice. However in
2001, Statistics Canada released the report, *Visible Minorities in Canada,*

Figure 4.9   Aboriginal Youth Highly Represented in Admissions to All Types of
Correctional Services, 2002/2004[1]

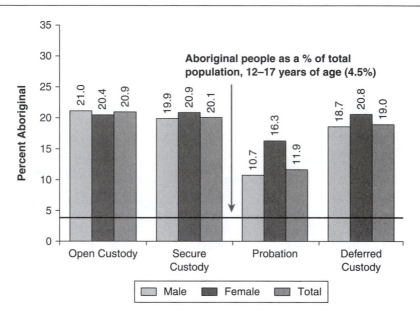

SOURCE: Statistics Canada, Canadian Centre for Justice Statistics, Youth Custody and
Community Services Survey, Demography Division, Census and Demographic Statistics.

NOTE:

1. Due to data unavailability, data for Prince Edward Island, Quebec, Saskatchewan, British
Columbia, Yukon, Northwest Territories and Nunavut are excluded.

which provided some insight on the topic. Using data from the 1999 General
Social Survey, the report was able to document some crime and justice information on visible minorities because "for the first time . . . respondents were
asked to self-identify their cultural or racial background" (*Visible Minorities,*
2001, p. 6).

The report found that 26% of visible minorities "were victims of household or personal crime one or more times in the previous year" (p. 6).
Moreover, it was noted that males and females experienced victimization at
similar rates. In general, the victimization rates of visible minorities were in
line with those of non-visible minorities. But when Canadians were queried
about their belief that their victimization was a result of their racial or ethnic
status, the findings illustrated that visible minorities perceived themselves to
be at an elevated risk for such victimization (19 per 1,000 versus 7 per 1,000).

Questions related to perceived crime trends in one's neighborhood found that visible and non-visible minorities alike held the view that crime in their neighborhood was lower than in other areas in Canada (*Visible Minorities,* 2001, p. 7). And in terms of one's feelings of safety, as illustrated in Table 4.9, there were slight differences between visible and non-visible minorities. Finally, the general satisfaction with the police and the courts were about the same, with visible minorities actually being less critical of the courts than non-visible minorities (*Visible Minorities,* 2001, p. 8). Both visible and non-visible minorities were rather critical of the prison and parole systems (p. 8).

Following this initial report, more recent reports highlighted the plight of visible minorities, crime, and justice. In 2004, a pilot survey on hate crimes revealed that "twelve major Canadian police forces reported a total of 928 hate crime incidents during 2001 and 2002" ("Pilot survey of hate crime," 2004, p. 1). Figure 4.9 reveals Jews were the most likely targets of hate crimes, while Blacks and Muslims were the second and third most likely targets, respectively. In general, racial/ethnic hate crimes comprised the largest share of the incidents. These encounters most often involved threats (49%) and physical violence (34%), with the other encounters involving knives/cutting weapons, other weapons, unknown weapons, and firearm-like weapons ("Pilot survey of hate crime," 2004, p. 3). It was also reported that the accused was located in only half of the incidents.

The 2004 General Social Science Survey also provides additional data on the topic, being one of the few places where racial/ethnic comparisons can be made. For example, in the area of victimization rates for violence, Highlight Box 4.1 illustrates the various rates among several racial/ethnic groups. These figures again illuminate the concerns related to Aboriginal people. As for visible minorities, their rate of victimization was slightly lower that non-visible minorities (98 versus 107 per 1,000 population) (Gannon & Mihorean, 2005, p. 8). Regarding the lower rate of immigrant victimization, the authors surmise that "the immigrant population tends to be older, a factor that reduces risk of victimization" (p. 8).

Though these figures provide some idea of the trend in victimization, they still do not disaggregate the figures by racial/ethnic group. Thus, it is likely misleading to believe that all of those groups collapsed into the visible minority category have the same victimization rates. Just by returning to the hate crime data in Figure 4.9 leads one to believe that they do have different experiences, which would likely lead to different outcomes as they relate to crime

Table 4.9　　　Feelings of Safety From Crime by Visible Minority Status,[1] 1999

	% of Population	
	Visible Minority Population	Non-Visible Minority Population
While waiting for/using public transportation alone after dark, how do you feel about your safety from crime?		
Not at all worried	51	54
Somewhat worried	39	39
Very worried	9	7
Don't know/Not stated	—	—
How safe do you feel from crime when walking alone in your area after dark?		
Very safe	33	45
Reasonably safe	50	45
Somewhat or very unsafe	16	10
Don't know/Not stated	—	—
While alone in your home in the evening or at night, how do you feel about your safety from crime?		
Not at all worried	74	80
Somewhat worried	22	18
Very worried	3	2
Don't know/Not stated	—	—
In general, how do you feel about your safety from crime?		
Very satisfied	33	46
Somewhat satisfied	56	46
Somewhat dissatisfied	5	4
Very dissatisfied	2	2
Don't know/Not stated	—	—

SOURCE: Statistics Canada, General Social Survey, 1999.

NOTE: Figures may not add to 100% due to rounding.

1. Includes only respondents who engaged in these activities.
– Amount too small to be expressed.

Figure 4.10   Targets of Hate Crimes in Canada

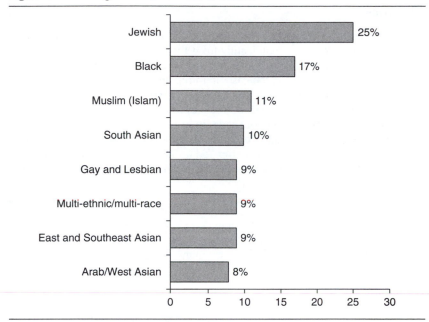

Violence Among Diverse Populations

Through the 2004 General Social Survey (GSS), it is possible to examine rates of violent victimization experienced by visible minorities, immigrants, including recent immigrants, and Aboriginal people, and to assess whether these segments of the population are at increased risk of being victimized.

Overall, Aboriginal people reported the highest rates of violent victimization compared to other minority populations and the non-Aboriginal population. Those who self-identified as being Aboriginal were three times more likely than the non-Aboriginal population to be the victim of a violent incident (319 people per 1,000 versus 101 per 1,000). Even when controlling for other factors such as age, sex, and income, Aboriginal people remained at greater risk of violent victimization.

Aboriginal women appeared particularly at risk of victimization. Rates for Aboriginal women were 3.5 times higher than the rates recorded for non-Aboriginal women, while rates for Aboriginal men were 2.7 times higher than those for non-Aboriginal men.

(Continued)

(Continued)

In the case of visible minorities, it was found that the risk of violent victi-
mizition did not differ significantly from their non-visible minority coun-
terparts (98 versus 107 per 1,000 population). This was true for both men
and women. However, in the case of immigrants, overall rates were lower
than that of non-immigrants (68 versus 116 per 1,000 population). The
reduced likelihood of victimization was even more pronounced when only
those who had immigrated to Canada since 1999 were included. For example, 71 per 1,000 population of those who immigrated prior to 1999 were
the victims of a violent crime, compared to 53 per 1,000 of those who had
immigrated in the past 5 year period. Again, these patterns were similar for
immigrant women and men.

One possible explanation for lower rates within the immigrant population
may be due to the fact that the immigrant population tends to be older, a
factor which reduces risk of victimization. According to the Census of the
Population, compared to immigrants, a higher proportion of non-immigrants
were under the age of 25 years, the most at-risk age group for violent
victimization.

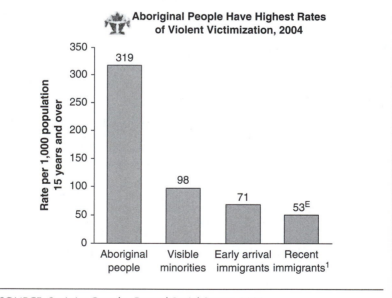

Aboriginal People Have Highest Rates of Violent Victimization, 2004

SOURCE: Statistics Canada, General Social Survey, 2004.

NOTE: Includes incidents of spousal sexual and physical assault. E = use with caution

1. Included are immigrants arriving between 1999 and 2004.

and justice. Further, Figure 4.9 suggests that, as in other countries, Blacks clearly have a different experience than other visible minorities. This trend is discussed further in the next section which highlights scholarship that has sought to contextualize racial/ethnic disparities in the Canadian criminal justice system.

EMERGING CRIME AND JUSTICE
SCHOLARSHIP ON ABORIGINAL AND VISIBLE MINORITIES

As evidenced by the above literature, the scholarship on the experiences of Aboriginals in the Canadian criminal justice system is more plentiful than what is available on other racial/ethnic groups. Roberts and Doob (1997) discuss this predicament by reviewing the long and arduous history of the debate surrounding the recording of race–crime statistics. The debate is believed to extend back at least to the late 1920s (Johnston, 1994). Over an extended period of time, Canadian citizens have resisted the movement to delineate crime statistics by race. Roberts and Doob (1997) write that: "Statistics Canada does not collect data on the racial or ethnic origin of suspects, accuseds, or convicted persons, though it does publish correctional statistics on Aboriginal people" (p. 483). In the early 1990s, Statistics Canada requested that police departments record such information, but Roberts and Doob note that few departments were willing or able to do so. In addition, they write that: "There was a negative response from Black community groups and many academics, all of whom had reservations about the utility of collecting such data" (Roberts & Doob, 1997, p. 483).

As a result of these collective factors, Statistics Canada stopped collecting the data; however, it did not stop the debate. Scholars across Canada began to debate the utility of the practice, with some arguing for the collection of data (Gabor, 1994) while others remained adamantly opposed to the practice (Doob, 1991; Roberts, 1994). Scot Wortley's (1999) review of the issue noted the three common arguments for and against the collection of race–crime statistics. In brief, he notes that those against the collection of such data point to: "(1) The poor quality of crime statistics; (2) the difficulty of measuring race; and (3) the possibility of race–crime statistics will be used to support racist theories of crime and subsequently justify discrimination against racial minorities" (p. 263). On the other side, he notes the following arguments in favor of recording race–crime statistics: "(1) This type of information is needed to identify whether or not minorities receive differential treatment within the justice system; (2) to challenge biological explanations of crime; and (3) because a ban will not prevent the spread of racist ideas" (p. 265). While good points were noted on each side, Wortley (1999) argued for a middle ground that might involve the production of special studies that would look at these issues. Such studies would explain in detail the limitations of the statistics presented. In recent years, Roberts (2002) has shown some support for this approach.

Taking a deep, historical view of the problem as it relates to Asians and Blacks in Canada, Clayton Mosher (1998, 1999) provides clear evidence that, at least in Ontario, there have been long-standing issues with these groups securing justice in the legal and criminal justice systems. Examining both jail records and newspaper accounts, Mosher found that Asians and Blacks were the targets of considerable legislation to restrict their full participation in Canadian society. Moreover, impetuous newspaper accounts of crime incidents involving these groups served as a way to racialize crime or associate crime with a particular racial or ethnic group (Mosher, 1998). However, these exaggerated concerns were really an affront to economic competition concerns. Nevertheless, the tactic was effective in making persons believe that the chief criminal justice concerns in Canada in the late 1800s to the early 1900s involved Asians and Blacks. Table 4.10, though, clearly shows that the real crime problem involved *White* Canadians.

Prior to the early 1990s, except for the unfounded biological assertions regarding the innate criminality of Blacks asserted by the Canadian scholar J. Phillipe Rushton (see generally, Rushton, 1988, 1990, 1995; and more recently, Rushton & Whitney, 2002) and countered by Canadian scholars who were skeptical and alarmed by Rushton's thesis (Roberts & Gabor, 1990), there was very little serious scholarship related to race and crime concerns in Canada. Mosher (1998) surmised that this was a product of two key reasons. The first reason:

> [There was] an underlying belief that Canada is a kinder and gentler nation [than the United States] with respect to a number of issues; this notion includes the country's social welfare system and extends to the idea that Canada has historically not been overly severe in its treatment of minority groups in society in general, or in its criminal justice system in particular. (p. 42)

Notably, a large portion of Mosher's work debunks this falsehood. And second, Mosher (1998) also felt the lack of attention was the result of a lack

Table 4.10   Convicts in Federal Penitentiaries, by Race, 1896–1938

Year	Black	Chinese	White	Total
1896	56 (4.1)	14 (1.0)	1,306 (92.9)	1,376
1897	55 (4.0)	10 (0.7)	1,287 (93.6)	1,375
1898–1899	NOT AVAILABLE			
1900	75 (5.3)	12 (0.8)	1,306 (92.2)	1,415
1901	54 (3.9)	10 (0.7)	1,281 (93.3)	1,372
1902	49 (4.1)	8 (0.7)	1,106 (92.5)	1,195
1903	53 (4.2)	7 (0.6)	1,131 (90.4)	1,250
1904	54 (4.1)	11 (0.8)	1,207 (90.8)	1,328
1905	55 (4.0)	14 (1.0)	1,244 (91.0)	1,367
1906	51 (3.5)	16 (1.1)	1,325 (92.1)	1,439
1907	51 (3.6)	17 (1.2)	1,298 (91.2)	1,423
1908	54 (3.7)	20 (1.4)	1,357 (91.9)	1,476
1909	62 (3.5)	22 (1.2)	1,635 (92.6)	1,765
1910	53 (2.9)	20 (1.1)	1,738 (93.5)	1,859
1911	52 (2.8)	21 (1.1)	1,747 (93.7)	1,864
1912	52 (2.7)	27 (1.4)	1,777 (93.8)	1,895
1913	62 (3.2)	29 (1.5)	1,831 (93.0)	1,968
1914	57 (2.8)	41 (2.0)	1,867 (93.2)	2,003
1915	62 (3.0)	39 (1.9)	1,929 (93.5)	2,064
1916	63 (3.0)	47 (2.2)	1,970 (93.0)	2,118
1917	56 (3.3)	38 (2.3)	1,553 (92.0)	1,688
1918	64 (4.4)	29 (2.0)	1,333 (91.1)	1,462
1919	52 (3.1)	24 (1.4)	1,585 (94.0)	1,686
1920	57 (3.0)	22 (1.1)	1,820 (94.3)	1,931

(Continued)

Table 4.10 (Continued)

Year	Black	Chinese	White	Total
1921	67 (1.1)	25 (1.2)	2,019 (93.9)	2,150
1922	83 (3.1)	30 (1.1)	2,489 (94.3)	2,640
1923	87 (3.5)	49 (2.0)	2,303 (92.8)	2,483
1924	63 (2.8)	51 (2.3)	2,065 (92.9)	2,224
1925	54 (2.3)	40 (1.7)	2,198 (93.8)	2,343
1926	48 (1.9)	44 (1.8)	2,327 (94.1)	2,473
1927	42 (1.7)	41 (1.7)	2,354 (94.9)	2,480
1928	43 (1.7)	58 (2.3)	2,409 (94.1)	2,560
1929	60 (2.2)	71 (2.6)	2,589 (93.5)	2,769
1930	60 (1.9)	80 (2.5)	2,995 (94.0)	3,187
1931	75 (2.0)	81 (2.2)	3,499 (94.2)	3,714
1932	79 (1.9)	81 (1.9)	3,923 (94.2)	4,164
1933	66 (1.4)	78 (1.7)	4,376 (95.4)	4,587
1934	50 (1.2)	51 (1.3)	4,068 (96.4)	4,220
1935	51 (1.4)	36 (1.0)	3,417 (96.2)	3,552
1936	45 (1.5)	24 (0.8)	2,972 (95.9)	3,098
1937	43 (1.3)	29 (0.9)	3,130 (95.9)	3,264
1938	58 (1.6)	30 (0.8)	3,426 (95.7)	3,580

SOURCE: *Canada Year Book, Report on Penitentiaries,* 1896–1938

NOTE: Figures in parentheses represent percentages of the totals and may not add up to 100 per cent because of unincluded groups and rounding error. Figures broken down by race are unavailable after 1938. Figures in 'Total' column may not equal sum of 3 columns because of missing data.

of data. Here, he seems to agree that, as a result of limited data, there were a limited number of studies on the topic. But, even from the limited studies available, Mosher concluded that "racism in the administration of justice in Canada is widespread and has existed throughout Canada's history" (p. 43).

Mosher's pioneering work was preceded 3 years earlier by the publication of reports by the *Commission on Systemic Racism in the Ontario Criminal Justice System* (1995). Many of these reports revealed that race was clearly a factor in criminal justice outcomes. Public opinion research revealed that residents felt that Blacks and Asians were not treated fairly by judges. But when defense attorneys and judges were surveyed, the results revealed mixed feelings on the topic. For example, 50% of defense attorneys felt Blacks and other minorities were treated the same as Whites. And the majority of the judges felt the same way (64% to 72% depending on the type of judge). Some judges felt that discrimination was an excuse for criminality, and if there was any discrimination it was economic (*Commission on Systemic Racism,* 1995). But these views were in stark contrast to the research studies in the report that showed a "race effect" was present and was a strong predictor of who did or did not get imprisoned (*Commission on Systemic Racism,* 1995).

The finding in the report regarding the drug trade and the treatment of Blacks sounded eerily familiar to the American context. The report indicated that "in 1992/93 the black pre-trial admissions rate for drug trafficking/importing charges was 27 times higher than the white rate" (*Commission on Systemic Racism,* 1995, p. iii). Moreover, Blacks convicted of drug charges were imprisoned at a higher rate than Whites (55% versus 36%). The report also highlighted the dramatic increase in imprisonment from 1986/87 to 1992/93. For example, while the increase in prison admissions of Whites to various Ontario institutions ranged from 25% to 667%, the increase in Black prison admissions over the same period ranged from 2,914% to 3,890% (pp. 78–79). These increases, which were a product of the Canadian "war on drugs," led to the phenomena where in the mid-1980s Whites had predominated correctional populations, to the 1990s when Blacks began to become considerably overrepresented in Ontario institutions. The report also dispelled the common argument concerning the potential role of prior records explaining this difference in sentencing outcomes.

The period leading up to the report and following its publication produced some heated debates regarding race and crime in Canada. Some research turned to interviews of Canadian citizens or police officers. In Vancouver, a survey of the police found that only 35.6% of them felt that discrimination against non-Whites was a problem. Given that when the same question was posed to the general Canadian population it resulted in 66% agreeing with the statement, it was obvious that Vancouver police officers saw things very differently. Most of the officers also suggested that race was used an excuse for wrongdoing (Ungerleider, 1994). These ideas were believed to be a possible indicator of the lack of empathy on the part of the officers. In the absence of such empathy, it is surmised that there might be more conflict between the police and non-Whites.

In the mid-1990s, the Angus Group conducted a poll of randomly selected Toronto area residents to determine if they felt that Blacks were prone to crime. The poll found that "nearly half (45%) believed that there was a relationship between a person's ethnicity or racial background and the likelihood that he (she) will be involved in crime" (Henry, Hastings, & Freer, 1996, p. 471). Seeking additional detail, the survey also revealed:

> Almost one half (46%) said that West Indians, such as Jamaicans Trinidadians, and others, were responsible. Another 19% thought that "blacks in general" were responsible and 18% mentioned Asians or Vietnamese. All told, 65% of the respondents who believed that there was a link between race and crime (45% of the total sample of respondents) thought that black people committed more crimes than other groups. The "culture, customs or background" of these groups was the most commonly asserted reason for their belief (54%). (p. 471)

The implications of such attitudes were clear. Many people viewed Blacks as the main criminal justice problem that would likely aggravate the problem of discrimination in their encounters with the police, courts, and during sentencing.

Besides this troubling situation regarding Blacks, as noted previously, Asians also were considered a problem in Toronto. To examine the specific views of Asians regarding crime and justice issues, Chow (1996) examined survey data from "189 randomly selected Chinese community organizations within Metro Toronto, of which 71 were returned" (p. 479). Even with the small sample size, the results provide some insight into the view of leaders within the Chinese community in Toronto. Some highlights of the findings presented by Chow (1996) include: 73% agreed or strongly agreed that "systemic racism is prevalent in the criminal justice system" (p. 479); 29% stated "that judges often treat Chinese people differently than whites" (p. 479); and 36.6% felt that "ethnic and racial minorities were more susceptible to discriminatory treatment in prisons" (p. 481). Thus, these Chinese residents of Toronto had some serious concerns about the Ontario justice system.

So, were similar concerns found in other Canadian cities? Yes. In Montreal, for example, Symons (1999, 2002) described the "racialization" of street gangs (for similar concerns regarding the racialization of crime in Canada, see Barnes, 2002; Chan & Mirchandani, 2002a; Dell, 2002; Doran,

2002; James, 2002; Jiwani, 2002; Wortley, 2002). To illustrate this, Symons notes how racial and ethnic gangs are referred to be their group of origin (e.g., Haitians, Jamaicans), while other gangs composed of Whites are referenced by their activities (e.g., Skinheads, Ku Klux Klan). While she readily acknowledges the challenges faced by the Montreal police, she also shows how racial and ethnic-based stereotypes have become too much of a focal point in dealing with the gang problem in Montreal.

In another study of Montreal, Ouimet (2000) illustrated how an integrated perspective using social disorganization and opportunity theory was useful for understanding the spatial distribution of juvenile delinquency in Montreal. More specifically, Ouimet's analysis of Montreal census tracts and neighborhoods, found:

> The ethnic composition of the population is the best predictor of the offender at both levels of analysis. Areas with newer immigrant groups have low delinquency rates (from Asia or India). . . . However, areas with many new immigrants mostly from Haiti, Jamaica, and French Africa have the highest delinquency rates. (p. 148)

After making these statements, Ouimet cautioned readers against making individual generalizations based on his aggregate analyses (the so-called ecological fallacy). Another concern that has arisen in Canada is racial profiling.

RACIAL PROFILING IN CANADA

In recent years, while there has been an increasing emphasis on race and the Canadian justice system (Chan & Mirchandani, 2002b; Manzo & Bailey, 2005; Wortley, 2002, 2003), there also has been a heavy focus on the practice of racial profiling. In Toronto, the *Toronto Star* newspaper instigated the dialogue. The paper printed an article that examined more than 480,000 stops by the Toronto police that were the result of a crime or a traffic violation. Following their analysis of the data, the authors concluded that "black Torontonians are highly over-represented in certain charge categories—including drug possession" (Wortley & Tanner, 2003, p. 367). The paper also noted that the discrimination did not stop at the arrest stage—it was pervasive throughout the front-end of the system (e.g., pretrial release). To top it off, the paper alleged that the Toronto Police Department was engaging in racial profiling. The product of this allegation was vociferous debate. The Toronto police not only denied the allegation, they hired their own expert to analyze the data, which as you can guess did not result in the same conclusions as the *Toronto Star* (see Harvey, 2003). Moreover, citizens and scholars alike weighed in on the controversy.

One of the first responses appearing in a scholarly journal was by Wortley and Tanner (2003). Their article actually challenged the reanalysis conducted by Edward Harvey, the expert brought in by the Toronto police. They point to five major errors in the reanalysis. These include: improperly defining racial profiling and ignoring the scholarly literature on the topic; making incorrect and misleading statements; using questionable data cleaning techniques, providing an incomplete reanalysis of the data, and most importantly, "providing no concrete evidence that can disprove the *Star's* allegation of racial bias" (Wortley & Tanner, 2003, p. 369). It is also important to note that Wortley and Tanner (2003) actually believe that many of Harvey's arguments "are completely consistent *with* [italics added] the racial-profiling argument" (p. 369).

The views of Wortley and Tanner were not, however, shared by Attorney Alan Gold (2003) and Gabor (2004). The primary focus here is on Gold's critique. His critique dissects the methods and principle of racial profiling. He notes that "statistics on police stops must obviously exclude stops involving the police looking for a racially identified perpetrator" (Gold, 2003, p. 395). Moreover, Gold also points to the scenario:

> [When] police activity is stepped-up in response to community concerns about local drug pushers or local speeders and that community (unsurprisingly) is economically disadvantaged and (equally unsurprising) is more heavily populated with visible minorities, the statistics will be skewed towards more police-minority interaction. (p. 395)

Put more succinctly, Gold argues that "good science" should "distinguish between situations in which the police are 'using race' and where they are 'finding race'" (p. 395). Responding to survey data on minority experiences with the police, presented by Wortley and Tanner (2003), Gold (2003) simply dismisses them as "anecdotes in bulk" (p. 397).

Gold closes noting that the *Star's* article lacked numerous aspects of serious scientific inquiry and represents "junk science." Gabor's (2004) critique follows a similar line of thinking, arguing that the allegations against the Toronto police were "baseless." He added that since crime is unevenly distributed in most jurisdictions, police deployment will be different across communities. Gabor's critique resulted in another reply from Wortley and Tanner (2005), who used survey data to show that Black youth are being profiled and disproportionately stopped. Just recently, Tator and Henry (2006) have produced a comprehensive volume highlighting the problem of racial profiling in Canada.

FINAL THOUGHTS ABOUT CANADIAN RESEARCH ON RACE AND CRIME

Scholars in Canada continue in earnest to research the relationship between race and crime. As a result, there has been a notable increase in the scholarship on Aboriginal (Latimer & Casey-Foss, 2005; McCarthy & Hagan, 2003) and Black youth (Manzo & Bailey, 2005); in addition, the increasing concerns regarding Aboriginal and Black women has also garnered scholarly attention (see contributions in Chan & Mirchandani, 2002; Schissel & Brooks, 2002). It is also interesting to note that Canadian scholars are following the American trend of trying to determine whether music associated with racial minorities (Rap) is linked to deviant behavior (Miranda & Claes, 2004). Such research sadly illustrates that the criminalization of Black culture, as seen in the United States, is well underway in Canada.

SUMMARY AND CONCLUSION

This chapter reviewed the beginnings of Canadian society. It showed the colonization practices that reduced the Aboriginal population from a majority to a minority. This colonization remains relevant to understanding the relationship, in numerous spheres including criminal justice, between the "new" owners of the country and the "old" ones. Further, the review showed that while Canada is largely a nation of immigrants, it has always welcomed some and spurned others. Fitting into the latter category are Blacks (particularly from the Caribbean) and, to a lesser extent, Asians who have been the long-standing targets of restrictive immigration legislation. The review of crime and justice information found that Aboriginal people and, based on the limited available research with race statistics, visible minorities are overrepresented in the Canadian justice system. This has resulted in a considerable increase in Canadian-based race and crime scholarship.

Even with the rise in the scholarship, Canada appears to be in a state of denial. Its resistance to collecting race–crime statistics obviously does nothing to solve the problem; but on the other hand, as seen in other countries, collecting them apparently does not either. Therefore, the sad fact is that crime in Canada has been already racialized—even without the widespread distribution of such statistics. And one must face the sobering reality that having studies on race and crime does not guarantee change will come. As David Cole (1999) so eloquently put it: "It is simply naïve on the part of those who press for change to assume that findings of differential outcome, however revelatory, will immediately galvanize politicians and powerful senior policy makers to redeploy scarce resources" (p. 431). In the end, irrespective whether there is a change to the Canadian race–crime statistics policy, it is clear that Canada is not "a kinder and gentler" nation to Aboriginals and visible minorities; especially in regard to crime and justice.

REFERENCES

Barnes, A. (2002). Dangerous duality: The "net effect" of immigration and deportation on Jamaicans in Canada. In W. Chan & K. Mirchandani (Eds.), *Crimes of colour: Racialization and the criminal justice system in Canada* (pp. 191–203). Plymouth, UK: Broadview Press.

Belanger, A. (Ed.). (2006). *Report on the demographic situation in Canada* (Juristat Catalogue No. 91–209-XIE). Ottawa: Statistics Canada.

Bothwell, R. (2002). *A traveller's history of Canada*. New York: Interlink Books.

Brzozowski, J. A., Taylor-Butts, A., & Johnson, S. (2006). *Victimization and offending among the Aboriginal population in Canada*. (Juristat Catalogue No. 85–002-XIE, Vol. 26, No. 3). Ottawa: Statistics Canada.

Calverley, D. (2006). *Youth custody and community services in Canada, 2003/2004*. (Juristat Catalogue No. 85–002-XPE, Vol. 26, No. 2). Ottawa: Statistics Canada.

Calverley, D. (2007). *Youth custody and community services in Canada, 2004/2005*. (Juristat Catalogue No. 85–002-XPE, Vol. 27, No. 2). Ottawa: Statistics Canada.

Chan, W., & Mirchandani, K. (2002a). From race and crime to racialization and criminalization. In W. Chan & K. Mirchandani (Eds.), *Crimes of colour: Racialization and the criminal justice system in Canada*. Plymouth, UK: Broadview Press.

Chan, W., & Mirchandani, K. (2002b). *Crimes of colour: Racialization and the criminal justice system in Canada*. Plymouth, UK: Broadview Press.

Chow, H. P. H. (1996). The Chinese community leaders' perceptions of the criminal justice system. *Canadian Journal of Criminology, 38*, 477–484.

Cole, D. (1999). Review of discrimination and denial: Systemic racism in Ontario's legal and criminal justice system, 1892–1961. *Canadian Journal of Criminology, 41*, 428–432.

Commission on Systemic Racism in the Ontario Criminal Justice System: A Community Summary. (1995). Toronto: The Commission.

Cook, R. (1997). The triumph and trials of materialism (1900–1945). In C. Brown (Ed.), *The illustrated history of Canada* (pp. 375–466). Toronto: Key Porter Books.

Crosby, A. W. (1972). *The Columbian exchange: Biological and cultural consequences of 1492.* Westport, CT: Greenwood Press.

Daunton, M., & Halpern, R. (Ed.). (1999). *Empire and others: British encounters with Indigenous peoples, 1600–1850.* Philadelphia: University of Pennsylvania Press.

Dell, C. A. (2002). The criminalization of Aboriginal women: Commentary by a community activist. In W. Chan & K. Mirchandani (Eds.), *Crimes of colour: Racialization and the criminal justice system in Canada* (pp. 127–137). Plymouth, UK: Broadview Press.

Dickason, O. P. (2006). *A concise history of Canada's first nations.* Toronto: Oxford Press.

Doob, A. (1991). *Workshop on collecting race and ethnicity statistics in the criminal justice system.* Toronto: University of Toronto, Centre of Criminology.

Doran, C. (2002). Making sense of moral panics: Excavating the cultural foundations of the "young, black mugger." In W. Chan & K. Mirchandani (Eds.), *Crimes of colour: Racialization and the criminal justice system in Canada* (pp. 157–175). Plymouth, UK: Broadview Press.

Gabor, T. (1994). The suppression of crime statistics on race and ethnicity: The price of political correctness. *Canadian Journal of Criminology, 36*, 153–165.

Gabor, T. (2004). Inflammatory rhetoric on racial profiling can undermine police services. *Canadian Journal of Criminology and Criminal Justice, 46*, 457–466.

Gannon, M. (2006). *Crime statistics in Canada, 2005.* (Juristat Catalogue No. 85–002-XIE, Vol. 26, No. 4). Ottawa: Statistics Canada.

Gannon, M., & Mihorean, K. (2005). *Criminal victimization in Canada, 2004.* (Juristat Catalogue No. 85–002-XPE, Vol. 25, No. 7). Ottawa: Statistics Canada.

Gold, A. D. (2003). Media hype, racial profiling, and good science. *Canadian Journal of Criminology and Criminal Justice, 45*, 391–399.

Harvey, E. (2003). An independent review of the *Toronto Star* analysis of criminal information processing system (CIPS). Available from Toronto Police Service Web site, www.torontopolice.on.ca

Henry, F., Hastings, P., & Freer, B. (1996). Perceptions of race and crime in Ontario: Empirical evidence from Toronto and the Durham region. *Canadian Journal of Criminology, 38*, 469–476.

James, C. E. (2002). Armed and dangerous! Racializing suspects, suspecting race. In B. Schissel & C. Brooks (Eds.), *Marginality and condemnation: An introduction to critical criminology* (pp. 289–307). Hailifax, NS: Fernwood Publishing.

Jiwani, Y. (2002). The criminalization of race, the racialization of crime. In W. Chan & K. Mirchandani (Eds.), *Crimes of colour: Racialization and the criminal justice system in Canada* (pp. 67–86). Plymouth, UK: Broadview Press.

Johnston, J. P. (1994). Academic approaches to race–crime statistics do not justify their collection. *Canadian Journal of Criminology, 36,* 166–173.

Kazemipur, A., & Halli, S. S. (1999). *The new poverty in Canada: Ethnic groups and ghetto neighborhoods.* Toronto: Thompson Educational Publishing.

Landry, L., & Sinha, M. (2008). *Adult correctional services in Canada, 2005/2006.* (Juristat Catalogue No. 85–002-XIE, Vol. 28, No. 6). Ottawa: Statistics Canada.

Latimer, J., & Casey-Foss, L. (2005). The sentencing of Aboriginal and non-Aboriginal youth under the young offenders act: A multivariate analysis. *Canadian Journal of Criminology and Criminal Justice, 47,* 481–500.

Li, G. (2007). *Homicide in Canada, 2006.* (Juristat Catalogue No. 85–002-XIE, Vol. 27, No. 8). Ottawa: Statistics Canada.

Manzo, J. F., & Bailey, M. M. (2005). On the assimilation of racial stereotypes among black Canadian young offenders. *The Canadian Review of Sociology and Anthropology, 42,* 283–300.

McCarthy, B., & Hagan, J. (2003). Sanction effects, violence, and native North American street youth. In D. F. Hawkins (Ed.), *Violent crime: Assessing race and ethnic differences* (pp. 117–137). Cambridge, UK: Cambridge University Press.

Miranda, D., & Claes, M. (2004). Rap music genres and deviant behaviors in French Canadian adolescents. *Journal of Youth and Adolescence, 33,* 113–122.

Morton, D. (1997a). *A short history of Canada* (3rd ed.). Toronto: McClelland & Stewart.

Morton, D. (1997b). Strains of affluence (1945–1996). In C. Brown (Ed.), *The illustrated history of Canada* (pp. 467–562). Toronto: Key Porter Books.

Mosher, C. J. (1998). *Discrimination and denial: Systemic racism in Ontario's legal and criminal justice systems, 1892–1961.* Toronto: University of Toronto Press.

Mosher, C. J. (1999). The reaction to black violent offenders in Ontario, 1892–1961: A test of the threat hypothesis. *Sociological Forum, 14,* 635–658.

Ouimet, M. (2000). Aggregation bias in ecological research: How social disorganization and criminal opportunities shape the spatial distribution of juvenile delinquency in Montreal. *Canadian Journal of Criminology, 42,* 135–156.

Pilot survey of hate crime. (2004, June 1). *The Daily.* Retrieved December 4, 2006, from www.statcan.ca/Daily/English/040601/d040601a.htm

Ray, A. (1997). When two worlds met. In C. Brown (Ed.), *The illustrated history of Canada* (pp. 17–104). Toronto: Key Porter Books.

Roberts, J. V. (1994). Crime and race statistics: Toward a Canadian solution. *Canadian Journal of Criminology, 36,* 175–185.

Roberts, J. V. (2002). Racism and the collection of statistics relating to race and ethnicity. In W. Chan & K. Mirchandani (Eds.), *Crimes of colour: Racialization and the criminal justice system in Canada* (pp. 101–112). Plymouth, UK: Broadview Press.

Roberts, J. V., & Doob, A. N. (1997). Race, ethnicity, and criminal justice in Canada. *Crime and Justice: A Review of Research, 21*, 469–522.

Roberts, J. V., & Gabor, T. (1990). Lombrosian wine in a new bottle: Research on race and crime. *Canadian Journal of Criminology, 32*, 291–313.

Rushton, J. P. (1988). Race differences in behaviour: A review and evolutionary analysis. *Personality and Individual Differences, 9*, 1009–1024.

Rushton, J. P. (1990). Race and crime: A reply to Roberts and Gabor. *Canadian Journal of Criminology, 32*, 315–334.

Rushton, J. P. (1995). Race and crime: International data for 1989–1990. *Psychological Reports, 76*, 307–312.

Rushton, J. P., & Whitney, G. (2002). Cross-national variation in violent crime rates: Race, r-K theory, and income. *Population and Environment, 23*, 501–511

Schissel, B., & Brooks, C. (2002). *Marginality and condemnation: An introduction to critical criminology.* Hailifax, NS: Fernwood Publishing.

See, S. W. (2001). *The history of Canada.* Westport, CT: Greenwood Press.

Silver, W. (2007). *Crime statistics in Canada, 2006.* (Juristat Catalogue No. 85–002-XIE, Vol. 27, No. 5). Ottawa: Statistics Canada.

Symons, G. L. (1999). Racialization of the street gang issue in Montreal: A police perspective. *Canadian Ethnic Studies, 31*, 124–138.

Symons, G. L. (2002). Police constructions of race and gender in street gangs. In W. Chan & K. Mirchandani (Eds.), *Crimes of colour: Racialization and the criminal justice system in Canada* (pp. 115–125). Plymouth, UK: Broadview Press.

Tator, C., & Henry, F. (2006). *Racial profiling in Canada: Challenging the myth of "a few bad apples."* Toronto: University of Toronto Press.

Ungerleider, C. S. (1994). Police, race and community conflict in Vancouver. *Canadian Ethnic Studies, 26*, 91–104.

Visible Minorities in Canada. (2001). Ottawa: Statistics Canada.

Wortley, S. (1999). A northern taboo: Research on race, crime, and criminal justice in Canada. *Canadian Journal of Criminology, 41*, 261–274.

Wortley, S. (2002). Misrepresentation or reality? The depiction of race and crime in the Toronto print media. In B. Schissel & C. Brooks (Eds.), *Marginality and condemnation: An introduction to critical criminology* (pp. 55–82). Hailifax, NS: Fernwood Publishing.

Wortley, S. (2003). Hidden intersections: Research on race, crime, and criminal justice in Canada. *Canadian Ethnic Studies, 35*, 99–117.

Wortley, S., & Tanner, J. (2003). Data, denials, and confusion: The racial profiling debate in Toronto. *Canadian Journal of Criminology & Criminal Justice, 45*, 367–389.

Wortley, S., & Tanner, J. (2005). Inflammatory rhetoric? Baseless accusations? A response to Gabor's critique of racial profiling research in Canada. *Canadian Journal of Criminology and Criminal Justice, 47*, 581–609.

Wynn, G. (1997). On the margins of empire (1760–1840). In C. Brown (Ed.), *The illustrated history of Canada* (pp. 189–278). Toronto: Key Porter Books.

Figure 5.1   Contemporary Map of Australia

FIVE

AUSTRALIA

———•◦•———

CHAPTER OVERVIEW

This chapter focuses on the Australian experience related to race and crime. To begin, the chapter reviews the rich history of Australia and its original people, referred to as Aboriginal people. This chapter also discusses European efforts and success at colonizing Australia, along with the impact of that colonization. Turning to the current state of affairs in Australia, the chapter reviews demographic information on the population, as well as the state of the Aboriginal people. The chapter continues, first with a brief review of Australian crime statistics, followed by a review of the state of Aborigines in relation to crime and justice. Here, the primary area of focus is the overrepresentation of Aborigines in the Australian justice system. Within this focus, the chapter discusses the various aspects of the overrepresentation, and the efforts to reduce it.

EARLY HISTORY

Australia is a continent of contrasts (see Figure 5.1). On the one hand, it is a continent that is both flat and dry; while on the other hand, approximately "40 percent of Australia lies within the tropics" (Chambers, 1999, p. 7). These contrasts continue as we consider the history and nature of its people. It comprises of six states, including Tasmania, Queensland, New South Wales, Victoria, Western Australia, and South Australia. For more than 50,000 years before the arrival of Captain James Cook, the British explorer who "discovered" Australia for the second time in 1788, it is believed that the Aboriginal people migrated to the continent from Asia. Therefore, as noted by Chambers (1999, p. 1), Australia also has two histories: pre-European colonization and the era following the introduction of European colonization. Prior to the arrival of Europeans, the Aboriginal people had distinct cultural traditions. Of the Aboriginal people and their traditions, Chambers (1999) wrote:

> Theirs is . . . the world's oldest continuous culture, with easily the world's oldest continuous religion. And their religion and culture were embedded in a way of life most subtly adapted to the environment and to the seasonal supplies of food. More than that, they had achieved a successful, almost symbiotic relationship with the land, living with it without destroying it or the other living species that depend upon it. (p. 11)

Their society was based on hunting and gathering in which they traveled in small groups and, even without having discovered the ability to write, they documented their culture and society by "[painting] complicated, often beautiful, symbolic murals in caves and on rocky outcrops" (Chambers, 1999, p. 11). At the arrival of the Europeans, who in 1788 brought with them 11 ships which included "736 convicts, women and guards" (Roberts, 1993, p. 366), it is estimated there were approximately 300,000 Aborigines on the continent (Knightley, 2000). By all scholarly accounts, as happened elsewhere across the globe, diseases brought by the Europeans killed many of the indigenous people (also generally referred to as Aborigines), which comprise of Aborigines (the first inhabitants of Australia), Tasmanian Aborigines, and Torres Strait Islanders who are from the Torres Strait Islands located in Queensland. In addition, Knightley writes that "the killing began early on" (p. 108). Another product of colonization, the brutalization and genocidal practices of the Europeans in Australia, are well documented. Describing this process and its ramifications, Knightley (2000) noted that:

> In many states in the early days the settlers cleared Aboriginals from their land as casually as kangaroos. They shot them, poisoned them and clubbed them. In Tasmania, they succeeded in wiping them out nearly entirely. The Black War from 1803 to 1830 reduced the Aboriginal Tasmanian population from a few thousand to less than 100. In the rest of the country over a period of 150 years the Aboriginal population declined from an estimated 300,000 to about 75,000. (p. 108; see also Turnbull, 1965)

As the Aboriginal population declined, there was a rise in the population of foreigners and White Australians. Within 50 years of arrival, the White settler population had grown to 100,000, and by 1860 it had grown to 1 million people (Roberts, 1993, p. 366). What caused such growth in the settler population? First, the British Empire continued to use Australia as a penal colony for convicts which, along with the increase in the White population, also served to bring a certain level of chaos to certain areas. For example, the rise of "bushraging" or the "lawlessness of escaped convicts and other bandits, who terrorized the more remote areas" (Langer, 1968, p. 928), contributed to such chaos. Even with such criminal and violent behavior from the convicts, once their sentences expired, they were granted 30 to 50 acres of land (Langer, 1968). By so doing, the convicts were free to populate the land and partake in the "brutal and rapid extermination of the natives" (Langer, 1968, p. 926). Second, in 1793 free settlers, "who received free passage, tools, convict service, and land grants" (Langer, 1968, p. 926), began to arrive in Australia. With such incentives, even with the impending uncertainty of the new land, settlers were willing to take their chances. So by 1840, when the last of the 60,000 to 75,000 convicts had arrived in New South Wales (the last convicts were actually sent to West Australia in 1867), there were more free settlers than convicts (Langer, 1968, p. 926). Finally, in 1851, gold was discovered. This development brought "gold diggers" from all over the world. While most of those who came were integrated into the gold rush, Chambers indicates that the 40,000 Chinese who came faced discrimination to the point that, at some point, there were limits placed on Chinese immigration (Chambers, 1999, p. 144). Notwithstanding the restrictions on Chinese immigration (there was also resistance to Japanese immigration), the gold rush was likely the largest contributor to the dramatic rise in the Australian population during the 19th century.

Just before the gold rush, Britain passed the Australian Colonies Government Act in 1850. The act was the first step towards independence. It allowed the Australian colonies to "constitute their own legislatures, fix the franchise, alter their constitutions, [and] determine their own tariffs, all subject to royal confirmation" (Langer, 1968, p. 929). It wasn't until 50 years later that Australia became independent and formed the Commonwealth of Australia in 1901. At that time, they created a Parliament comprised of a House of Representatives and a Senate. The governor-general was the title given to the person who represented the Queen, but the person who actually runs the country is referred to as the Prime Minister. And finally, a high court was developed to interpret the Australian Constitution (Chambers, 1999). So where did all this "progress" leave the Aboriginal people?

Well, during this period, the Aboriginal people were literally fighting for their survival. With 4 million people in Australia by the passage of the Constitution, and large numbers of them immigrants from England, Scotland, Ireland, and Wales, the Aborigines "were overwhelmed by the ever-growing, aggressive tide of white immigrants" (Woodruff, 2002, p. 67). In fact, according to Hanks (1984), the Constitution left the destiny of the Aborigines in the hands of the state. There was little concern about the Aborigines because it was widely believed that they were dying off (Hanks, 1984). Much of the concern in the Constitution was reserved for persons immigrating to Australia. Later on, though, the Commonwealth government passed acts that pertained to Aboriginals. For example, the Northern Territory Aboriginals Act was passed in 1910. This act turned the control of the Northern Territory over to the federal government of Australia. In general, however, the Commonwealth left the handling of the Aboriginals to the various states in which the population resided.

Throughout the 20th century Aboriginal issues were dealt with a measure of indifference. At various times, discussions took place about how to deal with them. For example, in the late 1930s, the emphasis from all levels of government was assimilation (Hanks, 1984). During this era, A. O. Neville, the chief protector of Aboriginals of Western Australia, came up with a strategy to handle Aboriginals. He presented a proposal called "The Destiny of the Race" at a conference that, according to Knightley (2000):

> called for the total absorption into the white community of all non-full-blood Aborigines. Taking part-Aboriginal children from their mothers and families by force was part of this ambition. Over the years various regulations had been invoked to make this possible. (p. 112)

Knightley (2000) writes that these "'half-caste' children were seized by the state and placed in institutions where they suffered physical mistreatment and sexual abuse" (p. 112). Moreover, Knightley describes these state-sanctioned kidnappings that took place well into the 1960s:

> White welfare officers, often supported by the police would descend on Aboriginal camps, round up all the children, separate the ones with light-coloured skin, bundle them into trucks and take them away. If their parents protested they were held at bay by the police. (p. 113)

Given that many Aboriginals didn't even vote until the early 1960s, they had little political influence to end this despicable policy, which took so-called child saving to another level (Platt, 1969). In fact, they weren't even recognized as being citizens until 1967 when, included within legislation that federalized the handling of Aboriginal affairs, the national census began to enumerate their population (Hanks, 1984, pp. 24–25). Citizenship was, in fact, one of a variety of things that Aboriginals pursued. Other pursuits included "improved conditions, recognition of equality and the rights of full citizenship, and concomitant dismantling of discrimination" (Merlan, 2005, p. 482).

CONTEMPORARY HISTORY

After the amendments to the Australian Constitution were passed, concerns remained regarding the Aboriginal people. Nevertheless, during the 1970s Aboriginals made notable strides, with some of them becoming senators, barristers, governors, and holding leadership positions within the religious ministry. Furthermore, taking a cue from the Black Power Movement in the United States, they became more socially active (see Clemons & Jones, 2001; Lothian, 2005). This period also saw the Australian government abandoning their assimilation policies and adopting a policy of "multiculturalism," whereby Aborigines and persons of other ethnic backgrounds were encouraged to celebrate their heritage. Chambers (1999) suggests that while the policy was ambitious, it spurred backlash from nationalists who believed that the policy "undervalued Anglo-Celtic heritage" (p. 278). Irrespective of these sentiments, the government pursued an open immigration policy that, for the first time in more than a century, welcomed Asian immigrants. In some ways, this was a strategic move because of Australia's increasing trade with Asian countries.

In the 1980s, the government created the Aboriginal and Torres Strait Islander Commission. The commission coordinated regional councils concerned with Aboriginal matters throughout Australia. In general, the commission increased the visibility of Aborigines, which led to their movement to reclaim Aboriginal lands. From this movement, "the first large transfer . . . 28,000 square miles of land (larger than Tasmania) at Maralinga in South Australia was handed back to Aboriginal ownership" (Chambers, 1999, p. 285).

Reconciliation was the theme of the 1990s. In 1991, the government formed the Council for Aboriginal Reconciliation Act (CARA), which would take the lead in "creating a new relationship between settler Australia and its indigenous peoples" (Merlan, 2005, p. 485). However, even with this Act in place, the government remained unwilling to offer an apology for the wrongs of early White settlers. Merlan (2005) observes that:

> Apology has remained an unresolved issue, and some indigenous spokes people have concluded that no apology is forthcoming. Thus, many contentious issues have continuously been laid on the public table and have made evident different views of history, responsibility, justice, and reparation. (p. 486)

Even with the call for an apology from Cathy Freeman, the Aboriginal Olympic gold medalist from the 2000 Sydney Olympics and a national hero whose grandmother was a victim of the government's earlier removal of Aboriginal children from their parents (Gardiner, 2003), the government remained steadfast in its decision to not offer an apology for past wrongs related to Aboriginals. Nevertheless, this decade saw the unearthing of the genocidal and racist practice of the past. Curiously, though, as these wrongs were being brought to the fore, in 2000 the CARA ended. It did, however, end on a high note with the holding of the People's Walk for Reconciliation in which an estimated 250,000 to 400,000 people crossed the Sydney Harbor Bridge to show their support for the process of reconciliation. In its final report delivered to the federal government in 2002, the authors wrote:

> Reconciliation has begun to enter the hearts and minds of the Australian people creating one of the most determined vibrant people's movements ever seen in the history of the nation. Aboriginal and Torres Strait Islander and other Australians are increasingly working together to recognize and help heal the wounds of the past and move on together. (Merlan, 2005, p. 487)

Clearly, the conclusions of the full report were not acceptable to the government because as Merlan reports, "It was not accepted by the federal government" (p. 487). Moreover, in 2004 the government closed down the Aboriginal and Torres Strait Islander Commission. This was another obvious sign that, within the government, "there [was] little collective will for institutional change" (Merlan, 2005, p. 487; for a similar conclusion, see Short, 2003). Remarkably, in 2008, the Australian government finally apologized to the Aboriginal people for the Australian government's participation in the "stolen generations" (Laurie, 2008). In addition, those Aboriginals who were taken from their families are seeking compensation for the abuse they suffered at the hands of their caretakers.

Today, while Aboriginals and foreigners are still not highly regarded, many of the more recent concerns have been directed at Muslim-Australians and Arab-Australians, which is likely a product of international events. But, in general, the emerging scholarly attitudinal research on Australians presents a clear picture of racism remaining a continuing problem in the country Down Under (Dunn, Forrest, Burnley, & McDonald, 2004; Fozdar & Torezani, 2008; Larson, Gillies, Howard, & Coffin, 2007; Leach, 2005; Paradies, 2005; Schweitzer, Perkoulidis, Krome, Ludlow, & Ryan, 2005). Such problems are likely to reveal themselves in social institutions throughout society (employment, criminal justice, etc.).

In the next section, I briefly note some current socio-demographics of Australia. Following this, the remainder of the chapter will examine the role of race in the administration of criminal justice in Australia.

OVERVIEW OF SOCIO-DEMOGRAPHICS IN AUSTRALIA

In 2001, the Australian census reported that nearly 19.5 million people lived in the country (the population has since surpassed the 21 million mark in 2007). Of these persons, 458,520 (2.4% of the total population) identified themselves as indigenous (Australian Bureau of Statistics, 2003). In general the indigenous population tends to be younger than the non-indigenous population. More specifically, the median age of the indigenous population is 20.5, while the figure is 36.1 for the non-indigenous population. Nearly 60% of the indigenous population resides in two areas of the Commonwealth: New South Wales (134,888) and Queensland (125,910). The remainder are scattered throughout the Commonwealth, with Western Australia (65,931) and the Northern Territory (56,875) being the other places where considerable numbers reside. Although the largest number of indigenous people live in major cities (30%), their representation in such areas is much less than that of non-indigenous people, two-thirds of whom reside in such areas. Moreover, while more than 25% of indigenous people reside in remote to very remote areas, only 2% of non-indigenous persons reside in these areas. Finally, the median age of death for indigenous persons was 54, while the corresponding figure for the Australian population was 78.5.

Moving on to educational and work statistics, we first find that the indigenous population is less formally educated than the non-indigenous population. Only 19% of the indigenous population has some educational qualifications, while nearly 46% of non-indigenous persons have such qualifications (Australian Bureau of Statistics, 2003). A likely consequence of such figures can be found in figures showing that 20% of indigenous persons were unemployed, while 7% of non-indigenous persons were unemployed. It is also important to note here that a large share of indigenous persons indicated they were not in the labor force at all (39.4% of males and 55.8% of females). Of those indigenous persons in the labor force, their primary areas of employment were laborers and related workers (23.5%); immediate clerical, sales, and service workers (18.1%); professionals (11.1%); and tradespersons and related workers (10.2%). Non-indigenous persons were found heavily in the ranks of professionals (18.4%); immediate clerical, sales, and service workers (16.5%); tradespersons and related workers (12.3%); and associate professionals (11.8%). Overall, the figures suggest that there is clearly more balance among the distribution of employment among non-indigenous persons.

In regard to income, the average household income for indigenous persons was $364 per week which, according to the Australian Bureau of Statistics, represented only 62% of the average income of non-indigenous persons ($585 per week). As one might expect, indigenous income decreased as their population became more remote or rural. It is notable, though, that from 1996 to 2001 the level of income among indigenous persons rose 11%. Indigenous persons were more likely to be renters (63%) than other persons (26.6%). In fact, only 33% of indigenous persons were either in the process of purchasing their homes or already owned their homes. The figures for non-indigenous persons revealed that 67% of them were either purchasing (27%) or already owned (40.4%) their homes.

The aforementioned figures provide a brief synapsis of the condition of indigenous people in Australia. We will now review crime and justice issues in general and as they pertain to Australian Aborigines.

OVERVIEW OF CRIME AND JUSTICE IN AUSTRALIA

Official Crime Data

At first glance, Australia appears to be a place with little crime. For a country of 21 million people to record only 319 homicides in 2006 (*Australian*

Crime, 2008, p. 8) is rather impressive—considering that one major city in the United States could have double that number. In fact, an examination of the trends for violent crimes from 1996 to 2006 reveals a fairly consistent pattern of fairly low violent crime levels (see Table 5.1). For some of the more violent offenses, these figures translate into the following rates per 100,000 persons in the population (see Figure 5.2): homicide (1.5 per 100,000), robbery (84 per 100,000), and kidnapping (3.8 per 100,000). Even with these low violent crime rates, the nature of such crimes appears to mirror that of other countries. For example, homicide victims were mostly males; male victims were in the 25 to 44 age group; and, according to *Australian Crime* (2008):

> Male victims in 2005–06 were more likely than female victims to be killed by a friend or acquaintance (38% and 16%, respectively), whereas female victims are more likely than male victims to have been killed by a family member (21% and 16% respectively). (p. 20)

Figure 5.3 highlights the victim–offender relationship of homicides in Australia.

Figure 5.2   Violent Crimes, 1996–2006 (rate per 100,000 persons)

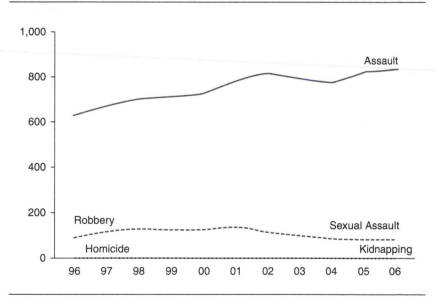

SOURCE: *Australian Crime: Facts and Figures 2007* (Australian Institute of Criminology, 2008).

NOTE: Homicide and kidnapping occur at rates of less than 5 per 100,000 each and are difficult to distinguish on this chart.

Figure 5.3   Homicide Victims, Relationship to Offender, 2005–2006 (percent)

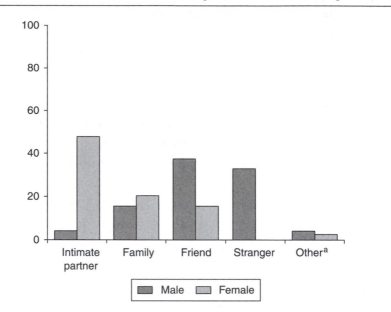

SOURCE: *Australian Crime: Facts and Figures 2007* (Australian Institute of Criminology, 2008).

NOTES:

a. Other includes business associates, employee/employer, colleagues and other relationships.

In most countries, though, the larger percentage of crimes can be found in property offenses. Predictably then, in 2006, Australia reported much higher rates for property crimes in the same 1996 to 2006 time period (see Figure 5.4). However, there has been a declining trend in this type of offense, which declined to its lowest point in 2004. While motor vehicle theft is also on the decline (see Figure 5.5), the most fascinating figure here is that 75% of stolen vehicles are actually recovered! Besides motor vehicle theft, other forms of theft such as pickpocketing, bag snatching, stealing, and theft from a motor vehicle, were also on the decline (see Figure 5.6). Two other types of offenses noted in the annual crime statistics are fraud and deception offenses (these include offenses such as check fraud, credit card fraud, forgery, etc.) and drug arrests. While the authors note that the former offenses are also decreasing, they caution readers that as much as 50% of such offenses go

Table 5.1   Victims of Violent Crimes, 1996–2006

	Homicide	Assault	Sexual Assault	Robbery	Kidnapping
1996	354	114,156	14,542	16,372	478
1997	364	124,500	14,353	21,305	564
1998	332	130,903	14,336	23,801	707
1999	386	134,271	14,104	22,606	766
2000	363	138,708	15,759	23,336	695
2001	346	152,283	16,897	26,591	767
2002	365	160,118	17,977	20,989	706
2003	341	157,280	18,237	19,709	696
2004	293	156,849	18,400	16,513	768
2005	295	166,499	18,172	16,787	730
2006	319	170,907	18,211	17,284	725

SOURCE: *Australian Crime: Facts and Figures 2007* (Australian Institute of Criminology, 2008).

NOTES:

- Between 1996 and 2003, the number of homicide victims fluctuated between 332 and 386, before dropping below 300 in 2004 and 2005. In 2006, homicide rose above 300 again, to 319.
- Continuing the trend of recent years, robbery offences increased in 2006.
- The number of recorded kidnappings fluctuates yearly. Over the period 1996–2004 kidnappings registered a general increase, but decreased between 2004 and 2006, from 768 to 725.
- The trend in recorded sexual assaults showed a steady increase over the period 1996–2004. A slight decrease in 2005 was followed by another increase in 2006.
- Assaults continue to represent the majority of recorded violent crimes. The overall trend since 1996 has been upward, with an increase of 50% between 1996 and 2006.

unreported (*Australian Crime*, 2008, p. 39). Drug arrests comprise the last set of figures. Here, it is observed that arrests have also declined. These arrests are categorized by consumers (users) and providers (dealers or sellers). And, like in other countries, consumers are the ones who tend to be arrested most frequently (see Figure 5.7).

Figure 5.4   Property Crimes, 1996–2006 (rate per 100,000 persons)

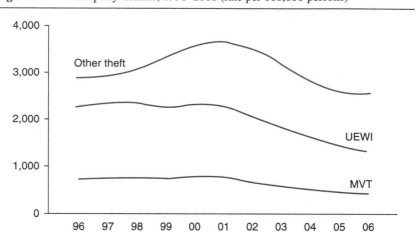

SOURCE: *Australian Crime: Facts and Figures 2007* (Australian Institute of Criminology, 2008).

Figure 5.5   Motor Vehicle Theft, by Month, 1995–2006 (number)

SOURCE: *Australian Crime: Facts and Figures 2007* (Australian Institute of Criminology, 2008).

Crime Victimization

In line with other countries, Australia contrasts official crime statistics with victimization surveys. The Australian Bureau of Statistics and the Australian Institute of Criminology (AIC) conducts such surveys. The 2005 survey

Figure 5.6 Other Thefts, 1995–2006 (number)

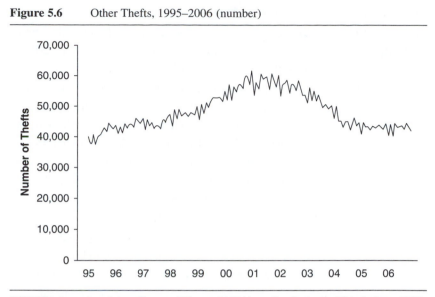

SOURCE: *Australian Crime: Facts and Figures 2007* (Australian Institute of Criminology, 2008).

Figure 5.7 Drug Arrests, Consumers and Providers, by Type of Drug, 2005–2006 (percent)

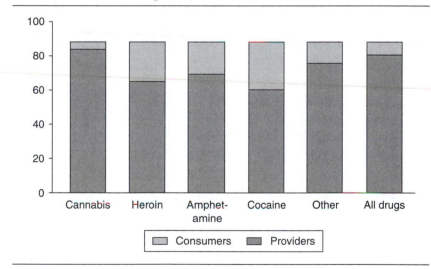

SOURCE: *Australian Crime: Facts and Figures 2007* (Australian Institute of Criminology, 2008).

conducted by the AIC comprised a sample of 7,700 Australians, age 16 and older (*Australian Crime*, 2008, p. 45). At an aggregate level, the survey found that, "In 2005, 5% of persons surveyed were victims of personal crime in the preceding 12 months" (*Australian Crime*, 2008, p. 45). Figure 5.8 shows the consistency of these low numbers over a 7-year period. Further, the survey found that there was a wide range of compliance in the reporting of crime to the police, with motor vehicle theft being the most reported and assault being the least reported (Figure 5.9). The respondents reported a variety of reasons why they did not report the criminal incident. These varied based on the type of incident. For example, in the case of burglaries, many respondents indicated they did not report the offense because they either felt the police could not do anything about the victimization and the loss was trivial or unimportant. In instances of assault the respondents did not report for reasons such as they did not think the incident was serious, and they felt it was a personal matter that they would handle themselves (*Australian Crime*, 2008, p. 48).

The fear of crime was another area investigated. In the aggregate, the data revealed that most citizens appear to feel safe walking close to home at night; however when the data is disaggregated by gender, it mirrors international trends, with females being more likely than males to report feeling unsafe (see Figure 5.10). Given this generally positive outlook of Australian crime and victimization, one wonders what race-related concerns would emerge? The next section answers this question.

Figure 5.8   Persons Aged 15 Years and Older Experiencing Personal Crime in the Previous Year, 1998–2005 (percent)

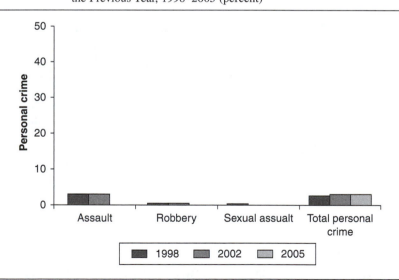

SOURCE: *Australian Crime: Facts and Figures 2007* (Australian Institute of Criminology, 2008).

Figure 5.9   Selected Crimes Reported to Police, 2005 (percent)

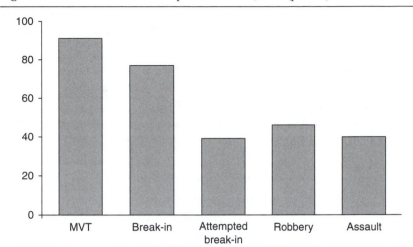

SOURCE: *Australian Crime: Facts and Figures 2007* (Australian Institute of Criminology, 2008).

Figure 5.10   Feelings of Safety Walking Alone in the Local Area After Dark by Gender, 2005 (percent)

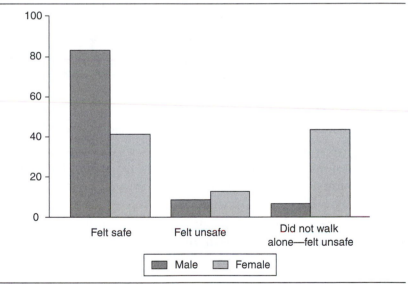

SOURCE: Australian Institute of Criminology National Police Custody Survey, 2002.

Aboriginal Justice in Australia

Recall that for nearly two centuries, Aborigines in Australia were the targets of genocidal aggression that left them a small minority group in a country in which they were once the dominant population. Consequently, very little attention was paid to their experience within the Australian justice system. In actuality, not until the formation of the Royal Commission into Aboriginal Deaths in Custody, that convened from 1987 to 1991 and published its results in five massive volumes in 1991, was there any serious interest or focus on Aboriginal justice concerns. Formed under public pressure from Aboriginal people and chaired by Commissioner Elliot Johnston, the commission's report was thorough and blunt in its openness regarding the problem. The problem centered on the deaths of 99 Aboriginal and Torres Strait Islanders between January 1980 and May 1989. In general, the commission noted that "Aboriginal people die in custody at a rate relative to their proportion of the whole population which is totally unacceptable and would not be tolerated if it occurred in the non-Aboriginal community" (Royal Commission, 1991, sect.1.3.3). Later in the report, the commission noted that during the same period, there were 383 non-Aboriginal deaths, 254 of which took place in prison and 129 in the custody of the police. In fact, the report argues that the real problem has to do with the fact that "Aboriginal people are in gross disproportionate numbers, compared with non-Aboriginal people, in both police and prison custody, and it is this fact that provides the immediate explanation for the disturbing number of Aboriginals deaths in custody" (Royal Commission, 1991, sect. 9.4.1).

Putting this aside, the commission still devoted considerable attention to determining the causes of death of the 99 Aboriginals. After carefully analyzing the cases, the commission concluded that most of the deaths occurred in police custody, with others occurring while the persons were in the custody of the prison system. The commission stated up front that there was no "foul play" in the deaths. According to the commission, the investigation found that 37 were from disease (primarily heart and respiratory tract ailments); 30 occurred as the result of suicide (self-inflicted hangings); 23 were the result of external trauma (mostly head injuries); and 9 were associated with alcohol or drug abuse. Even with the overall conclusion that "foul play" was not involved, the commission wrote:

> The finding that foul play on the part of police and prison officials was not
> implicated in the deaths in no way diminishes the seriousness of the problem
> of Aboriginal deaths in custody, nor does it undermine the reasons for the
> establishment of the Royal Commission. Indeed, the finding that the life styles
> of the Aboriginal people who died in custody, along with the procedures
> adopted by custodians and others, are the central determinants of their deaths

(rather than foul play on the part of custodial officials) highlights the importance of the Royal Commission's broad enquiry into the position of Aboriginal people in Australia today and the ways that Aboriginal people are handled by the police and criminal justice systems. (Royal Commission, 1991, chap. 3)

This was an important statement that indicated some level of commitment to get at the heart of the problem. Doing so led the commission to examine things such as the nature and condition of the cells in which the deaths took place; the medical care received by the deceased; the level of training given to those who handled the deceased; the adequacy of investigations into the deaths prior to the convening of the commission; and the rights of the deceased's family.

Part B of Volume 1 of the commission's report examined more generally the nature of the overrepresentation of Aborigines in custody:

The Royal Commission's Research Unit conducted a National Police Custody Survey during the month of August 1988. The survey obtained basic information on each occasion on which a person was taken into police custody during August 1988 and was physically lodged in a police cell. (Royal Commission, 1991, sect. 6.1.2)

Data from 1989 also were acquired during the period of this report. Results of the 1989 survey are presented in Table 5.2. The survey shows some parity in terms of the percentages of Aborigines and non-Aborigines represented in each age group; however, given their overall numbers in the population, Aborigines are clearly overrepresented in the figures. These figures also reveal that Aboriginal women (21%) were more often in police custody than non-Aboriginal women (8%). Table 5.3 shows that in several jurisdictions, as with police custody, Aborigines were heavily overrepresented in prison custody. Specifically, Aborigines also were overrepresented in the prison custody figures, where they accounted for 14% of those in custody across Australia. For example, in the Northern Territory, 69% of the prisoners in police custody were Aboriginals, with Western Australia (35.6%) having a large percentage of overrepresentation as well.

Turning to the reasons why persons were in custody, the report indicated that most people were arrested without a warrant (55%). The remainder of the persons were arrested with warrants and were incarcerated in protective custody due to public drunkenness, which in most jurisdictions was not a criminal offense. It is with the latter situation where "a far higher proportion of the Aboriginal cases were placed in protective custody because of public intoxication

Table 5.2   Persons Taken Into Police Custody August 1988, by Age Group

| Age group | Aboriginal | | Non-Aboriginal | | Total | |
	Number	Percent	Number	Percent	Number	Percent
0–14	103	1	199	1	302	1
15–19	1,487	19	3,805	19	5,292	19
20–24	1,840	23	5,701	29	7,541	27
25–29	1,427	18	3,902	20	5,329	19
30–34	974	12	2,289	12	3,263	12
35–39	714	9	1,415	7	2,129	8
40–44	483	6	920	5	1,403	5
45–49	379	5	585	3	964	4
50–54	235	3	325	2	560	2
55–59	126	2	254	1	380	1
60–64	64	1	148	1	212	1
65+	48	1	102	1	150	1
Total	7,880	100	19,645	100	27,525	100

SOURCE: Royal Commission into Aboriginal Deaths in Custody: National Report (1991).

where it is not an offence compared with non-Aboriginal cases (21% compared with 8%)" (Royal Commission, 1991, sect. 7.1.5). This situation was more pronounced with females where "19% of the Aboriginal females were for public intoxication where it was not an offence compared with only 6% of the non-Aboriginal females" (Royal Commission, 1991, sect. 7.1.5). When the commission examined the nature of the most serious offenses for which persons were in prison in April 1989, the most striking figure, as is seen in Table 5.4, is that 39.5% of Aborigines were there because they defaulted on a fine. In general, the report was successful in providing a benchmark dataset to determine the nature and scope of overrepresentation of Aborigines in the Australian justice system. In fact, the report included more than 300 recommendations, all aimed at reducing Aboriginal overrepresentation. A few of

Table 5.3   Prisoners in Custody, By Jurisdiction, 30 June 1989

Jurisdiction	Aboriginal	Non-Aboriginal	Not stated	Total	Percent Aboriginal
NSW (b)	415	4,861	7	5,283	7.9
Vic	86	2,156	14	2,256	3.8
Qld	412	1,855	122	2,386	18.2
WA	558	1,010	–	1,568	35.6
SA	102	761	8	871	11.8
Tas	9	215	21	245	4.0
NT	243	109	–	352	69.0
Aust	1,825	10,967	172	12,964	14.3

SOURCE: Royal Commission into Aboriginal Deaths in Custody: National Report (1991).
NOTES:
a. Percentage of those prisoners for whom Aboriginality or non-Aboriginality was stated in the census.
b. Including ACT.

these included developing diversion programs, regularly conducting police surveys to monitor the progress in reducing overrepresentation, investing in programs to deal with alcoholism, and committing to the process of reconciliation. So how is Australia doing?

National Police Custody Survey

The 2002 National Policy Custody Survey provides some of the most recent data to answer that question. The survey is conducted with the cooperation of Australian police services throughout the country. More specifically, according to Taylor and Bareja (2005):

> [The survey] attempted to cover every occasion in which a person was taken into police custody and physically lodged in a police cell, at any location in Australia, during the month of October 2002. This means that the survey did not cover *all* people arrested, as only a proportion of such people are placed into cells. (p. 18)

Table 5.4   Most Serious Offence of Sentenced Prison Receptions, Aboriginal
and Non-Aboriginal, April 1989

	Aboriginal		Non-Aboriginal	
Offence	*Number*	*Percent*	*Number*	*Percent*
Homicide	4	1.2	13	1.0
Assault	40	11.9	87	6.6
Sex Offences	11	3.3	42	3.2
Other Against Person	1	0.3	13	1.0
Robbery	1	0.3	28	2.1
Break and Enter	25	7.4	144	11.0
Fraud	2	0.6	71	5.4
Theft	28	8.3	212	16.2
Property Damage	14	4.2	19	1.4
Fine Default	133	39.5	258	19.7
Justice Procedures	18	5.3	110	8.4
Good Order Offences	11	3.3	39	3.0
Drug Offences	3	0.9	60	4.6
Traffic Offences	37	11.0	204	15.5
Other	9	2.7	12	0.9
Total	337	100.0	1312	100.0

SOURCE: Royal Commission into Aboriginal Deaths in Custody: National Report (1991).

In total, more than 27,000 incidents were examined. This was an increase from the 1995 survey but was lower than the first one completed in 1988 (see Figure 5.11). The figures from the survey reveal that indigenous persons remain overrepresented in police custody (see Table 5.5). Such over-representation is most pronounced in the Northern Territory and Western Australia where they represent 81.6% and 45.9% of those in police custody, respectively (Taylor & Bareja, 2005, p. 22). To punctuate the scope of the overrepresentation, Table 5.6 shows the rates of indigenous and non-indigenous custody along with the ratios of overrepresentation. Here, Western Australia (27.0%), Southern Australia (25.3%), and Australian Capital Territory (21.7%), each show high ratios of overrepresentation (p. 23). A trend analysis reveals that these figures are actually an improvement over earlier periods (see Table 5.7). The figures are quite telling. Western Australia's overrepresentation ratio, for example, went down from 50.3% in 1988 to 27.0% in 2002. On the whole, Australia went down from a ratio of 28.6% to 17.0%.

An important additional analysis is to determine whether any reductions in indigenous overrepresentation ratios are "due to either a reduction in rates of Indigenous custody *or* an increase in rates of non-Indigenous custody" (Taylor & Bareja, 2005, p. 25). In general, the authors noted that such reductions were a product of both situations. As one might expect, both indigenous and non-indigenous custody incidents involve males who are 25 years of age and older. There also was, however, considerable overrepresentation for indigenous youth under age 17 (see Table 5.8). So why are indigenous persons and other persons being taken into police custody?

Figure 5.11   Numbers of Police Custody Incidents for Surveys Conducted in
1988, 1992, 1995, and 2002

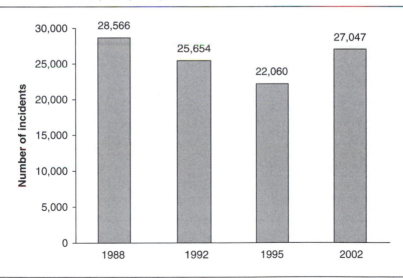

SOURCE: Australia Institute of Criminology National Police Custody Survey 2002 [computer file]; Carcach & McDonald 1997; McDonald 1992, 1993.

Table 5.5   Number of Incidents of Police Custody by State/Territory and
Indigenous Status

	Indigenous		Other		Total	
	N	%	N	%	N	%
New South Wales	1,738	16.3	8,935	83.7	10,673	100
Queensland	1,416	24.4	4,387	75.6	5,803	100
Western Australia	1,755	45.9	2,072	54.1	3,827	100
South Australia	710	27.6	1,865	72.4	2,575	100
Victoria	187	8.2	2,099	91.8	2,286	100
Northern Territory	1,250	81.6	282	18.4	1,532	100
ACT	36	19.3	151	80.7	187	100
Tasmania	19	11.6	145	88.4	164	100
Australia	7,111	26.3	19,936	73.7	27,047	100

SOURCE: Australian Institute of Criminology National Police Custody Survey 2002.

Table 5.6   Rates of Indigenous and Non-Indigenous Custody by Jurisdiction

	Indigenous	Other	Over-Representation
New South Wales	1,693.2	158.2	10.7
Queensland	1,483.1	141.4	10.5
Western Australia	3,468.0	128.4	27.0
South Australia	3,605.3	142.4	25.3
Victoria	861.1	49.9	17.2
Northern Territory	2,841.9	234.9	12.1
ACT	1,187.7	54.7	21.7
Tasmania	144.2	86.6	3.9
Australia	2,028.7	119.6	17.0

SOURCE: Australian Institute of Criminology National Police Custody Survey 2002: ABS 2003,
2004.

NOTE: Number of incidents of police custody per 100,000 population aged 10 years and over.

Table 5.7 Percentage of Custody Incidents Involving Indigenous Persons and Over-Representation Ratios by Jurisdiction for 1988, 1992, 1995 and 2002 Surveys

	1988		1992		1995		2002	
	%	Over-rep	%	Over-rep	%	Over-rep	%	Over-rep
New South Wales	14.3	15.4	16.2	12.6	21.0	17.0	16.3	10.7
Queensland	28.8	17.9	23.6	10.9	32.3	17.6	24.4	10.5
Western Australia	54.2	50.3	57.3	48.3	52.8	40.3	45.9	27.0
South Australia	21.8	28.3	19.5	19.6	25.1	27.1	27.6	25.3
Victoria	4.1	12.4	3.8	9.7	4.8	12.0	8.2	17.2
Northern Territory	76.3	10.4	80.0	10.9	80.0	11.3	81.6	12.1
ACT	5.0	11.2	2.7	3.6	17.0	24.8	19.3	21.7
Tasmania	7.5	4.8	5.4	2.2	12.1	5.0	11.6	3.9
Australia	28.6	28.6	28.8	22.4	31.1	25.2	26.3	17.0

SOURCE: ABS 1993, 1994, 1998a, 1998b, 2003, 2004.

Table 5.8   Custody Incidents by Age and Indigenous Status

	Indigenous		Other		Total	
	N	%	N	%	N	%
Less than 17	904	12.7	1,346	6.8	2,250	8.3
17–19	920	12.9	2,683	13.5	3,603	13.3
20–24	1,176	16.5	4,213	21.1	5,389	19.9
25–34	2,387	33.6	6,281	31.5	8,668	32.0
35 and over	1,724	24.3	5,414	27.2	7,138	26.4
Total	7,111	100.0	19,936	100.0	27,047	100.0

SOURCE: Australian Institute of Criminology National Police Custody Survey 2002.

Table 5.9 indicates that the most frequent reason why all persons were being taken into custody was arrest. For indigenous persons, protective custody for cases involving public drunkenness followed next, while for non-indigenous persons, the second most frequent reason they were brought into custody was for investigation. Overall, indigenous persons were more likely to be in custody for public order offenses, assault/intent to injure, or justice offenses (see Table 5.10 for all definitions). For all youth, burglary/theft/property damage represented the largest share of the more serious offenses for which they were taken into police custody (see Table 5.11). Of particular concern is the rate at which indigenous persons are taken into custody for public drunkenness. Presently, about "19 percent of all custody incidents were for public drunkenness whereas this figure was only eight percent for non-Indigenous persons" (Taylor & Bareja, 2005, p. 40). Separating these figures out by jurisdiction reveals wide variations in terms of public drunkenness custody incidents for indigenous and non-indigenous persons (see Figure 5.12).

Further analysis of the police custody data provides insights into the length of custody and the reasons for release from custody. In general, there are very few differences between the length of time in custody for indigenous and non-indigenous persons. As one would expect, those offenders who are being held for the more serious offenses are more likely to spend longer periods

Figure 5.12   Percentage of All Public Drunkenness Incidents Within Each
Jurisdiction by Indigenous Status

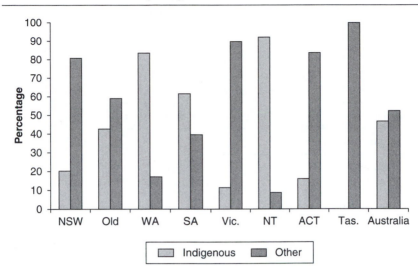

SOURCE: Australia Institute of Criminology National Police Custody Survey, 2002.

of time in police custody. Moreover, for public drunkenness, in general, indigenous people were held longer (7 hours) than non-indigenous persons (5 hours). But, as before, this varied by jurisdiction. Describing this variation, Taylor and Bareja (2005) write: "In Western Australia and the Northern Territory Indigenous people were detained longer than non-Indigenous people. However in Victoria . . . detention periods were significantly shorter for Indigenous people than non-Indigenous people" (p. 46). Finally, there were limited data on reasons for release, but from what is available, most persons were released from custody on bail. It is noteworthy that many indigenous persons were released after being freed from protective custody (related to drunkenness) and after being sent on to the courts or prison (Taylor & Bareja, 2005).

In general, these figures reveal some progress. Even so, other problems such as suicide have emerged as a concern among Aboriginals (Elliott-Farrelly, 2004). But, the two areas that remain of particular concern are the level of overrepresentation as it pertains to Aboriginal women and juveniles. These two issues are explored briefly in the next two sections.

Table 5.9   Reasons for Being in Custody

	Indigenous		Other		Total	
	N	%	N	%	N	%
Arrest	3,904	54.9	10,198	51.2	14,102	52.1
Warrant	784	11.0	2,521	12.6	3,305	12.2
Remand	158	2.2	217	1.1	375	1.4
Protective custody[a]	939	13.2	383	1.9	1,322	4.9
For investigation[b]	654	9.2	3,676	18.4	4,330	16.0
Other[c]	668	9.4	2,908	14.6	3,576	13.2
Not stated	4	0.1	34	0.2	38	0.1
Australia	7,111	100.0	19,936	100.0	27,047	100.0

SOURCE: Australian Institute of Criminology National Police Custody Survey 2002.

NOTES:

a. Protective custody incidents were comprised almost entirely of public drunkenness. Persons taken into protective custody for public drunkenness were in New South Wales, Western Australia, South Australia, Northern Territory, Tasmania and the ACT where public drunkenness is not an offence.

b. Includes questioning

c. Includes awaiting transit to/from court, awaiting extradition, breaches of court orders and fine defaults (where the persons was not arrested)

Aboriginal Women, Crime, and Justice

Scholars from across the globe have continued to note the intersection of race, class, gender, and crime (Agozino, 1997; Barak, Flavin, & Leighton, 2006; Reasons, Conley, & Debro, 2002; Schwartz & Milovanovic, 1996; Sudbury, 2005). This "articulation," as Agozino (1997) refers to it, suggests that when one studies race and crime, it is essential to take into account issues pertaining to class and gender. Without doing so, researchers risk missing what might be the key variables when examining race and crime. That is, a relationship that on the surface might be accounted for by race might actually be

Table 5.10 Most Serious Offence Associated With Being in Custody

Reason for Custody[a]	Indigenous		Other		Total	
	N	%	N	%	N	%
Homicide	15	0.3	51	0.4	66	0.4
Assault/intent to injure*	737	16.2	1,643	12.6	2,380	13.6
Sexual assault	48	1.1	176	1.4	224	1.3
Dangerous acts	184	4.0	480	3.7	664	3.8
Abduction	4	0.1	39	0.3	43	0.2
Robbery/extortion	45	1.0	177	1.4	222	1.3
Break and enter*	364	8.0	697	5.4	1,061	6.0
Theft*	377	8.3	1,394	10.7	1,771	10.1
Deception/fraud*	28	0.6	340	2.6	368	2.1
Drug offences*	93	2.0	717	5.5	810	4.6
Weapons	59	1.3	164	1.3	223	1.3
Property damage	151	3.3	402	3.1	553	8.2
Public order offences*[b]	1,069	23.5	2,212	17.0	3,281	16.7
Traffic offences[b]	351	7.7	1,329	10.2	1,680	9.6
Justice offences[c]	499	11.0	1,228	9.4	1,727	9.8
Miscellaneous	77	1.7	202	1.6	279	1.6
Other not definable	448	10.0	1,744	13.4	2,192	12.5
Not stated[d]	1,156	–	5,529	–	6,685	–
Not applicable[e]	1,407	–	1,411	–	2,818	–
Total	7,111	100.0	19,936	100.0	27,047	100.0

SOURCE: Australian Institute of Criminology National Police Custody Survey 2002.

NOTES: *difference significant to $p < .05$

a. Most serious offence coded according to The Australian standard offence classification (ABS 1997).

b. Public order offences include trespass, offensive language, offensive behaviour, criminal intent, conspiracy, disorderly conduct, betting and gambling offences, liquor and tobacco offences, censorship offences, prostitution offences and other public order offences.

c. Offences against justice include breaches of justice orders, subverting the course of justice, resisting or hindering police or government officials, offences against government security and operations.

d. These incidents were not included in the calculation of percentages.

e. Includes incidents of protective custody for those states where public drunkenness is not an offence, as well as where the word 'arrest' or 'warrant' was written but nothing else. These incidents were not included in the calculation of percentages.

Table 5.11   Percentage of Most Serious Offence Type Within Each Age Group

	<17 years		17–19		20–24		25–34		35 or over	
	Ind	*Other*	*Ind*	*Other*	*Ind*	*Other*	*Ind*	*Other*	*Ind*	*Other*
Assault	7.6	10.5	14.7	11.1	16.0	11.3	18.7	13.0	18.3	14.6
Burglary/theft/property damage	48.1	42.1	28.5	26.2	20.0	19.9	13.1	17.5	7.5	12.2
Justice offences	15.5	12.0	12.2	6.8	10.1	9.2	10.0	9.6	9.7	10.2
Public order	10.6	10.3	17.8	22.6	21.5	19.2	24.2	15.1	34.6	16.0
Traffic offences	1.2	2.0	6.1	7.7	9.1	11.4	9.5	11.0	8.6	11.4
Drug offences	0.9	1.1	2.0	3.3	2.7	5.5	1.9	6.4	2.3	6.4
Other personal[a]	4.6	6.3	3.0	4.8	1.9	2.6	2.3	2.3	1.6	4.0
Other[b]	11.5	15.7	15.6	17.4	18.5	20.9	20.3	24.9	17.3	25.3
Total	100.0	100.0	100.0	100.0	100.0	100.0	100.0	100.0	100.0	100.0

SOURCE: Australian Institute of Criminology National Police Custody Survey 2002.

NOTE: Excludes instances where offence information was not stated or was not applicable

a. Includes homicide, sexual assault, abduction and robbery
b. Includes dangerous acts, deception/fraud, weapon offences, miscellaneous and other not definable

a function of class and/or gender. In the case of Australia, it is clear that, because of intersecting class and gender issues, Aboriginal females are being negatively impacted by the Australian justice system and too often the targets of abuse by their Aboriginal partners (Homel, Lincoln, & Herd, 1999; Ogilvie & Lynch, 2002; Payne, 1993). At one level, Aboriginal women feel as though they have to deal with several types of law. These include: "'white man's law, traditional law and bullshit law,' the latter being used to explain a distortion of traditional law used as a justification for assault and rape of women . . ." (Payne, 1993, p. 71).

Regarding domestic violence, Sharon Payne, a member of the Aboriginal and Torres Strait Islander Commission, wrote that numerous studies had been done on the problem of domestic abuse and, in her words: "Data from those studies expose a level of death by homicide among Aboriginal women by their spouses, sons, grandsons, uncles, and the list goes on to include all male relatives, at a rate which rivals that of all Aboriginal deaths . . ." (Payne, 1993, p. 68). Other scholarship has continued to note the abuse, struggles, potential relevance for feminist theory, and the few triumphs of Aboriginal women, as they relate to the Australian justice system (Adler, 1995; Kilroy, 2005; Kina, 2005; Mackay & Smallacombe, 1996; Payne, 1990; Sarre, 1996).

Aboriginal Youth and Crime

Well before the Royal Commission was convened, scholars were concerned about the overrepresentation of Aboriginal youth in custody (Bird, 1987; Eggleston, 1976; Gale, 1985). Fay Gale's (1985) work was among the first to make use of multivariate techniques to isolate the potential causes of their overrepresentation. From her research, Gale reported several important findings. First, as Aboriginal youth go through the system, they develop a cumulative disadvantage. Gale (1985) writes:

> A clear increase in the disproportionate degree of over-representation of Aboriginal youth can be seen within the legal system from the point where they made up some 4 per cent of all youth going through the cautioning procedure of Aid Panels to 14 per cent of those appearing in Court and almost 32 per cent of all youth being sentenced to a detention centre. (p. 3)

When examining why so many Aboriginal youth were arrested in the first place, Gale found that while race did play a minor role in police officers' decisions to make an arrest, other factors such as employment status and family structure were stronger predictors of police actions. On this point, Gale (1985) notes:

> Aboriginal youth are being discriminated against by the police but only marginally because they are black. Primarily it is because, being Aboriginal, they belong to those social categories of people such as unemployed youth living in multiple households in poorer areas. White youths from such social situations are also treated differently from the "middle class" employed youths from nuclear households in areas of home ownership. (p. 9)

In short, Gale (1985) identified "structural racism" as the problem—not individual racism. In a similar vein, more recent studies have found that arrest records significantly reduce the employment opportunities of indigenous persons (Hunter & Borland, 1999). Goodall (1990) has made a compelling argument that researchers should also consider the important role of the genocidal Australian "child saving" movement as a key contributor to the overrepresentation of aboriginal youth in welfare and juvenile justice systems.

On the whole, though, researchers have continued to take notice of the problem of Aboriginal youth overrepresentation (Maunders, 2001; O'Conner, Daly, & Hinds, 2002; Walker & McDonald, 1995). The challenge now has been to find viable strategies to reduce their overrepresentation in custody. On this front, Homel, Lincoln, and Herd (1999) have argued that a developmental approach (beginning early in life and continuing through adulthood) is necessary to prevent crime and violence in Aboriginal communities. They are in favor of initiatives that take into consideration Aboriginal risk factors such as "racism, group powerlessness, and the conflicting demands of different cultures" (Homel et al., 1999 p. 184). Moreover, they believe culturally specific approaches are essential to the success of any prevention program involving Aborigines (see also Chantrill, 1998). Blagg (1997) supports this contention by noting the weaknesses of the conferencing or Reintegrative Shaming Model that was popularized by Braithwaite (1989) and have been adopted in New Zealand and parts of Australia. However, more recent research has shown some support for conferencing in Australia (Hayes & Daly, 2003).

The final section of the chapter provides some brief closing thoughts concerning race, crime, and justice in Australia.

SUMMARY AND CONCLUSION

This chapter revealed that Australia is a country that has a history of genocidal actions against its indigenous people. Such a history, and its crime-related
consequences, as stated in the Introduction, is best contextualized by the colonial model. Other observers of the Australian experience have also pointed to
the colonial model as being important to understanding the overrepresentation
of indigenous persons in the Australian criminal justice system. Bird (1987),
for example, writes that "Aboriginal crime must be analyzed in its specific historical site and that the racial tensions exhibited in the construction of crime
are bound up with the colonial experience" (p. 45). A decade later, Broadhurst
(1997) pointed to "frontier culture," conflict theory, and socioeconomic factors, as potential explanations for Aboriginal imprisonment (pp. 456–463).
Five years later, though, Broadhurst (2002), again focusing on Aboriginal
overrepresentation, noted the importance of the colonial model, writing that:

> Differences in social and economic capital of Aboriginal groups have arisen for
> many reasons. These include the impact of colonization (especially the devel-
> opment of remote areas), differential employment opportunities (associated
> with decline in pastoral and seasonal work), and the structure of Aboriginal
> governance. These differences challenge current explanations of Aboriginal
> over-involvement in crime, which are largely predicated on a (largely) uniform
> experience of social and economic disparity with "White" Australia. Variations
> in the intensity and nature of criminalization among the Indigenous population
> suggests that "racialisation" and social deprivation explanations over predict
> their involvement in crime . . . Thus if we are to account for these extremes,
> variation in the colonial and post-colonial experience of Aborigines appear to
> be relevant factors, as well as judicial practices. (p. 257)

Moving the discussion to another level, Davis (1999) argued that in order
to solve the problems related to the overrepresentation of Aborigines in custody, there needs to be the development of "Indigenous Australian Criminology" (p. 2). Because as he sees it, while traditional criminologists might
have some interactions with Aboriginals, they "won't have had any first hand
experience of our cultures" (p. 2). Davis argues that a paradigm shift must take
place in which courses in Indigenous Criminology would become core or
required courses. If all of this sounds familiar, it represents the same move
towards educating students about the problem on the socio-historical context
of race and crime. So, while the setting has changed, the objective remains the

same. Further, the call for more culturally specific programs rings familiar as well. Aborigines in Australia, like racial and ethnic minorities around the world, continue to seek out remedies that reconnect them to their past. In the coming years, it will be interesting to see the impact of the efforts by Australians to reduce the overrepresentation. Unlike other countries, they have been fairly aggressive in trying to divert indigenous persons out of the system. Only time will tell whether the gains that have been made are continued and expanded.

REFERENCES

Adler, C. (1995). Feminist criminology in Australia. In N. H. Rafter & F. Heidensohn (Eds.), *International feminist perspectives in criminology: Engendering a discipline* (pp. 17–38). Buckingham: Open University Press.

Agozino, B. (1997). Is chivalry colour-blind? Race–class–gender articulation in the criminal justice system. *International Journal of Discrimination and the Law, 2*, 199–216.

Australian Bureau of Statistics. (2003). *Population characteristics of Aboriginal and Torres Strait Islander Australians: 2001 Census* [Media release]. Retrieved September 10, 2006, from www.abs.gov.au

Australian crime: Facts and figures 2007. (2008). Canberra: Australian Institute of Criminology.

Barak, G., Flavin, J. M., & Leighton, P. S. (2006). *Class, race, gender, and crime: Social realities of justice in America* (2nd ed.). Lanham, MD: Rowman & Littlefield.

Bird, G. (1987). *The "civilizing mission": Race and the construction of crime.* Victoria: Monash University.

Blagg, H. (1997). A just measure of shame? Aboriginal youth and conferencing in Australia. *The British Journal of Criminology, 37*, 481–501.

Braithwaite, J. (1989). *Crime, shame, and reintegration.* Melbourne: Cambridge University Press.

Broadhurst, R. G. (1997). Aborigines and crime in Australia. *Crime and Justice: An Annual Review of Research, 21*, 407–468.

Broadhurst, R. G. (2002). Crime and indigenous people. In A. Graycar & P. Grabosky (Eds.), *The Cambridge handbook of Australian criminology* (pp. 256–280). Cambridge, UK: Cambridge University Press.

Chambers, J. H. (1999). *A Traveller's history of Australia.* New York: Interlink Books.

Chantrill, P. (1998). Community justice in indigenous communities in Queensland: Prospects for keeping young people out of detention. *Australian Indigenous Law Reporter, 18*. Retrieved September 10, 2006, from AustLII Databases: www.austlii .edu.au/au

Clemons, M. L., & Jones, C. E. (2001). Global solidarity: The Black Panther Party in the international arena. In K. Cleaver & G. Katsiaficas (Eds.), *Liberation, imagination and the Black Panther Party* (pp. 20–39). New York: Routledge.

Davis, B. (1999). *The inappropriateness of the criminal justice system—Indigenous Australian criminological perspective.* Paper presented at the 3rd National Outlook Symposium on Crime in Australia, Canberra.

Dunn, K. M., Forrest, J., Burnley, I., & McDonald, A. (2004). Constructing racism in Australia. *Australian Journal of Social Issues, 39*, 409–430.

Eggleston, E. (1976). *Fear, favor, and affection.* Canberra: Australian National University Press.

Elliott-Farrelly, T. (2004). Australian Aboriginal suicide: The need for an Aboriginal suicidology? *Australian e-Journal for the Advancement of Mental Health, 3*, 1–8.

Fozdar, F., & Torezani, S. (2008). Discrimination and well-being: Perceptions of refugees in Western Australia. *The International Migration Review, 42*, 30–63.

Gale, F (1985). *Aboriginal youth and the law: Problems of equity and justice for black minorities.* London: Institute of Commonwealth Studies.

Gardiner, G. (2003). Running for country: Australian print media representation of indigenous athletes in the 27th Olympiad. *Journal of Sport & Social Issues, 27*, 233–260.

Goodall, H. (1990). Saving the children: Gender and the colonization of Aboriginal Children in NSW, 1788 to 1990. *Aboriginal Law Bulletin.* Retrieved September 10, 2006, from AustLII Databases: www.austlii.edu.au/au

Hanks, P. (1984). Aborigines and government. In P. Hanks & B. Keon-Cohen (Eds.), *Aborigines and the law: Essays in memory of Elizabeth Eggleston* (pp. 19–49). Sydney: George Allen & Unwin.

Hayes, H., & Daly, K. (2003). Youth justice conferencing and reoffending. *Justice Quarterly, 20*, 725–764.

Homel, R., Lincoln, R., & Herd, B. (1999). Risk and resilience: Crime and violence in prevention in Aboriginal communities. *The Australian and New Zealand Journal of Criminology, 32*, 182–196.

Hunter, B., & Borland, J. (1999). *The effects of arrest on indigenous employment prospects.* Sydney: NSW Bureau of Crime and Statistics Research.

Kilroy, D. (2005). Sisters inside: Speaking out against criminal injustice. In J. Sudbury (Ed.), *Global lockdown: Race, gender, and the prison-industrial complex* (pp. 285–294). New York: Routledge.

Kina, R. (2005). Through the eyes of a strong black woman survivor of domestic violence: An Australian story. In J. Sudbury (Ed.), *Global lockdown: Race, gender, and the prison-industrial complex* (pp. 67–72). New York: Routledge.

Knightley, P. (2000). *Australia: A biography of a nation.* London: Jonathan Cape.

Langer, W. L. (1968). *An encyclopedia of world history: Ancient, medieval, and modern* (4th ed.). Boston, MA: Houghton Mifflin Company.

Larson, A., Gillies, M., Howard, P. J., & Coffin, J. (2007). It's enough to make you sick: The impact of racism on the health of Aboriginal Australians. *Australian and New Zealand Journal of Public Health, 31*, 322–329.

Laurie, V. (2008, March 16). Pay the debt: stolen generations need help. *The Australian*. Retrieved March 18, 2008, from www.theaustralian.news.com.au

Leach, C. W. (2005). Against the notion of "new racism." *Journal of Community & Applied Social Psychology, 15*, 432–445.

Lothian, K. (2005). Seizing the time: Australian Aborigines and the influence of the Black Panther Party, 1969–1972. *Journal of Black Studies, 35*, 179–200.

Mackay, M., & Smallacombe, S. (1996). Aboriginal women as offenders and victims: The case of Victoria. *Aboriginal Law Bulletin*. Retrieved September 10, 2006, from AustLII Databases: www.austlii.edu.au/au

Maunders, D. (2001). Excluded or ignored: Issues for young people in Australia. *Development Bulletin, 56*, 70–73.

Merlan, F. (2005). Indigenous movements in Australia. *Annual Review of Anthropology, 34*, 473–494.

O'Conner, I., Daly, K., & Hinds, L. (2002). Juvenile crime and justice in Australia. In N. Bala, J. Hornick, H. Snyder, & J. Paetsch (Eds.), *Juvenile justice systems: An international comparison of problems and solutions* (pp. 221–254). Toronto: Thomson Educational Publishing.

Ogilvie, E., & Lynch, M. (2002). Gender, race, class, and crime in Australia. In A. Graycar & P. Grabosky (Eds.), *The Cambridge handbook of Australian criminology* (pp. 196–210). Cambridge, UK: Cambridge University Press.

Paradies, Y. (2005). Anti-racism and indigenous Australians. *Analyses of Social Issues and Public Policy, 5*, 1–28.

Payne, S. (1990). Aboriginal women and the criminal justice system. *Aboriginal Law Bulletin*. Retrieved September 10, 2006, from AustLII Databases: www.austlii.edu.au/au

Payne, S. (1993). Aboriginal women and the law. In P.W. Easteal & S. McKillop (Eds.), *Women and the law* (pp. 65–75). Canberra: Australian Institute of Criminology.

Platt, A. M. (1969). *The child savers: The invention of delinquency.* Chicago: University of Chicago Press.

Reasons, C. E., Conley, D. J., & Debro, J. (Eds.). (2002). *Race, class, gender, and justice in the United States.* Boston: Allyn & Bacon.

Roberts, J. M. (1993). *A short history of the world.* New York: Oxford University Press.

Royal commission into Aboriginal deaths in custody: National report. (1991). Retrieved September 10, 2006, from www.austlii.edu.au/au/special/rsjproject/rsjlibrary/rciadic

Sarre, R. (1996). Aboriginal Australia: Current criminological themes. In M. D. Schwartz & D. Milovanovic (Eds.), *Race, gender, and class in criminology: The intersection* (pp. 193–217). New York: Garland Publishing.

Schwartz, M. D., & Milovanovic, D. (Eds.). (1996). *Race, gender, and class in criminology: The intersection.* New York: Garland Publishing.

Schweitzer, R., Perkoulidis, S., Krome, S., Ludlow, C., & Ryan, M. (2005). Attitudes towards refugees: The dark side of prejudice in Australia. *Australian Journal of Psychology, 57*, 170–179.

Short, D. (2003). Reconciliation, assimilation, and the indigenous peoples of Australia. *International Political Science Review, 24*, 491–513.

Sudbury, J. (Ed.). (2005). *Global lockdown: Race, gender, and the prison-industrial complex.* New York: Routledge.

Taylor, N., & Bareja, M. (2005). *2002 National police custody survey.* Canberra: Australian Institute of Criminology.

Turnbull, C. (1965). *Black war: The extermination of the Tasmanian Aborigines.* Melbourne: Landsdowne Press.

Walker, J., & McDonald, D. (1995). *The over-representation of indigenous people in custody in Australia.* Canberra: Australian Institute of Criminology.

Woodruff, W. (2002). *A concise history of the modern world: 1500 to the present.* New York: Palgrave Macmillan.

Figure 6.1   Contemporary Map of South Africa

SIX

SOUTH AFRICA

————◦•◉•◦————

CHAPTER OVERVIEW

This chapter begins with a review of South African history. This history includes a discussion of the Dutch and British colonization of the country. The discussion will consider the mayhem and destruction produced by the colonization of the native people and their land. With the discovery of gold and diamonds, the chapter will examine the "mad scramble" to South Africa that further divided the country along racial lines. This division, which was codified by the apartheid system, is also discussed, along with the long and bloody struggle that overturned the system. Finally, we will examine the nature of post-apartheid South Africa and its crime-related challenges.

EARLY HISTORY

The history of pre-colonial life in South Africa has not been well documented. There have been archeological finds that support the existence of people having resided in the region 115,000 years ago (see Figure 6.1). Early inhabitants, known as "bushmen" or "San," belonged to hunting and gathering societies, and lived in areas where there was a ready supply of food and water (Ross, 1999, p. 8). The early San society, as in other early societies, used cave and rock paintings to document their existence. The Khoi or Khoikhoi represent another early group of indigenous people in South Africa. Their life was more pastoral which required them to move around seasonally to locate "suitable pasture for their cattle" (Mason, 2004, p. 13). Because of their nomadic practices, the Khoi and San oftentimes interacted with one another. As a result of this interaction, the groups intermingled and became the Khoisan or Khoikhoi-San (Elphick, 1985).

In the 1400s, the indigenous South African population's existence was threatened by the increasing exploration of the Cape or the landmass around the peninsula of South Africa. In fact, Portuguese explorer Bartolomew Dias was credited with being the first European to see South Africa. In an attempt to find India and "capture for Portugal the markets of the East," Dias was caught in a storm that brought him to South Africa (Mason, 2004, p. 19). Others also tried to reach South Africa, but it was difficult to navigate the Cape. In addition, Mason (2004) wrote that "the local population . . . was mostly unwelcoming, or more properly put, resistant to the likelihood of exploitation. There were numerous recordings of landing crews being ambushed before they could begin to barter for food and water" (p. 21). Nevertheless, Europeans continued to venture to South Africa, with the British arriving in 1591, the Dutch in 1595, and the French and Scandinavians in the 1600s. In most cases, the Cape was a place where trade occurred. Travelers stopped there to resupply their ships and trade. Interestingly, it was by accident that the Dutch came to believe that the Cape would be a good place to develop a settlement. After their ship crashed trying to navigate the cape in 1648, Dutch sailors adapted to the Cape and, with the help of the indigenous people, survived long enough so that persons from the homeland saw this as a place for colonization and settlement (Mason, 2004, pp. 23–24).

In 1652, the Vereenigde Oost-Indisch Compagnie (VOC), or more commonly known as the Dutch East India Company, sent three ships with 90 men to establish a Dutch settlement. After some early setbacks the settlers, under the commandment of Jan van Riebeeck, worked hard to keep the settlement viable. In 1657, Mason (2004) noted that:

> Nine individuals were granted land rights outside the fortified perimeter of the colony . . . Although these were the first of the so-called free burghers, in reality these men only had a modicum of liberty (they were, for example, still subject to VOC rules and regulations). (p. 27)

Out of the initial and new settlements, Cape Town emerged and became the center of most commerce.

The expansion of the colonial settlements by Europeans gradually began to displace the indigenous people. Lacking the organization to repel this disturbing trend, the indigenous people were overwhelmed by the European colonization. Over time, though, more burghers existed in the colony, with a sizeable number of immigrants coming from Germany, Scotland, and England. This additional growth of immigrants resulted in the Khoisan feeling a need to adjust to the inevitable: White colonization and domination. In time, though, the growing White population required additional labor to increase the profitability of the land. Following other colonial settings, they turned to slavery as a way to fill the labor shortage gap. And in the late 1650s, the first slaves were imported from Dahomey and Angola (Thompson, 2001). From that point forward, as noted by Thompson, "The Cape had become a slaveholding society" (p. 36).

In contrast to the American slave trade, slaves in the Cape originated from a variety of places including Mozambique, Madagascar, Indonesia, India, and Ceylon (Sri Lanka). After a while, slaves actually outnumbered the free burgher population. And though the slave system in South Africa did not take on the character of the American slave system, the society did become dependent on the system. In all, during the 150 years of slavery, it is believed that 63,000 slaves were imported into the Cape. Like the American slave system, few slaves were ever manumitted because the White populace was concerned about having too many "free Blacks" in society.

Another aspect of the American system that developed in South Africa involved the increasing legislation that dictated the movement of "free Blacks." Describing the impact of this legislation, Thompson (2001) wrote: "The free blacks initially had the same rights as the white settlers, but the law began to discriminate against them in the 1760s, and by the 1790s they were obliged to carry passes if they wished to leave town" (p. 37). In general, the slave system served as a proxy for the racial hierarchy that developed in the Cape. On this point, Mason (2004) wrote: "The only strata of society lower than slaves and Khoi-San were convicts and political prisoners. . . . Slavery acted as a catalyst for the brutalization of, and discrimination against, all blacks in the Cape" (p. 37). And as one might have expected, "Violence and discrimination on racial grounds were increasingly practiced at every level of society" (Mason, 2004, p. 38).

Skirmishes continued between the indigenous people and the settlers. The trekkers or trekboers (later known as Boers) were migrant farmers who ventured outside of Cape Town. In time, they adapted some of the native cultures and abandoned many European practices. They also developed their own language, Afrikaans, which integrated English, Portuguese, and African dialects with Dutch. But as the trekkers headed further east, they encountered African societies who were resistant to the encroachment onto their lands. This led to continual warring that produced instability in their new settlements. And with little aid coming from the Cape, the trekkers rebelled against the rule of the VOC, leading to further unrest in Cape Town. Nearing financial ruin in the late 1700s, the British took over the Cape in 1795. Even though the British made numerous and positive changes in terms of land rights and the curtailing of trading monopolies often practiced by the Dutch, in 1803 with the "British occupancy having no clear legal basis," rule was returned to Dutch. The Dutch's rule was brief but memorable. Educational systems were improved and political systems were made more inclusive. Nevertheless, by 1805, the British had returned to rule, with more changes ahead.

The changing shifts in colonial powers also resulted in changes in the landscape of the indigenous people. During the 1820s and 1830s, The Mfecane or "the crushing," was a "time of much destruction and great suffering in which many thousands died violent deaths and many more were displaced while war-induced famine and starvation apparently drove some to cannibalism" (Afolayan, 2004, p. 32). This process also resulted in tribes merging and the development of stronger tribes such as the well-known Zulu Kingdom, brought to fame by their legendary military ruler Shaka Zulu. Known for his brilliance and visionary leadership (Afolayan, 2004), it was Shaka's ruthlessness and unrelenting quest to quash other chiefdoms, that led to his assassination in 1828.

The 1800s saw South Africa continue to be a society pulled apart because of the various groups struggling for control. This struggle resulted in race playing a prominent role in the developing hierarchy within the country. Battles between Africans and Whites did little to settle the issues but in many cases hardened feelings on all sides. In the 1850s, after a long, unsuccessful struggle to fight off White settlers, the Xhosa (a Bantu-speaking people of southeast South Africa) turned to their ancestors to aid in their struggle. Based on a vision by a teenage girl, the Xhosa were directed to kill their cattle to rid themselves of White settlers. This action produced a hardship that actually resulted in widespread starvation and the migration of the survivors to settler areas where they could find work and sustenance.

This was the beginning of a trend whereby many Africans headed to urban areas looking for work and, out of desperation, reluctantly giving in to colonialism. During the 1800s, the British outlawed slavery with the passage of the

Abolition Act of 1833. Though not popular among many Dutch South Africans, they still held sway in controlling African labor albeit through labor contracts which, as in the United States, maintained labor through oppressive systems such as sharecropping.

Eventually, the Dutch trekkers felt a need to escape from British rule, so they headed away from Cape Town. The "Great Trek," as it is referred to, took them into land occupied by the Ndebele, and later the Zulu. Over time, they defeated both groups and laid claim to some of their lands. In time, though, the battles over land between Whites and Africans continued. Even with the abolition of slavery, White settlers still insisted on creating a society in which Africans had little to no authority. This began to take shape in the mid-1850s, in the coastal area of Natal. Though the British tried to ensure that Africans had some standing in the area, Mason (2004) writes it was clear that:

> The settlers had no time for the ideal of equality, and resisted all measures introduced by the British to protect African interests. Racist attitudes were as clearly discernible at the surface of Natal society as they were in Boer republics. The locals organized themselves to oppose local polities and, in the early 1860s, to campaign against the arrival of migrant labourers from South Asia. (pp. 100–101)

Unfortunately, the views of the racists prevailed and resulted in the first attempt to legally segregate Africans from White settlers. In fact, Africans were eventually allocated "reserves," which amounted to 2 million acres being set aside for Africans to reside and practice their customs. In the meantime, Whites allocated prime land settlements to themselves.

The relationship between Africans and Whites became even more strained with the discovery of diamonds and gold in South Africa. The discovery of diamonds in Kimberly, South Africa, "the diamond city," produced a "mad scramble" to the region. In 1870, 5,000 persons lived in the area, but by 1872, 20,000 Whites and 30,000 Africans resided there (Thompson, 2001, p. 115). With the consolidation of much of the diamond mining industry by Cecil Rhodes and his company De Beers, the industry stabilized. Nevertheless, disparate treatment in terms of White and Black miners was prevalent, with Black miners being reduced to the lowest positions and worst treatment. For a time, there was a movement to eliminate Black diggers and to give authorities the discretion to search Blacks without a warrant. If that was not enough, a committee of Whites wanted Blacks to receive 50 lashes if they were found with diamonds. While not all of this was enacted, it was clear that Whites were concerned about the competition being aroused by having Blacks in the mining labor force. In the end, White racists won out and Blacks were subjected to degrading strip searches and confined to unsanitary mining camps, which produced high death rates (Thompson, 2001).

The discovery of gold outside of Pretoria a little more than a decade later (in 1886) led to the development of another racially split mining labor force. Here, White workers earned eight times as much as African workers, and Blacks were subjected to "severe discipline imposed by African foremen responsible for white managers. They were clustered together, as many as fifty to a room, where they slept without beds in double-decker concrete bunks" (Thompson, 2001, p. 121). The increasing wealth of South African society, at least for Whites, became an issue that would lead to the push for South African independence. This push resulted in the South African War (1899–1902). Ironically, the war was between White South Africans and the White British, who were fighting over a land that was primarily populated by Black Africans. Africans, in fact, were, at times, caught in the cross fire of the dispute.

The brutal war produced the first concentration camps. Created by the British, the camps were segregated by race and involved terrible living conditions, in which Africans received less rations than Whites. The result of such treatment was the death of 28,000 Afrikaners (another term used to refer to White South Africans) and 14,000 Africans, mostly from measles, dysentery, and other diseases (MacKinnon, 2004). The outrage over the camps helped end the war, resulting in the British turning over the reign of power to the Afrikaners. So what did Africans gain from the war? MacKinnon (2004) summed it up best:

> Although the Africans had participated in and suffered from the war, they gained little in the end. The war was fought to settle white concerns about power, and the overall effect on the Africans was their increasing subordination to the imperatives of white supremacy and capitalism. (p. 173)

Very little changed after the full cessation of British rule, following the passage of the South Africa Act of 1909 that made South Africa an independent country. This was despite the fact that there was a considerable population imbalance in favor of Africans. Specifically, at the time of independence, there were 4 million Africans, 500,000 coloureds (of mixed race), 150,000 South Asians, and 1.275 million Whites in South Africa (Thompson, 2001, p. 153). Even with Africans comprising the largest share of the populace of the country, by 1913, the White minority had moved to fully segregate Africans from the fruits of their native land.

The Natives' Land Act of 1913 was the start of state-sanctioned segregation. The Act limited African land ownership to reserves. Highlighting the serious implications of the Act, Mason (2004) wrote:

> The Act outlawed the renting or purchase of land by Africans anywhere outside areas designated as reserves. The reserves covered a mere 7 per cent of the land total of South Africa, that is 22 million acres, and were both removed from areas of white land ownership and deliberately placed away from the most desirable areas of agricultural commerce. Land was demarcated as "white" or "native" and there could be no change between the two categories. So, in effect, African cultivators were banned from some 93 per cent of the land of the Union (or, viewed another way, 67 per cent of the population [was] restricted to 7 per cent of the country's land mass). (p. 165)

Such legislation was typical of 20th-century South Africa. Increasingly, Africans headed into urban areas looking for work. This trend was punctuated by the hardships brought on following World War I. Because of the economic downturn after the war, even more Africans headed to urban centers. But, as in other areas, Whites soon became resentful of the increasing African presence and competition for jobs. Thus in 1923, the Urban Areas Act was passed that required Africans to be segregated into separate urban areas and restricted their right to own property in urban areas. The act also had a "catch all" provision that stated that "Africans should only be permitted within municipal areas in so far and for so long as their presence is demanded by the wants of the white population" (Mason, 2004, pp. 175–176). Other acts would follow that either further restricted Africans or made minimal concessions in order to quell potential disturbances. Eventually, though, moderate African groups began to more aggressively agitate for change. But following World War II, the rise of apartheid caused massive changes in South Africa.

The creation of a governmental system based on apartheid was clearly the product of decades of little steps towards the inevitable (Mason, 2004). Thus, it was no surprise when the National Party of South Africa won the 1948 election on a platform based on the institution of a segregationist government. The legislation that helped move the segregationist practices along included the 1950 Population Registration Act that created categories for each segment of society. Therefore, the population was now divided into four racial groups: White, Coloured, Asiatic, or Native. And one's classification would determine "what individuals could and could not do, where they lived, and which laws were applied to their lives" (Mason, 2004, p. 194).

CONTEMPORARY HISTORY

The second half of the 20th century produced an ongoing struggle to end apartheid. Some of this struggle would be led by the African National Congress (ANC) and other activist groups in and out of South Africa. International outrage was widely reported in media outlets around the globe. Nevertheless, South Africa drifted further into a society of have's and have not's. Such a development resulted in skirmishes, massacres, and other attempts by the government to maintain the status quo; and on the other side, Africans continued to do all they could to share in the fruits of their native land. Not until the 1970s did the efforts of numerous protestors and martyrs result in the so-called demise of apartheid. The highly publicized 1977 killing of Black Consciousness Movement leader Stephen Biko sparked a nationwide protest and resulted in an estimated 200 to 500 deaths across South Africa. Again, the international community expressed outraged at these events. Consequently, the United Nations imposed an arms embargo on South Africa. Countries around the world also halted or restricted trade with South Africa. In the end, it was not until the 1990s, under the rule of F. W. De Klerk, that some of the apartheid legislation started to be repealed. In 1990, De Klerk released all political prisoners, including Nelson Mandela, who had been incarcerated for 27 years. Further, in 1991, the Population Registration Act was repealed. In addition, many of the government's covert activities that had been put in place to undermine anti-apartheid movements were ceased. Even so, the tensions within the country remained high.

With the repeal of apartheid legislation and practices, Africans became increasingly impatient in their quest for equality and full citizenship. Ongoing negotiations during this period attempted to minimize the violence that had already spread across the country. As leader of the ANC, Mandela along with De Klerk in 1992 signed the Record of Understanding, which allowed for open negotiations to resolve some of the more divisive issues. In the end, the discussions resulted in the 1994 multi-racial democratic elections, which resulted in Nobel Peace prizes for Mandela and De Klerk. Given their mass numbers, the ANC, now a political party, secured victory in the national elections. And in May 1994, Mandela was sworn in as president of South Africa.

Following his election as president in 1997, Mandela signed into law a new constitution that was formulated by the combined efforts of the National Party and ANC. Also, from 1996 to 1998, the Truth and Reconciliation Commission (TRC) was enacted and run by Bishop Desmond Tutu to bring to the fore the travesties perpetrated during the apartheid regime. In return for "telling the truth," perpetrators of the brutal offenses were provided amnesty from prosecution. One of the most controversial aspects of the new government, the commission's work was meant to bring closure to the long-standing, state-sanctioned repression. Whether the commission has achieved its objective has resulted in considerable debate (for an excellent discussions of this debate, see Herwitz, 2005; Rotberg & Thompson, 2000; Terreblance, 2002).

After Mandela left office in 1999, one of his deputies, Thabo Mbeki, ascended to the presidency. South Africa continues to struggle with its past, but with Africans playing a larger role in their own destiny, even with the serious challenges ahead, in the last decade the country has clearly taken a small step in the right direction. Next, the chapter examines the most recent figures on the characteristics of South Africans.

OVERVIEW OF SOCIO-DEMOGRAPHICS IN SOUTH AFRICA

Mid-year population figures from 2007 reveal that South Africa is a country of more than 47 million people, with Black Africans representing 79.6% (38 million) of the population. White South Africans represent 9.1% of the population and Indian/Asians represent 2.5% (see Table 6.1). The Kwazulu-Natal province has nearly 20.9% of the population (Table 6.2). In regard to life expectancy, South African men averaged 48.4 years of life, while females averaged 51.6 years of life (*Mid-Year Population Estimates*, 2007). With an HIV-prevalence rate at 11% (5.3 million persons infected), the virus has clearly had an impact on South African life expectancy figures.

CRIME AND JUSTICE IN SOUTH AFRICA

So how much crime is there in South Africa? As in other countries, South Africa's crime figures can be ascertained through their national police force, the

Table 6.1   Mid-Year Estimates for South Africa by Population Group and Sex, 2007

Population Group	Male		Female		Total	
	Number	% of Total Population	Number	% of Total Population	Number	% of Total Population
African	18,775,600	79.7	19,304,300	79.5	38,079,900	79.6
Coloured	2,081,500	8.8	2,163,500	8.9	4,245,000	8.9
Indian/Asian	574,900	2.4	598,800	2.5	1,173,700	2.5
White	2,130,600	9.1	2,221,500	9.1	4,352,100	9.1
Total	**23,562,600**	**100.0**	**24,288,100**	**100.0**	**47,850,700**	**100.0**

SOURCE: *Mid-year population estimates 2007.* (2007).

Table 6.2   Percentage Distribution of the Estimated Provincial Share of the Total Population, 2007

Eastern Cape	Free State	Gauteng	Kwazulu-Natal	Limpopo	Mpumalanga	Northern Cape	North West	Western Cape	Total
14.4	6.2	20.2	20.9	11.3	7.4	2.3	7.1	10.1	100.0

SOURCE: *Mid-year population estimates 2007.* (2007).

South African Police Service. And while it would be nice to track crime trends in South Africa pre- and post-apartheid, figures "for the pre-1994 period show that crime rates for most of the country have been increasing since the mid-1980s . . . because these statistics exclude crime incidents in the apartheid era . . . they are widely regarded as inaccurate" (du Plessis & Louw, 2005, p. 428). Table 6.3 presents the six most recent years of crime data for the country. These figures represent recorded crime and, as with other crime sources around the world, do not provide information on unrecorded or unreported crime. In general, the most frequent crimes occurring in South Africa are theft-related. For example, from the earliest period provided (2001/2002), to the most recent period (2006/2007), the number of thefts in the "all thefts not mentioned elsewhere" category were the categories with the largest share of crime. In the more familiar categories, in 2006/2007, there were 65,489 shoplifting offenses (a slight increase over the previous year); 71,156 common robberies (a significant decline over previous years); 58,438 burglaries at nonresidential premises (an increase over the previous year, but a significant decline over earlier years in the time series); 126,558 robberies with aggravating circumstances (an increase over the previous year); and 249,665 burglaries at residential premises (a decline over previous years). As for murder, there were 19,202 in the 2006/2007 time period, a slight increase from 2005/2006. Rapes decreased slightly to 52,617, while drug-related crime increased by nearly 10%. In fact, it reached its highest point at 104,689 incidents, which amounted to more than 50,000 additional drug-related crimes than in 2001/2002.

Moving to corrections, in March 2008 a total 165,840 people were incarcerated in South African prisons. Of these persons, 113,178 had been sentenced, and another 52,662 had not. Table 6.4 shows the racial and gender composition of the South African correctional population. The Black population represented the largest share of those incarcerated. Coloureds also were a sizeable portion of the inmate population at 29,136. Whites and Asians accounted for the smallest share of the inmate population (www.dcs.gov.za). As for the death penalty in South Africa, when used, it has long been largely reserved for Black Africans (Turrell, 2004).

Victimization Surveys in South Africa

In the late 1990s, following the lead of other countries, South Africa conducted its first victimization survey (*National Victims of Crime Survey,* 1998).

Table 6.3 Serious Crime Between the 2001/2001 and 2006/2007 Financial Years With the Percentage Increases/Decreases in Crime Between 2005/2006 and 2006/2007

Crime Category	Incidence of Crime per 100,000 of the Population							Raw Figures/Frequencies						
	2001/ 2002	2002/ 2003	2003/ 2004	2004/ 2005	2005/ 2006	2006/ 2007	% Increase/ Decrease	2001/ 2002	2002/ 2003	2003/ 2004	2004/ 2005	2005/ 2006	2006/ 2007	% Increase/ Decrease
Contact Crimes														
Murder	47.8	47.4	42.7	40.3	39.5	40.5	2.4	21,405	21,553	19,824	18,793	18,528	19,202	3.5
Rape	121.1	115.3	113.7	118.3	117.1	111.0	-5.2	54,293	52,425	52,733	55,114	54,926	52,617	-4.2
Attempted murder	69.8	78.9	64.8	52.6	43.9	42.5	-3.0	31,293	35,861	30,076	24,516	20,571	20,142	-2.0
Assault with the intent to inflict grievous bodily harm	589.1	585.9	560.7	535.3	484.0	460.1	-4.9	264,012	266,321	260,082	249,369	226,942	218,030	-3.9
Common assault	584.3	621.6	605.7	575.0	485.3	443.2	-8.7	261,886	282,526	280,942	267,857	227,553	210,057	-7.7
Indecent assault	17.1	19.4	20.1	21.7	20.9	19.8	-5.5	7,683	8,815	9,302	10,123	9,805	9,367	-4.5
Robbery with aggravating circumstances	260.5	279.2	288.1	272.2	255.3	267.1	4.6	116,736	126,905	133,658	126,789	119,726	126,558	5.7
Common robbery	201.3	223.4	206.0	195.0	159.4	150.1	-5.8	90,205	101,537	95,551	90,825	74,723	71,156	-4.8
Contact-Related Crimes														
Arson	19.5	20.2	19.0	17.6	16.3	16.6	2.0	8,739	9,186	8,806	8.184	7,622	7,858	3.1
Malicious damage to property	324.5	345.6	341.2	323.7	307.7	302.5	-1.7	145,541	157,070	158,247	150.785	144,265	143,336	-0.6

Crime Category	Incidence of Crime per 100,000 of the Population							Raw Figures/Frequencies						
	2001/ 2002	2002/ 2003	2003/ 2004	2004/ 2005	2005/ 2006	2006/ 2007	% Increase/ Decrease	2001/ 2002	2002/ 2003	2003/ 2004	2004/ 2005	2005/ 2006	2006/ 2007	% Increase/ Decrease
Property-Related Crimes														
Burglary at non-residential premises	675.3	704.0	645.2	592.8	559.9	526.8	-5.9	302,657	319,984	299,290	276,14	262,535	249,665	-4.9
Burglary at residential premises	194.4	162.8	139.3	120.3	116.0	123.3	6.3	87,114	73,975	64,29	56,048	54,367	58,438	7.5
Theft of motor vehicles and motorcycles	216.1	204.9	190.0	180.0	183.3	182.1	-0.7	96,859	93,133	88,144	83,857	85,964	86,298	0.4
Theft out of or from motor vehicles	444.6	431.0	370.8	318.8	296.6	261.7	-11.8	199,282	195,896	171,982	148,512	139,090	124,029	-10.8
Stock-theft	92.9	102.7	89.0	70.1	61.3	60.8	-0.8	41,635	46,680	41,273	32,675	28,742	28,828	0.3
Crimes Heavily Dependent on Police Action for Detection														
Illegal possession of firearms and ammunition	34.6	34.8	36.3	33.3	28.7	30.3	5.6	15,494	15,839	16,839	15,497	13,453	14,354	6.7
Drug-related crime	118.0	118.4	135.1	180.3	204.1	220.9	8.2	52,900	53,810	62,689	84,001	95,690	104,689	9.4
Driving under the influence of alcohol or drugs	54.8	48.7	53.7	64.2	70.6	80.7	14.3	24,553	22,144	24,886	29,927	33,116	38,261	15.5

(Continued)

Table 6.3 (Continued)

Crime Category	Incidence of Crime per 100,000 of the Population							Raw Figures/Frequencies						
	2001/ 2002	2002/ 2003	2003/ 2004	2004/ 2005	2005/ 2006	2006/ 2007	% Increase/ Decrease	2001/ 2002	2002/ 2003	2003/ 2004	2004/ 2005	2005/ 2006	2006/ 2007	% Increase/ Decrease
Other Serious Crimes														
All theft not mentioned elsewhere	1286.7	1364.6	1307.4	1151.1	922.7	876.0	–5.1	576,676	620,240	606,460	536,281	432,629	415,163	–4.0
Commercial crime	130.4	123.7	120.4	115.8	115.6	130.2	12.6	58,462	56,232	55,869	53,931	54,214	61,690	13.8
Shoplifting	152.6	151.8	155.0	142.8	137.5	138.2	0.5	68,404	69,005	71,888	66,525	64,491	65,489	1.5
Some Subcategories of Aggravated Robbery Already Accounted for Under Aggravated Robbery Above[*]														
Carjacking	–	–	–	–	–	–	–	15,846	14,691	13,793	12,434	12,825	13,599	6.0
Truckjacking	–	–	–	–	–	–	–	3,333	986	901	930	829	892	7.6
Robbery of cash in transit	–	–	–	–	–	–	–	238	374	192	220	383	467	21.9
Bank robbery	–	–	–	–	–	–	–	356	127	54	58	59	129	118.6
Robbery at residential premises	–	–	–	–	–	–	–	–	9,063	9,351	9,391	10,173	12,761	25.4
Robbery at business premises	–	–	–	–	–	–	–	–	5,498	3,677	3,320	4,387	6,689	52.5

SOURCE: South African Police Service (2007).

NOTE: [*] The ratios for the subcategories of aggravated robbery in this table are too low to calculate meaningful percentage increases or decreases.

Table 6.4   Inmate Gender and Racial Composition as on the Last Day of
March 2008

Races			*Unsentenced*	*Sentenced*	*All Sentence Groups*
Asian	Female		30	35	65
	Male		171	527	698
	All Genders		201	562	763
Coloured	Female		247	455	702
	Male		7,985	20,449	28,434
	All Genders		8,232	20,904	29,136
Black	Female		771	1,800	2,571
	Male		42,823	87,724	130,547
	All Genders		43,594	89,524	133,118
White	Female		49	222	271
	Male		586	1,966	2,552
	All Genders		635	2,188	2,823
All Races	**All Genders**		**52,662**	**113,178**	**165,840**

SOURCE: Department of Correctional Services, http://www.dcs.gov.za/webstatistics.

Since then, there has been considerable discussion about a variety of crime and victimization issues, but it makes sense to first highlight the results from this pioneering survey. Based on a sample of 4,000 randomly selected South Africans (16+ years old), the survey was constructed for three purposes:

1. Provide an accurate picture on the nature, extent, and patterns of crime in the country, from the victim's perspective

2. Determine victim risk and victim proneness so as to inform the development of crime prevention and public education programs

3. Assess people's perceptions of services provided by the police and the courts as components of the criminal justice system

The survey found that, in 1997, 21% of all South African households "had experienced at least one household crime, and 15 percent of individuals aged

16 years and more had experienced one individual crime" (*National Victims of Crime Survey*, 1998, p. 1). Housebreaking and burglary were the most common incidents experienced by households (7%). On the whole, South Africans are most often the victims of theft of property and assault. The racial characteristics of individual victimization reveal Coloureds at 16.8%, followed by Whites at 16.5%. Africans/Blacks were close behind at 14.1%.

Income was also a significant factor when examining individual victimization. South Africans with the highest level of income were most likely to report having experienced victimization at least once. Considering the trends with cross-national data, men (16.4%) were also more likely than women (12.9%) to report having been victimized. Cross-national trends also held true regarding the ages most prone to have experienced victimization, with ages 16 to 25 and ages 26 to 35 reporting the highest levels of victimization. Victimizations occurred in a variety of settings. For example, assaults were most likely to occur in dwellings, while robberies were most likely to occur outside a shop or on the street. Nearly half of all sexual offenses occurred inside a dwelling and nearly 32% of theft of personal property offenses occurred in the same place.

White households (4.3%) experienced household victimizations at a higher rate than Africans/Blacks (2.7%), and Coloureds (2.4%). Of those households that experienced at least one victimization, Indian/Asians (26.2%) had the highest incidence of nonviolent crime victimization. Whites fell in line next (24.4%), with Coloureds (17.9%), and Africans/Blacks (16.1%) next. It was interesting to find that Africans and Coloureds both experienced violent crime victimization at the same rate (7%), while Whites (5%) and Indian/Asians (3.35%) reported fewer such instances.

Reporting practices was another area explored by the survey. Here, the survey found that the theft of cars (95%) was the most reported offense, while the theft of livestock (59.9%) was the least reported offense. The reporting of offenses differed by race. For example, most groups do not even report instances of corruption. In fact, only Africans/Blacks bothered to report them. And, among them, only 6.9% did so. The reporting also was sporadic for more serious offenses such as robbery, where most groups reported in the upper 30% range, but Whites reported 62% of their victimizations. The reasons for not reporting the offenses also varied. For some offenses, such as robbery and assault, most stated the crime was not serious enough to report. But for sexual offenses, the most noted reason for not reporting the offense was fear of reprisal by the offender.

The final part of the survey sought to capture the level of satisfaction with the South African police force. Separating the responses by type of crime and

accounting for the years 1993 to 1997, South African households were most dissatisfied with how the police handled murders and housebreaking and burglary
offenses. When queried about why they were dissatisfied with the police, the
most frequent responses for hijacking/attempted hijacking, housebreaking and
burglary, and murder were: "Police did insufficient to solve case," "Police lack
interest," and "Police failed to make an arrest." The one difference among the
offenses was that for those who had their vehicle stolen, for obvious reasons, not
recovering the vehicle was the second strongest reason for dissatisfaction.
Finally, when comparing the level of satisfaction with the police by race, the
Coloureds reported the highest level of satisfaction with the police (50.6%), followed by Whites (41.9%), Africans/Blacks (36.6%), and Indians/Asians (30.2%).

So what has been the trend since this pioneering study? In 2003, the
Institute for Security Studies (ISS) replicated the survey (see Burton,
du Plessis, Leggett, Louw, Mistry, & Van Vuuren, 2004) and, based on the
reporting, found that "nearly one quarter of all South Africans (22.9%) had
been a victim of crime" (Burton et al., 2004, p. 103). This was a slight decrease
from 1998 (see Table 6.5). In addition, only two crimes (housebreaking and
theft of motorbike) had slight increases. Even with these promising figures,
concerns remain related to crimes being reported to the police. As a consequence of these figures, South Africans remain fearful of crime, which has
severely impacted their quality of life (Lemanski, 2006; Powdthavee, 2005).

To mediate their concerns regarding crime, some communities have enlisted
private security firms, while others have relied on vigilante groups. About 60%
of the respondents indicated there was some sort of volunteer anti-crime group
in their community. Approximately 25% of the respondents reported a vigilante
group in their community. Of this group, Blacks (76%) and Coloureds (70%)
were much more likely than Indians (43%) and Whites (19%) to report their
existence (Burton et al., 2004, p. 69). Another notable finding was that Blacks
had to travel farther than Whites to get to the nearest police station. Specifically,
27% of Blacks had to travel "between 30 minutes and one hour to their police
station, while only 3% of whites travelled in excess of one hour to their nearest
station" (Burton et al., 2004, p. 72). Also, after having contact with the police,
Blacks and Coloureds were more likely than Whites and Indians to indicate their
opinion of the police improved. Figure 6.2 shows that Blacks were more likely
than other groups to believe that the police were doing a good job. Respondents
also were asked what the government should do to make their area safe. Here
again, this varied by race. Figure 6.3 reveals that Blacks and Coloureds wanted
the government to invest more in social development, while Indians wanted

Table 6.5   Comparative Victimization Rates, 1998 and 2003 (%)

	1998	2003
Any crime	24.5	22.9
Housebreaking	7.2	7.5
Corruption*	–	5.6
Theft of personal property	4.8	4.7
Stock theft	4.9	2.5
Theft out of vehicle	2.5	2.5
Assault	4.2	2.2
Robbery	2.4	2.0
Deliberate damage to vehicle	1.3	1.3
Bicycle theft*	–	1.2
Car theft	1.2	1.0
Deliberate damage to buildings	1.1	0.9
Fraud	3.0	0.8
Crop theft*	–	0.7
Car hijacking**	1.4	0.5
Other crime	1.6	0.2
Murder	0.5	0.2
Theft of motorbike	–	0.1
Sexual assault/rape	0.4	0.1

SOURCE: Burton, P., et al. (2004).

NOTES: *Crime types not covered in the 1998 survey
**In the 1998 survey the category "car hijackings" included attempted and "successful" hijackings, while in the 2003 survey only successful hijackings were recorded. This probably accounts for the decrease in the hijacking rate between 1998 and 2003 reflected here.

Figure 6.2   Respondents' Rating of the Police in Their Area, by Race

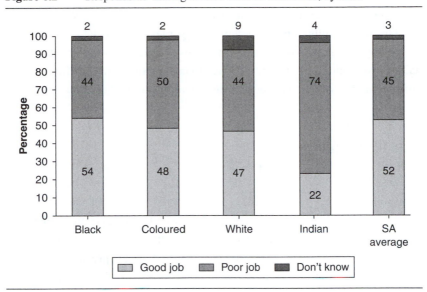

SOURCE: Burton, P., et al. (2004).

Figure 6.3   Which One of the Following Should Government Spend Money on to Make Your Area Safe From Violent Crime? (By Race)

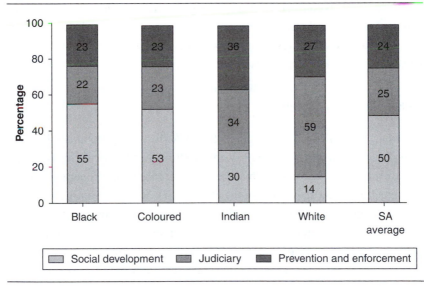

SOURCE: Burton, P., et al. (2004).

them to mostly invest in prevention and enforcement, and most Whites wanted the government to invest in the judiciary.

Given the results from the victimization surveys and the data on crime and prison populations, the next section provides a review of what scholars have had to say about crime in South Africa. Because of the unreliability of early crime data, this section will focus primarily on post-apartheid South Africa.

SCHOLARSHIP ON CRIME
AND JUSTICE IN SOUTH AFRICA

Crime and justice in South Africa has garnered significant attention from scholars. Just as South Africa is a desired tourist attraction, criminologists and other scholars also are enamored with crime in the country. Why? It is likely that because of the furor surrounding South Africa's previous apartheid regime, people want to see how the country has emerged from that system (Singh, 2008). Also, it is likely that because it is such a popular tourist destination, people want to understand the magnitude and scope of its crime-related issues. Perhaps, though, as Steinberg has pointed out, like other countries, South Africa always believes it is in the middle of a crime wave (Steinberg, 2001, pp. 2–4). Nevertheless, there are legitimate concerns related to crime and justice. Thus, scholarly observers have keyed in on several areas such as gangs, organized crime, crime in post-apartheid South Africa, and sexual violence. The following sections examine these areas.

South African Gang Activity

Shaw (2002) traced the origin of South African gangs to about 1900. In his estimation, by that time gangs were in all of South Africa's major cities. Their evolution was explained by "the massive social and economic dislocation experienced by many African societies" (p. 7). Moreover, during this same period, gangs served as a unifying force for ethnic groups involved in mining (Kynoch, 2000). Often referred to as the Tsotsis (gangster/thug), gangs became of particular concern in the 1950s and have continued to be a concern into present times. Though there are many reasons why citizens joined the gangs, the obvious one was economics—but, in another sense, joining a gang in South Africa also served as a way for Blacks to resist White oppression.

Fenwick (1996) also discusses the role of Hollywood movies, as well as the role of South Africa's popular media, in the large-scale adoption of gangsterism in South Africa. More specifically, he makes a compelling argument that *The African Drum* (later renamed the *Drum*) helped to glorify gang life presented in American movies, which in turn had an impact on Black South Africans. This was accomplished through an increased focus on gangs and also a change in focus from highlighting tribal issues and native topics, to urbanization and a continuing focus on gangs and gangsterism (Fenwick, 1996).

As a result of continuing economics concerns, continued White oppression, and the change in the emphasis in the media, gangs became even more institutionalized in South Africa. Unfortunately, as they became more prevalent, they reproduced themselves. Thus, when a gang developed in an area and became a problem in that particular area, another gang might form to protect themselves from the initial gang. Shaw (2002) describes this pattern as it happened in Soweto (located in Johannesburg) in the 1960s. The 1970s however saw residents becoming fed up with the escalating violence and victimization produced during this cycle. Consequently, while the response to gangs varied by jurisdiction, in Soweto residents banded together to fight off the gang presence. Of this practice, Shaw (2002) writes: "During the 1970s, middle-aged men in Soweto established civil guards, which eventually came together into an umbrella organization called the 'Moakgotla,' which attacked the gangs" (p. 8). Even with these efforts, gangs continued to wield power in Soweto. Glaser (1998) presents an analysis of Soweto's gangs in which he shows how gangs and high school students engaged in conflicts from the late 1960s to the mid-1970s. Because gangs were attractive to downtrodden youth, they competed with high schools for their attention. In some ways, both institutions attempted to accomplish the same aim: Overcome oppression and become self-sufficient but through different means.

The Black Consciousness Movement led by Steven Biko in a number of ways mirrored the Black Power Movement in the United States. The movement was integrated into the Soweto schools and had a profound impact on the youth. This movement produced the 1976 Soweto uprising, which essentially were riots that protested the apartheid government's practices. In the last decade, scholars have also noted that, as in other parts of the world, gangs are prevalent in South African prisons (Houston & Prinsloo, 1998). Though not new, these gangs which in some extreme instances represent as much as 60% or more of prison populations in South Africa (Houston & Prinsloo, 1998, p. 48) have presented similar challenges in South Africa, as they have in the United States and other industrialized countries. Such challenges include dealing with the gang/prison code, which often results in institutional problems (i.e., violence) and other management issues. Be it gangs or other crime-related activities, one thing is clear, since the change from an apartheid government, crime in South Africa has become the number one priority of the government. This trend is discussed below.

Crime and Justice in Post-Apartheid South Africa

It was only natural that following the transition to democratic rule in South Africa, scholars would be interested in the status of crime and justice in post-apartheid South Africa (see Dixon & van der Spuy, 2004; Leggett, 2005; Shanafelt, 2006; Singh, 2005, 2008). This interest, though, has led scholars to point to different causes for the continuing crime problem. Kynoch (2005) notes that the following explanations (that cover social and political factors) had been proffered to explain crime in South Africa: "poverty and joblessness, a new criminal-friendly constitution, a corrupt and ineffective national police force, and the post-apartheid influx of African immigrants" (p. 493). However, Kynoch (2005) debunks these notions by presenting a deep historical analysis of South African history that, among other things, shows that historically there have been high levels of violence in South Africa. Logically, then, violent crime in post-apartheid South Africa is not solely a product of the wide-reaching changes that followed the transition to democratic rule. In fact, Kynoch (2005) argues that the long-standing existence of violence in South Africa has resulted in a "culture of violence" within the country (p. 498).

Others who have written about the decade following the transition to democratic rule present overwhelmingly positive portraits of the handling of crime in the South Africa. For example, du Plessis and Louw (2005) point to the discrepancy between the victimization and crime data (from police) that actually shows that crime had decreased in the country. To emphasize the point further, they turn to South African homicide statistics that show an appreciable decline since 1994. They also highlight the fact that crime in South Africa is regional and that serious crime concerns do not exist everywhere in the country. These positive assertions are then followed by a review of how post-apartheid South Africa responded to crime. In short, the authors point to critical policies and legislation that were enacted. As an example, the National Crime Prevention Strategy (NCPS) was put in place in 1996 to help reduce crime. Included in this approach was the belief that to reduce crime, the following were necessary:

- Improve the functioning of the criminal justice system
- Consider crime prevention through environmental design
- Focus on community values and education
- Focus on transnational crime.
  (du Plessis & Louw, 2005, p. 430)

Other efforts during the mid-1990s included the South African Police Service Act, which sought to unify the police into a national force, to investigate complaints against the police force, and to ensure that Community Police Forums (CPFs) were being used as a means for the police to connect with the community (du Plessis & Louw, 2005). Four years after the NCPS was conceived, the South African Police Services produced the National Crime Combating Strategy (NCCS). This approach had two foci. First, it employed the "hotspots" approach that was popularized in the United States; and second, it was also concerned with the investigation of organized crime activity.

On the flip side of all these positives, it has been recognized that there have been continuing challenges, such as trying to strike a balance between enforcement and prevention, maintaining true oversight of the police force and, as in other countries, trying to get criminal justice agencies to work collectively to address crime and justice concerns (du Plessis & Louw, 2005). In addition to the aforementioned, organized crime and violence against women have both remained challenges.

Organized Crime in South Africa

Suppressing organized crime has been difficult in South Africa. Given that during the apartheid rule the government itself had engaged in "state lawlessness" (Omar, 1990) that paralleled and sanctioned the activities of organized crime (Standing 2004), one can see why there might be some difficulty conjuring up the support and moral fortitude required to aggressively attack the problem. Going further, Standing (2004) clearly shows that in contrast to the belief that the increased activity in organized crime in post-apartheid South Africa was primarily a product of the opening of the country's borders, other factors also contributed to the problem. Such factors included a reduction in law enforcement and improvements in communication and banking. Further, in some instances, certain state officials continued to work in conjunction with organized criminals, while in other places organized crime served as a form of criminal governance.

In short, if the state could not take care of its citizens, in some jurisdictions organized criminals (gangsters) stepped in and used their illicitly acquired wealth to
provide "philanthropy" for needy citizens (Standing, 2004, pp. 42–44). Such a
contradiction has been beautifully illustrated by Altbeker (2001), who wrote
about his experience attending the funeral of a Soweto gangster. At the funeral,
he was surprised to find out how revered the gangster was because of his "gen-
erosity" with the fruits from his criminal activity.

Sexual Violence in South Africa

Sexual violence has been referred to as an epidemic in South Africa. Moffett
(2006) writes that "survey after survey . . . [has found that] South Africa has the
higher level of rape of women and children than anywhere else in the world not
at war or embroiled in civil conflict" (p. 129). So how prevalent is rape in South
Africa? Numerous studies have estimated that *1 in 3* South African women will
at some point in their lifetime become a rape victim (Moffett, 2006). In addition,
children and infants also have been targeted for sexual violence with some scholars reporting that between 1992 and 2002 there was a 400% increase in violence
against these populations (Meier, 2002, p. 532).

With such startling figures, scholars have attempted to understand why sexual violence is so prevalent in South Africa and what can be done about it. (For
an excellent summary on the critical issues surrounding this topic, see Jewkes &
Abrahams, 2002.) Some believe many of the explanations used to explain this
troubling trend fall short of the mark and have been labeled "excuses" (Moffett,
2006). The most prevalent explanation is that because the apartheid regime sup-
pressed Black masculinity, in the post-apartheid period, they used their freedom
to exert their masculinity against the only population they could—their
women—through sexual and domestic violence. (On the struggles concerning
domestic violence, see Smythe & Paranzee, 2004; Vetten & Bhana, 2005). An
additional notion of this thesis is that colonization and the apartheid system normalized violence (Britton, 2006); so therefore the perpetrators of sexual violence
do not feel they will be penalized for their actions. Using a feminist framework,
Britton (2006) elaborates on the South African situation:

> Gender-based violence is often linked to patterns of patriarch and systems of
> oppression that are in accord with those found during the colonial period in
> South Africa. The patterns of exploitation did not end with colonialism but
> were extended within the apartheid system of white-minority rule. (p. 148)

Britton goes on to note that such systems did not cease with the end of apartheid rule; they continue in South Africa with gender-based violence—*at all levels of society*—in the form of "rape, domestic violence, sexual harassment, 'corrective rape' against gays and lesbians, virginity testing and sexual assaults . . ." (p. 149). Britton (2006) closes by arguing that South African women's organizations need to play a critical role in pushing for an end to what she refers to as "the growing menace of violence against women" (p. 163).

Another explanation for the high incidence of sexual violence includes those who suggest that rapes occur in South Africa because of the mythology that "[having] sex with a child or baby will cure AIDS" (Meier, 2002, p. 533). The same mythology also surrounds having sex with a young virgin (Madu & Peltzer, 2000). Other observers have suggested that, because of the dire economic situation in South Africa, women turn to sex work and, as a result, are placed at an increased risk for HIV/AIDS and sexual violence (Wojcicki & Malala, 2001).

Fighting the problem of sexual violence in South Africa is extremely difficult. Why? Because studies suggest that in far too many instances the attitudes of South African men towards their women have all but normalized sexual violence among a segment of the male population (see Kalichman, Simbayi, Kaufman, Cain, Cherry, Jooste, & Mathiti, 2005; Kalichman, Simbayi, Cain, & Cherry, 2007; Peterson, Bhana, & McKay, 2005). A recent study by Jewkes and her colleagues found that 16.3% of a sampling of young South African men admitted to having raped a non-partner or participated in a gang rape or "streamlining," as it is referred to in South Africa (Jewkes, Dunkle, Koss, Levin, Nduna, Jama, & Sikweyiya, 2006). Of these participants, 8.3% had also engaged in sexual violence towards an intimate partner (Jewkes et al., 2006).

Peer relations were highly associated with engaging in non-partner rapes. Such relations "included (mostly criminal) gang membership . . . and perceiving peer pressure to have sex" (Jewkes et al., 2006, p. 2958). In addition, Jewkes and her colleagues found that heavy alcohol consumption and drug use were associated with rape. Other research has also noted that when South African men witness abuse of their mothers during childhood, they are more likely to engage in intimate partner violence (including sexual) as adults (Abrahams & Jewkes, 2005). While many of these findings mirror international findings, all observers would agree that any populace with a male population in which 20% admit to rape is a serious concern. Even so, we should remember that 80% of the men did not report engaging in any form of sexual violence.

SUMMARY AND CONCLUSION

South Africa represents another country in which Tatum's colonial model rings true. From the earliest stages of colonization, European colonizers sought to control the country's resources "by any means necessary." By so doing, they engaged in genocidal actions that left Blacks on the margin of the country. Black South Africans still have not recovered from the ravages of colonialism and, more recently, the reign of the brutal apartheid regime. Following the trend of all societies where severe economic and social depressions are found, crime has flourished in South Africa's recent history. And though some of the recent crime and justice statistics have shown a positive trend, the increasing prison populations and the prevalence of gangs and organized crime remain serious challenges. Moreover, one can only agree with an early observer of the sexual violence crisis: "South Africa is a society at war with its women" (Carol Bower as quoted in Ramsay, 1999, p. 2018). And taking into consideration South Africa's other crisis regarding HIV/AIDS transmission, bringing this war to an end is among the most critical challenges facing the country.

REFERENCES

Abrahams, N., & Jewkes, R. (2005). Effects of South African men having witnessed abuse of their mothers during childhood on their level of violence in adulthood. *American Journal of Public Health, 95*, 1811–1816.

Afolayan, F. (2004). *Culture and customs of South Africa.* Westport, CT: Greenwood Press.

Altbeker, A. (2001). Who are we burying? The death of a Soweto gangster. In J. Steinberg (Ed.), *Crime wave: The South African underworld and its foes* (pp. 88–94). Johannesburg: Witwatersrand University Press.

Britton, H. (2006). Organising against gender violence in South Africa. *Journal of South African Studies, 32*, 145–163.

Burton, P., du Plessis, A., Leggett, T., Louw, A., Mistry, D., & Van Vuuren, H. (2004). *National victims of crime survey: South Africa 2003.* Pretoria: Institute for Security Studies. (ISS Monograph Series No. 101)

Dixon, B., & Van der Spuy, E. (2004). (Eds). *Justice gained? Crime and crime control in South Africa's transition.* Devon, UK: Willan Publishing.

Du Plessis, A., & Louw, A. (2005). Crime and crime prevention in South Africa: 10 years after. *Canadian Journal of Criminology and Criminal Justice, 47*, 427–446.

Elphick, R. (1985). *Khoikhoi and the founding of white South Africa.* Johannesburg: Ravan Press.

Fenwick, M. (1996). Tough guy, eh? The gangster-figure in the *Drum. Journal of South African Studies, 22*, 617–632.

Glaser, C. (1998). "We must infiltrate the Tsotsis": School politics and youth gangs in Soweto, 1968–1976. *Journal of South African Studies, 24*, 301–323.

Herwitz, D. (2005). The future of the past in South Africa: On the legacy of the TRC. *Social Research, 72*, 521–548.

Houston, J., & Prinsloo, J. (1998). Prison gangs in South Africa: A comparative analysis. *Journal of Gang Research, 5*, 41–52.

Jewkes, R., & Abrahams, N. (2002). The epidemiology of rape and sexual coercion in South Africa: An overview. *Social Science & Medicine, 55*, 1231–1244.

Jewkes, R., Dunkle, K., Koss, M. P., Levin, J. B., Nduna, M., Jama, N., Sikweyiya, Y. (2006). Rape perpetration by young, rural South African men: Prevalence, patterns and risk factors. *Social Science & Medicine, 63*, 2949–2961.

Kalichman, S. C., Simbayi, L. C., Cain, D., Cherry, C. (2007). Sexual assault, sexual risks and gender attitudes in a community sample of South African men. *AIDS Care, 19*, 20.

Kalichman, S. C., Simbayi, L. C., Kaufman, M., Cain, D., Cherry, C., Jooste, S., & Mathiti, V. (2005). Gender attitudes, sexual violence, and HIV/AIDS risk among men and women in Cape Town, South Africa. *The Journal of Sex Research, 42*, 299–305.

Kynoch, G. (2000). Politics and violence in the "Russian zone": Conflicts in Newclare South, 1950–1957. *Journal of African History, 41*, 267–290.

Kynoch, G. (2005). Crime, conflict and politics in transition-era South Africa. *African Affairs, 104*, 493–514.

Leggett, T. (2005). Just another miracle: A decade of crime and justice in democratic South Africa. *Social Research, 72*, 581–604.

Lemanski, C. (2006). Residential responses to fear (of crime plus) in two Cape Town suburbs: Implication for the post-apartheid city. *Journal of International Development, 18*, 787–802.

MacKinnon, A. S. (2004). *The making of South Africa: Culture and politics.* Upper Saddle River, NJ: Pearson/Prentice Hall.

Madu, S., & Peltzer, K. (2000). Risk factors and child sex abuse among secondary school students in the Northern Province, South Africa. *Child Abuse & Neglect, 24*, 259–268.

Mason, D. (2004). *A traveller's history of South Africa.* New York: Interlink Books.

Meier, E. (2002). Child rape in South Africa. *Pediatric Nursing, 28*, 532–535.

Mid-year population estimates 2007. (2007). Pretoria: Statistics South Africa.

Moffett, H. (2006). These women, they force us to rape them: Rape as narratives of social control in post-apartheid South Africa. *Journal of Southern African Studies, 32*, 129–144.

Omar, D. (1990). An overview of state lawlessness in South Africa. In D. Hansson & D. van Zyl Smit (Eds.), *Towards justice: Crime and state control in South Africa* (pp. 17–27). Cape Town: Oxford University Press.

Peterson, I., Bhana, A., & McKay, M. (2005). Sexual violence and youth in South Africa: The need for community-based prevention interventions. *Child Abuse & Neglect, 29*, 1233–1248.

Powdthavee, N. (2005). Unhappiness and crime: Evidence from South Africa. *Economica, 72*, 531–547.

Ramsay, S. (1999). Breaking the silence surrounding rape. *The Lancet, 354*, 2018.

Ross, R. (1999). *A concise history of South Africa.* Cambridge, UK: Cambridge University Press.

Rotberg, R. I., & Thompson, D. (2000). *Truth v. justice: The morality of truth commissions.* Princeton, NJ: Princeton University Press.

Shanafelt, R. (2006). Crime, power, and policing in South Africa: Beyond protected privilege and privileged protection. In N. Pino & M. D. Wiatrowski (Eds.), *Democratic policing in transitional and developing countries* (pp.149–164). Aldershot, UK: Ashgate.

Shaw, M. (2002). *Crime and policing in post-apartheid South Africa: Transforming under fire.* Bloomington, IN: Indiana University Press.

Singh, A. (2005). Some critical reflections on the governance of crime in post-apartheid South Africa. In J. Sheptycki & A. Wardak (Eds.), *Transnational and comparative criminology* (pp. 117–134). London: Glasshouse Press.

Singh, A. (2008). *Policing and crime control in post-apartheid South Africa.* Aldershot: Ashgate Publishing.

Smythe, D., & Parenzee, P. (2004). Acting against domestic violence. In B. Dixon & E. Van der Spuy (Eds.), *Justice gained? Crime control in South Africa's transition* (pp. 140–162). Devon, UK: Willan Publishing.

Standing, A. (2004). Out of the mainstream: Critical reflections on organized crime in the Western Cape. In B. Dixon & E. Van der Spuy (Eds.), *Justice gained? Crime control in South Africa's transition* (pp. 36–57). Devon, UK: Willan Publishing.

Statistics South Africa and Secretariat for Safety and Security. (1998). *National victims of crime survey.* Pretoria: Author.

Steinberg, J. (Ed.). (2001). *Crime wave: The South African underground and its foes.* Johannesburg: Witwatersrand University Press.

Terreblance, S. (2002). *A history of inequality in South Africa, 1652–2002.* Scottsville, SA: University of Natal Press.

Thompson, L. (2001). *A history of South Africa.* New Haven, CT: Yale University Press.

Turrell, R. (2004). *White mercy: A study of the death penalty in South Africa.* Westport, CT: Praeger.

Vetten, L., & Bhana, K. (2005). The justice for women campaign: Incarcerated domestic violence survivors in post-apartheid South Africa. In J. Sudbury (Ed.), *Global lockdown: Race, gender, and the prison-industrial complex* (pp. 255–270). New York: Routledge.

Wojcicki, J. M., & Malala, J. (2001). Condom use, power and HIV/AIDS risk: Sex-workers bargain for survival in Hillbrow/Joubert Park/Berea, Johannesburg. *Social Science & Medicine, 53*, 99–121.

❈ SEVEN ❈

CONCLUSION

———◆•◆•◆———

I had two aims when I began this work. First, I wanted to see the depth of the race and crime problem across the globe. To do so, I selected five countries and examined their early and contemporary histories in an effort to contextualize the experiences of the various racial and ethnic groups. Using the colonial model as a framework for understanding the nature of race, ethnicity, and crime proved fruitful. In each of the countries profiled, colonization has had its hand in shaping the society. Further, the colonization process produced long-standing inequalities that, in each society, undoubtedly contributed to race and ethnic groups being overrepresented in their respective criminal justice systems. It is important to state here that the problems related to race, ethnicity, crime, and justice in these countries only scratched the surface of the problems across the globe. Thus, even a cursory review of the literature will reveal similar pressing race, ethnicity, crime and justice-related issues in the Caribbean (Mahabir, 1988; Mahabir, 1996); Italy (Angel-Ajani, 2002; Melossi, 2003; Quassoli, 2004); Bulgaria (Gounev & Bezlov, 2006); Sweden (Bunar, 2007; Lööw, 1995, 2000; Pettersson, 2003); Israel (Fishman, Rattner, & Turjeman, 2006; Rattner & Fishman, 1998); Denmark (Holmberg & Kyvsgaard, 2003); Norway (Sollund, 2006); Nigeria (Saleh-Hanna, 2008), France (Jackson, 1997; Schneider, 2008; Zauberman & Levy, 2003); Germany (Albrecht, 1997); and South America (Mars, 2002). In some places, such as Antarctica, the colonization process simply wiped out the entire native population. Of this, criminologists Mueller and Adler (2004) write: "The indigenous people do not commit crimes, because they are gone" (p. 408).

Unfortunately, such genocidal actions tied to colonialism are only now receiving serious scholarly attention from criminologists (for example, see Hagan & Rymond-Richmond, 2008). I could go on, but you should now understand why race, ethnicity, and crime must be seen as an international dilemma.

My second aim in writing this book was to examine the similarities and differences of the experiences of racial and ethnic minorities across the globe. To examine some of these similarities, let's return our discussion to the countries profiled in the last five chapters. A review of the general history and of the race and crime issues in these countries speaks volumes about the importance of understanding colonialism and to the utility of Tatum's articulation of the colonial model. Qualitatively, the perspective clearly has applicability to the profiled countries. From the means used to invade and "take over" countries to the race-based societies that develop after colonization has taken hold, almost every one of the societies profiled developed under similar circumstances. Further, after the colonial system is put in place, the native's culture is marginalized, they have very little political power, and, in the end, the criminal justice system (and military) becomes the societal institution that keeps them in their place. England, however, represented a unique case study. It is rather ironic that the country that led the way in colonizing countries around the world had only a trace of ethnic minorities in their own society. Mulling over this fact, one wonders why would there be any appreciable number of ethnic minorities (particularly Blacks) in a society that only saw such people as cogs in a global system of slavery and exploitation? Consequently, it should be no surprise that when Blacks and other ethnic minorities began to arrive in the land of the colonizer, they would receive the same treatment they received in their homelands. And, in short order, they would become "the problem." The colonial model speaks to this pattern. The model also tells us that, at some point, racism will be legitimized through legislation. Thus, legislation is the key to maintaining the racist colonial systems and, conversely, down the line when adequate pressure is placed on governments (forcibly or otherwise), it also helps to begin the dismantling of racist colonial practices.

Unfortunately, though, there has only been modest progress in the "recovery" from colonization, considering that far too many Blacks and indigenous people around the globe still remain in the lower-stratum of post-colonial societies. Moreover, in a post-9/11 context, there has been a steady move away from the embrace of multiculturalism or related philosophies that have the aim of bringing people together in multiethnic and post-colonial societies (see

Gilroy, 2005). Nonetheless, it is promising that Barack Obama was elected president of the United States in 2008. This suggests that there have been some improvements in race relations in America. Even so, considering the long-standing inequalities in the United States and around the globe, the election of a minority person at this level does not guarantee that the plight of racial and ethnic minorities in America or elsewhere will change in the immediate future.

So what now? How do we use the finding that colonialism can, in fact, contextualize the etiology of race and crime across the globe? Scholars who have considered this very question have pointed to the need of the colonized to reconnect with their origins—a process referred to as the "decolonization of the mind" or rooting out the belief that everything related to the colonized is inferior or bad (see Akbar, 1982, 1998; Chinweizu, 1987; Wa Thiongo, 1986; Wilson, 1998)—before any substantive progress can be made towards solving social problems that can be traced to the colonization process. Moreover, post-colonial societies need to understand and acknowledge the far-reaching effects of colonization. The Australian government's recent apology for the stolen generations is a step in the right direction. Along with this acknowledgement must come reparations to compensate for the endless tragedies and injustices under the colonial system. In short, to deny or ignore the colonial foundations of a society does nothing to rectify centuries of injustice.

OPENING THE DIALOGUE AND DEALING WITH THE "ELEPHANT IN THE ROOM"

One final point needs to be discussed here. Whenever one talks about race and crime, at least in my experience, there is always the proverbial "elephant in the room." This relates to the fact that some Whites tend to feel that they are blamed for all the problems around the world (even though people of color would debate that this is their badge). In a sense, such thinking must be tempered with an understanding that colonization around the globe was primarily spearheaded by White people under the belief of White supremacy and, in some isolated instances, moved along with the assistance of unwitting people of color and others looking to also benefit from the fruits of the colonial machinery. To be sure, history tells us this time and time again. So, in essence, even though Whites are descendants of colonizers from long ago, White students today should not feel that they are the "colonizers." However, they must understand what colonization has done for them. It has placed them, more often than not, in positions of privilege. As an example, I held a class discussion one day where I asked one of my more vocal White students if he felt privileged as a White person. He said he had heard such a supposition before but "he didn't feel it." As I thought about his response, the reality is that most White people will never "feel it." Why? In short, because such privilege is something they take for granted, but Blacks and other groups can't. And, in case you're wondering, it is not just about how much money is in your bank account. Thus, when two people (one Black and one White) head into a store to make a purchase and the Black person is followed out of "suspicion" while the White person is not, why would the White person feel privileged in this scenario? During their visit to the store, they simply carry on their shopping activities, oblivious to what is going on behind the scenes. But, even though they do not "feel it," they must understand that it exists, and, to use a tired adage, they "should be part of the solution not part of the problem." This involves taking a stance when they see such obvious discriminatory practices. To do otherwise, in my view, condones those practices that criminalize people of color and give Whites the "benefit of the doubt" in certain situations.

On the other side, minorities need to also understand that just because Whites "don't feel it" doesn't make them all racists or the enemy. Given the colonial histories reviewed in the earlier chapters, it is understandable that some people of color would have animosity toward the White race—even if the Whites of today are not the ones who put the colonial machinery into place. Even so, as a product of their exposure to the history of the brutality of colonization and the equally brutal system of slavery, the Whites they see and interact with daily are the ones that, for better or worse, will likely shape their perceptions as to whether contemporary Whites are fair, trustworthy, etc. Even with the extra societal burden imposed on Blacks and other persons of color, it is important to understand that, though tough, overcoming the status of being underprivileged is possible. The examples of success are too numerous to provide here. But as is usually the case, it requires the collective to stand against the evils of colonialism, racism, and sexism wherever they may exist. It is important to take such a stance because, as evidenced by the contents of this book, Panayi (1994) might be onto something when he writes:

> All minorities in all societies in all historical periods have endured hostility from the government and the majority populations in which they live. The differentiating factor from one example to another is the intensity and ways in which racism manifests itself. (p. 102)

FUTURE DIRECTIONS FOR RACE, ETHNICITY, AND CRIME SCHOLARSHIP

In closing, one question remains: Where should race and crime research go next? It seems as though we have studied the same topics over and over and over again. It is time for scholars to investigate new directions in this area. Two areas that are in need of serious scholarly attention among those interested in race and crime (at least in the United States) include a serious examination of White criminality in its varied forms and also the nature and scope of crime and violence in the Asian American community (for a discussion of this oversight as it relates to the study of Asian American violence, see Hawkins, 1999, pp. 199–200). I agree with a few colleagues who served on an author-meets-critic panel at the 2006 Academy of Criminal Justice Sciences meeting in Baltimore, where one panelist, with the concurrence of the others, noted: "White people tend to get a pass when we examine race and crime." Just as the number of crime and justice texts devoted to Blacks, Hispanics, and Native Americans are on the rise, the same should happen for Whites and Asian Americans. In the case of Whites, after all, they commit most of the crimes in the United States and in other countries such as Great Britain, so taking a cue from race and crime scholars (see Russell-Brown, 2009 specifically Chapter 7; Bowling & Phillips, 2002, pp. 27–30; Webster, 2008) there should likely be more of an emphasis (maybe even a subfield) among race and crime scholars on White crime. This only makes sense.

Finally, I would be remiss if I didn't mention the critical issue of gender-related violence targeted at women across the globe. While the recently edited volumes by Sudbury (2005) and Bosworth and Flavin (2007) have already opened up the international dialogue on crime and justice-related problems facing women of color across the globe, more needs to be done. I must admit that by reviewing the international literature on the topic, I have become more sensitized to the diversity of issues they face. Furthermore, after taking stock of these issues, it has left me firmly believing that the true measure of the stature and civility of any society in the world should be how they treat their women. Need I say more?

REFERENCES

Akbar, N. (1982). *From miseducation to education.* Jersey City, NJ: New Mind Productions.

Akbar, N. (1998). *Know thyself.* Tallahassee, FL: Mind Productions & Associates.

Albrecht, H. (1997). Minorities, crime, and criminal justice in the federal republic of Germany. In I. H. Marshall (Ed.), *Minorities, migrants, and crime: Diversity and similarity across Europe and the United States* (pp. 86–109). Thousand Oaks, CA: Sage.

Angel-Ajani, A. (2002). Diasporic conditions: Mapping the discourses of race and criminality in Italy. *Transforming Anthropology, 11,* 36–46.

Bosworth, M., & Flavin, J. (Eds.). (2007). *Race, gender, and punishment: From colonialism to the war on terror.* New Brunswick, NJ: Rutgers University Press.

Bowling, B., & Phillips, C. (2002). *Racism, crime, and justice.* London: Longman.

Bunar, N. (2007). Hate crimes against immigrants in Sweden and community responses. *American Behavioral Scientist, 51,* 166–181.

Chinweizu. (1987). *Decolonising the African mind.* Lagos, Nigeria: Pero Press.

Fishman, G., Rattner, A., & Turjeman, H. (2006). Sentencing outcomes in a multinational society: When judges, defendants, and victims can be either Arabs or Jews. *European Journal of Criminology, 3,* 69–84.

Gilroy, P. (2005). *Postcolonial melancholia.* New York: Columbia University Press.

Gounev, P., & Bezlov, T. (2006). The Roma in Bulgaria's criminal justice system: From ethnic profiling to imprisonment. *Critical Criminology, 14,* 313–338.

Hagan, J., & Rymond-Richmond, W. (2008). *Darfur and the crime of genocide.* Cambridge, UK: Cambridge University Press.

Hawkins, D. F. (1999). What can we learn from data disaggregation? The case of homicide and African Americans. In M. D. Smith & M. A. Zahn (Eds.), *Homicide: A sourcebook of social research* (pp. 195–210). Thousand Oaks, CA: Sage.

Holmberg, L., & Kyvsgaard, B. (2003). Are immigrants and their descendants discriminated against in the Danish criminal justice system? *Journal of Scandinavian Studies in Criminology and Crime Prevention, 4,* 125–142.

Jackson, P. I. (1997). Minorities, crime, and criminal justice in France. In I. H. Marshall (Ed.), *Minorities, migrants, and crime: Diversity and similarity across Europe and the United States* (pp. 130–150). Thousand Oaks, CA: Sage.

Lööw, H. (1995). Racist violence and criminal behavior in Sweden: Myth and reality. In T. Bjorga (Ed.), *Terror from the extreme right* (pp. 119–161). London: Cass.

Lööw, H. (2000). Incitement of racial hatred. *Journal of Scandinavian Studies in Criminology and Crime Prevention, 1,* 109–120.

Mahabir, C. (1985). *Crime and nation building in the Caribbean.* Cambridge, MA: Schenkman.

Mahabir, C. (1988). Crime in the Caribbean: Robbers, hustlers, and warriors. *International Journal of Sociology of Law, 16,* 315–338.

Mahabir, C. (1996). Rape, prosecution, culture, and inequality in postcolonial Greneda. *Feminist Studies, 22,* 89–117.

Mars, J. (2002). *Deadly force, colonialism, and the rule of law: Police violence in Guyana.* Westport, CT: Greenwood Press.

Melossi, D. (2003). "In a peaceful way": Migration and the crime of modernity in Europe/Italy. *Punishment & Society, 5,* 371–397.

Mueller, G. O. W., & Adler, F. (2004). No crime in no-man's land? An Antarctic exploration. *Criminal Justice Studies, 17,* 405–409.

Panayi, P. (1994). *Immigration, ethnicity and racism in Britain, 1815–1945.* Manchester, UK: Manchester University Press.

Pettersson, T. (2003). Ethnicity and violent crime: The ethnic structure of networks of youths suspected of violent offenses in Stockholm. *Journal of Scandinavian Studies in Criminology and Crime Prevention, 4,* 143–161.

Quassoli, F. (2004). Making the neighbourhood safer: Social alarm, police practices and immigrant exclusion in Italy. *Journal of Ethnic and Migration Studies, 30,* 1163–1181.

Rattner, A., & Fishman, G. (1998). *Justice for all? Jews and Arabs in the Israeli criminal justice system.* Westport, CT: Praeger.

Russell, K. (2009). *The color of crime (2nd ed.).* New York: New York University Press.

Saleh-Hanna, V. (Ed.). (2008). *Colonial systems of control: Criminal justice in Nigeria.* Ottawa: University of Ottawa Press.

Schneider, C. L. (2008). Police power and race riots in Paris. *Politics & Society, 36,* 133–159.

Sollund, R. (2006). Racialisation in police stop and search practice: The Norwegian case. *Critical Criminology, 14,* 265–292.

Sudbury, J. (Ed.). (2005). *Global lockdown: Race, gender, and the prison-industrial complex.* New York: Routledge.

Wa Thiongo, N. (1986). *Decolonising the mind: The politics of language in African literature.* London: James Currey Ltd.

Webster, C. (2008). Marginalized white ethnicity, race, and crime. *Theoretical Criminology, 12,* 293–312.

Wilson, A. N. (1998). *African-centered consciousness versus the new world order: Garveyism in the age of globalism.* New York: Afrikan World Infosystems.

Zauberman, R., & Levy, R. (2003). Police, minorities, and the French Republican ideal. *Criminology, 41,* 1065–1100.

INDEX

ABOUT THE AUTHOR

Shaun L. Gabbidon is professor of Criminal Justice in the School of Public Affairs at Penn State Harrisburg. He earned his PhD in Criminology at Indiana University of Pennsylvania. Dr. Gabbidon has served as a fellow at Harvard University's W. E. B. Du Bois Institute for Afro-American Research and as an adjunct associate professor in the Center for Africana Studies at the University of Pennsylvania. His areas of interest include race and crime, private security, Black studies, and criminology and criminal justice pedagogy. The author of numerous peer-reviewed articles, his recent publications have appeared in *Criminal Justice and Behavior*, *American Journal of Criminal Justice*, *Journal of Criminal Justice*, *Journal of Criminal Justice Education*, and *Journal of Black Studies*.

Dr. Gabbidon is the author or editor of 10 books. He has also co-authored two books with Dr. Helen Taylor Greene: *African American Criminological Thought* (2000; State University of New York Press) and *Race and Crime*, 2nd edition (2009; Sage). He has also co-edited three books, *African American Classics in Criminology and Criminal Justice* (2002; Sage), co-edited with Dr. Helen Taylor Greene and Dr. Vernetta Young; *Race, Crime, and Justice: A Reader* (2005; Routledge), co-edited with Dr. Helen Taylor Greene; and *Race and Juvenile Justice* (2006; Carolina Academic Press), co-edited with Dr. Everette B. Penn and Dr. Helen Taylor Greene. Dr. Gabbidon's latest books are *W. E. B. Du Bois on Crime and Justice: Laying the Foundations of Sociological Criminology* (2007; Ashgate), *Criminological Perspectives on Race and Crime* (2007; Routledge), and *Encyclopedia of Race and Crime* (2009; Sage), co-edited with Dr. Helen Taylor Greene. Dr. Gabbidon currently serves as the book series editor of Routledge's *Criminology and Justice Studies Series* and SUNY Press's *Race, Ethnicity, Crime and Justice Series*. Professor Gabbidon can be reached at slg13@psu.edu.